SIN CITY GANGSTERS

SIN CITY GANGSTERS

The Rise and Decline of the Mob in Las Vegas

Jeffrey Sussman

ROWMAN & LITTLEFIELD

Lanham • Boulder • New York • London

Published by Rowman & Littlefield
An imprint of The Rowman & Littlefield Publishing Group, Inc.
4501 Forbes Boulevard, Suite 200, Lanham, Maryland 20706
www.rowman.com

86-90 Paul Street, London EC2A 4NE, United Kingdom

British Library Cataloguing in Publication Information Available

Library of Congress Cataloging-in-Publication Data
Names: Sussman, Jeffrey, author.
Title: Sin City gangsters : the rise and decline of the mob in Las Vegas / Jeffrey Sussman.
Description: Lanham : Rowman & Littlefield, [2023] | Includes bibliographical references and index. | Summary: "Sin City Gangsters is an exciting page-turner about how the mob created and controlled modern Las Vegas and then lost it to Corporate America"—Provided by publisher.
Identifiers: LCCN 2022013296 (print) | LCCN 2022013297 (ebook) | ISBN 9781538161234 (hardcover) | ISBN 9781538161241 (epub)
Subjects: LCSH: Gangsters—Nevada—Las Vegas—History—20th century. | Organized crime—Nevada—Las Vegas—History—20th century. | Las Vegas (Nev.)—History—20th century.
Classification: LCC GT6611.L37 S87 2023 (print) | LCC GT6611.L37 (ebook) | DDC 364.10609793/135—dc23
LC record available at https://lccn.loc.gov/2022013296
LC ebook record available at https://lccn.loc.gov/2022013297

To my wife and best friend, Barbara.

CONTENTS

ACKNOWLEDGMENTS

There are a number of people who provided valuable information for my dive into the role of the mob in Las Vegas. They are Gary Jenkins, an intelligence unit detective who worked closely with the FBI in uncovering the Chicago Outfit's skimming of several casinos in Vegas. Meyer Lansky II, Suzanne Dalitz, Jay Sarno, and September Sarno, all of whom were forthright in their interviews with me. Tony Napoli, who told me about his time at the Sands Hotel and Casino and the fight between Frank Sinatra and Carl Cohen. Former organized crime detective Anthony Celano, who made available information from his library of crime information. Steven Spataro, chief reference librarian at the East Hampton Library, for digging up old newspaper and magazine articles. My editor, Becca Buerer, for her steadfast support. And, of course, my wife, Barbara, who read each word of the manuscript and offered valuable suggestions.

INTRODUCTION

Following talks about my books, I am often asked "What motivated you to write this book?" My initial interest is invariably sparked by having met and spoken with individuals whose stories fascinated me. Here are brief descriptions of three chance encounters that fed my interest in Las Vegas and the men who ran the casinos.

The first was Big Julie Weintraub, known as the King of the Las Vegas Junkets. He was as big and imposing as a heavyweight boxer. His gregarious affability was apparent from the easy grin that lit up his face. He wore his charm on a towering 6'5", 250-pound frame. His broken nose added perfection to his appearance as a Damon Runyon character. He owned a jewelry store in New York, but gambling was his true vocation, especially craps.

I asked him to explain how he put together his junkets. He explained that he would organize a group of high rollers and arrange to have them flown first class to Vegas. Treated to champagne or other wines or liquors and fed prime steak or roast beef or king crab legs during their flight, they would be primed to hit the gaming tables at the Dunes. From the airport, they were driven in sleek, swiftly moving limos to the Dunes Hotel and Casino. At the hotel, they were shown to their comped suites, then it was into the casino. They bought chips as eagerly as kids buying popcorn at movie theaters. "And, of course, you got a commission," I said. "What do you think?" he responded, looking at me as if I were slow to understand.

I also learned that he was obsessed by craps and so junkets were a means for supporting his obsession. He hit the craps table often before his customers began their gambling ventures. He was so successful at running junkets that his customers crowned him with the sobriquet King of the Junkets. He was a casino entrepreneur who saw an opportunity and successfully capitalized on it.

A few years later, I was at a New Year's Eve party in a house on the grounds of La Costa, a resort in Southern California. An elderly man, looking as benign as a Norman Rockwell grandfather, stood next to me as we were served drinks. "I have to sit down. My back is killing me," he said. I sat down beside him and we filled the air with our small talk. His name was Morris Kleinman, an innocuous-sounding name that had no resonance for me. After a few minutes, I asked him what he did for a living. "I was part owner of the Desert Inn. You know Howard Hughes moved in, taking up the top two floors. He had an army of Mormons who worked for him. They didn't drink, didn't gamble. Their rooms on the top floors were usually reserved for high rollers. We were losing money because of him. We told him to leave. He wouldn't go, so we told him to buy the place. He asked what we wanted and we gave him a price that was too high. He agreed to pay it," he said matter-of-factly. Not thinking how to respond, I simply said, "Wow." Two stories, two characters. My interest was jet fuel propelled.

Kleinman had obviously been an important player in Vegas. I wanted to know a little more and later discovered that Moe Kleinman was a mobster originally from Cleveland, where he, Moe Dalitz, Sam Tucker, and Louis Rothkopf (known as the Cleveland Four and members of the Cleveland Crime Syndicate) had made fortunes during Prohibition. From Prohibition they branched out into gambling, first in Kentucky, then in Vegas. Though Kleinman was not as well-known as his partner Dalitz, who became one of the most prominent mobsters and philanthropists in Vegas, he was integral to the mob that ran Vegas in the 1950s and 1960s. (Please see chapter 4.)

One more encounter was all it took to fully engage my interest in Sin City. It occurred in Chicago. I was promoting a book on a morning TV show and visiting a friend who owned a trucking company. He invited me to dinner at his club one night. I arrived a few minutes early. My friend was standing at the bar, talking to another man. I approached and my friend said he would join me in the dining room. "Just mention my name to the maître d' and he'll seat you." Before I turned to go, my friend, not wanting to be rude, quickly introduced me to his companion. "Tony, I would like you to meet Jeff Sussman." We shook hands, and I said, "Nice to meet you." "Nice to meet you too," he said, his face wrinkling with a kindly smile. I walked into the dining room and was seated. I ordered a glass of red wine and was soon joined by my friend. He handed me a large metallic button with a man's face pictured on it; around his countenance was a message in colorful letters: HAPPY BIRTHDAY BIG TUNA. "Hey, is that the guy you were just talking to?" I asked. "Who is he? And why Big Tuna." "He's Tony Accardo, and he told me not to worry about my trucks being hijacked or pilfered. He's known as Big Tuna because he likes to fish and once caught an immense tuna, so I've been told. Wear this button in the Loop or on Michigan Avenue and no one will bother you."

As with my curiosity about Kleinman, I wanted to know more about Tony Accardo. He turned out to be an on-again, off-again boss of the Chicago Outfit, Al Capone's old gang, and a not-so-secret owner of slot machines, who also had interests in Vegas casinos. Capone called him "Joe Batters" for using a baseball bat to beat to death three gang members who had betrayed the Outfit. When I met him, he seemed like a polite, well-dressed businessman.

Having written about two of Las Vegas' first casino gangsters, Bugsy Siegel and Meyer Lansky, in an earlier book, *Big Apple Gangsters*, I had additional motivation to write this book. I had known that Siegel and Lansky were original visionaries who turned a cowboy town with a few sawdust casinos into a thriving casino-centered resort that would make billions of dollars for its investors. Siegel had opened the Flamingo Hotel and Casino in 1946 with money that Lansky and partners, such as Lucky Luciano and Frank Costello, had provided. The Flamingo was the first resort hotel on the Vegas Strip. It had luxurious rooms and suites and provided guests with amenities not available in Vegas at that time. The hotel advertised a world-class spa and health club, a golf course, a nightclub as good as any in Hollywood, a top-flight restaurant, and a Monaco-style casino. Siegel was convinced that the hotel's luxury and the excitement of its gaming tables would attract famous Hollywood stars, directors, and producers. What was not said publicly was a comment made by Lansky that "the winners are those who control the game and all players are suckers." I explore more about Lansky in chapter 3, and Siegel is the subject of this book's first chapter.

Another chapter of the book deals with Gus Greenbaum and Moe Sedway, both of whom were chosen to run the Flamingo Hotel and Casino following Siegel's assassination. Sedway was a low-key operator who never made any waves and so lived unmolested into old age. Greenbaum, however, was addicted to drugs and uncontrolled gambling. He also skimmed money from the mob. But he was a superb manager who turned the

Flamingo into a fountain of money. Though he had a Midas touch, he could not resist the freedom he had to skim money from the mob. That alone should have resulted in a death sentence; however, the mob was willing to forgive him his skimming if he returned the money and undertook the management of other casinos for them. He refused, and so the mob sent two thugs to slit his throat while he slept. Unfortunately, his wife was at home at the time of the murder, and she was similarly murdered.

There were others a lot cagier than Greenbaum. One of the smartest of them was Moe Dalitz, who not only owned casinos but also was a political powerhouse in Vegas. When he arrived in Vegas, he discovered that banks would not lend money for the building of casinos. So Dalitz turned to Jimmy Hoffa, president of the Teamsters Union. The union's Central States Pension Fund became Dalitz's source of funding for the building of his casinos in the 1950s and 1960s. The relationship between Dalitz and Hoffa had started years earlier in Detroit, where Dalitz's family-owned laundry businesses had been targeted by union organizers. To keep the unions at bay, Dalitz asked Hoffa to effect deals that would keep the laundries union free. In a world of reciprocal favors, both men benefitted from helping each other. Once he had his first casino, the Desert Inn, up and running, he made slot machines his hottest money generator. He packed in as many as space would allow and gave the one-armed bandits the best locations. Tourists dropped more than $200 million into his slots. Dalitz couldn't rake in money fast enough. It was a deluge. But he didn't stop there. He not only made his Desert Inn into one of the hottest casinos in Vegas, he also built others just as successful. He also knew that by building edifices other than casinos he would assure himself the goodwill of politicians and citizens. He built churches, synagogues, shopping malls, and a hospital. He gave large sums of money to politicians, who protected his interests. He proved to be a classic American case of the man who starts out as a mobster, attains wealth and power, and buys a clean new reputation by doing good deeds. Before his death of natural causes, he was named Mr. Las Vegas and was the recipient of numerous awards. He is even honored as the first casino boss to hire Frank Sinatra in 1951 when the singer's career was fast sinking and he couldn't find work in nightclubs. Sinatra remained forever grateful to Dalitz.

By 1959, Vegas had become such a dominant destination for gamblers that the city decided it needed a special welcoming sign. The sign, WELCOME TO FABULOUS LAS VEGAS, was the creation of Vegas resident Betty Willis. Clark County paid her $4,000 for the sign, which still stands on an island median at the southern tip of the Strip.

Dalitz didn't know it, but his Desert Inn was a treasure that Howard Hughes intended to scoop up and add to his portfolio. Hughes arrived in Vegas in 1966 in a sealed, germ-free train car and was whisked as elusive as a ghost to the Desert Inn. He took over the top two floors, one for himself and one for his army of Mormon helpers, known as the Mormon Mafia. Not only did he buy the Desert Inn, but he went on a buying spree that enriched mobsters all across the Strip who sold their casinos to him. He bought the Sands, the Landmark, the New Frontier, and the Castaways; then because he found the neon sign of the Silver Slipper annoying, he bought that hotel and casino as well. Hughes was seen as a white knight who had driven the mob out of Vegas. His efforts resulted in new state legislation called the Second Corporate Gaming Act, which allowed corporations to own casinos. That meant that Wall Street and banks could now enter the gaming industry. Local government officials were thrilled. The media jumped on board and began promoting Vegas as a mob-free city, a safe, legitimate playground for families. Hughes, however, had no interest in making Vegas a Disneyland for gambler families. He wanted something more glamorous as if imagining a Hollywood movie. He wanted to attract handsome men in bespoke tuxedoes and beautiful diamond-adorned women in furs, arriving in Rolls-Royces. Vegas, however, would always be a city for the masses. Yet the changes he effected were considerable and all executed without leaving his suite, where the drapes were never opened and finally rotted to dangling threads and dust like those of Miss Havisham's in *Great Expectations*.

In that darkened suite, Hughes lived a life preoccupied by his health and diet. He developed an inordinate love for Baskin-Robbins' banana nut ice cream, which was stored in buckets in the hotel's freezer. Some days he would eat nothing but that ice cream. So in love was he with that banana nut ice cream that he had his factotums order hundreds of gallons of it. However, Baskin-Robbins had discontinued that flavor. Hughes was indignant, beside himself with frustration. He demanded that his aides find some. They contacted executives at Baskin-Robbins, and the company was able to find 350 gallons of the ice cream. It was shipped to the Desert Inn. But when it arrived, Hughes—like an impetuous child—said he didn't want it anymore. He now wanted only French vanilla ice cream. For one year, the management of the Desert Inn distributed free banana nut ice cream to its casino customers. However, they couldn't give it all away; thirty years later, there was still some banana nut ice cream left in the hotel's freezer.

Hughes, who was suffering from numerous physical maladies, was also becoming increasingly paranoid. He couldn't trust anyone. He thought people were out to get him. He was also furious that he was regularly constipated. He spent hours sitting on his toilet, but he refused to alter his diet. Las Vegas was not turning out to be the glamorous city of his imaginings. Angry and frustrated, he decided in 1970 to leave. He did so as the owner of numerous hotel-casinos and the city's largest employer. He had no idea how much he was admired by the general populace.

Though Howard Hughes did much to make Vegas attractive to those who would otherwise have felt vulnerable living in a city run by mobsters, there were hundreds of thousands of tourists who were still drawn to the city by its reputation for being a mob hangout. And the principal entertainer who seemed to embody the mob's swagger and indifference to commonplace rules was Frank Sinatra. He was cool and hip, and he generated an aura of excitement and danger. He was the hottest, most popular entertainer in Vegas. Whenever he appeared in the Sands' Copa Room, tickets were scooped up almost as soon as they were printed. Fans offered hundreds, even thousands, of dollars for tickets to Sinatra's sold-out performances. And when he appeared with the Rat Pack (Dean Martin, Sammy Davis Jr., Joey Bishop, and Peter Lawford), fans offered anything for seats. One man even offered his wife to the Copa Room's manager. Sinatra was the first to begin the metamorphosis of Vegas into the entertainment capital of the world.

Though Sinatra was a magnetic presence on stage, he could be a menace off stage. With one hand, he could tip a bellhop $100, and with the other he could fling a hamburger not cooked to his liking against a wall then demand that the waiter who served him and the chef who cooked the hamburger be fired. Some said his irrational fits of fury were caused by his alcoholism, others that he expected to be treated like the greatest singer in the world. Regardless of the cause, Sinatra was a man to be avoided when his furies took control of him. Yet, he was the hottest draw in the casinos. When he gambled, others flocked to his side. "I played blackjack with Sinatra" was a common boast that many tourists uttered back at home.

He was a privileged gambler. Though he might win thousands of dollars playing blackjack, he would never pay off his markers and his gambling losses. The house wrote off its losses to Sinatra because he brought in so many tourists who gambled away hundreds of thousands of dollars. The Sands and later Caesars Palace and the Golden Nugget paid him hundreds of thousands of dollars a week as an investment. Sinatra even got a two-points ownership stake in the Sands, followed by another seven, though it was rumored that the additional points were really owned by mobsters who couldn't get licensed in Vegas. It didn't matter: Sinatra brought in the high rollers. And it wasn't just his singing and joking with the Rat Pack that attracted huge audiences, it was his whispered connections with the mob, especially with Sam Giancana of Chicago's Outfit. Those connections stuck to Sinatra from early in his career when he had delivered an attaché case containing $1 million to an exiled Lucky Luciano in Havana. Sinatra added to the impression that he was connected to the mob when he told Eddie Fisher that he would rather be a Mafia godfather than the president of the United States.

Because Sinatra was treated like royalty at hotel-casinos where he performed, he acted like a privileged monarch for whom the casinos were his principality. One night, after losing thousands of dollars playing blackjack at the Sands, he demanded a $50,000 marker. The manager and part owner of the Sands, Carl Cohen, would not give it to him because Hughes (who had recently bought the resort) said no more markers for gamblers who already owed money to the house, and Sinatra reportedly owed the Sands $200,000. Sinatra was infuriated that he was denied an extension of credit. He threatened hotel workers, smashed telephones, destroyed furniture, threw sundry items against walls, and drove a golf cart through a plate glass door. Finally, he demanded to see Carl Cohen. They met in the coffee shop of the Sands. Sinatra harangued Cohen and finally called him a dirty kike. Cohen grabbed Sinatra by his shirt collars and punched his face, knocking out two of the singer's capped teeth. Because Sinatra had treated hotel and casino workers so badly, they disliked him, and the next day posters went up around town with a photo of Sinatra with his two front teeth blacked out. At the top of the poster was the message, "Carl Cohen for Mayor." Though disliked by the working class of Vegas, Sinatra continued to be the most popular entertainer in Vegas until the era of Elvis arrived.

Though Sinatra was referred to as the Chairman of the Board, Elvis was called The King. Elvis appealed to a younger, less hip audience than those who came to see and hear Sinatra. After a shaky start in Vegas, Elvis began drawing in huge audiences of more than one hundred thousand fans for his concerts. As valuable as Elvis was to Vegas, he was paid only $125,000 per week compared to Sinatra getting $400,000 a week. Over a seven-year period, Elvis drew in an audience totaling more than seven million fans. He became such a Vegas institution that Elvis wedding chapels sprang up like mushrooms after his sold-out performances, and casinos even installed Elvis slot machines. The International, where hundreds of thousands of fans watched Elvis perform, put a larger-than-life-size statue of the singer in the lobby. One could not walk a few blocks in Vegas without seeing two or three Elvis impersonators. He embodied Vegas like no other entertainer. There are movies, documentaries, TV shows, and record albums that have focused on his career in Vegas. Between 1969 and 1977, Elvis played Las Vegas exclusively at the International, which became the Las Vegas Hilton. Elvis played 837 shows in all—becoming Vegas' biggest icon. Colonel Tom Parker, Elvis's manager, said that his client loved Vegas for two reasons: the friendly people and the check he got every week.

Not all entertainers saw their names in lights, yet they were as traditional and integral to Vegas as slot machines. They are the showgirls, tall statuesque beauties, whose extravagant costumes and alluring dance numbers have never lost favor. They have added glamour, titillation, and sensuality that have made gambling more exciting than it might otherwise have been. While individual entertainers come and go, the showgirls remain a permanent part of the Vegas entertainment experience.

Entertainment, however, was not the primary focus of the Outfit when it moved into Vegas. Though many of the old-time gangsters had sold their casinos to Howard Hughes, there were other casinos that were owned by the Chicago mob and its subsidiaries in Cleveland, Kansas City, Detroit, and Milwaukee. And no account about the Outfit's involvement in Vegas would be complete without including Tony "the Ant" Spilotro. A diminutive gangster with a taste for murder, he received his nickname from FBI agent Bill Roemer, who referred to Spilotro as a "little pissant," which the media shortened to "the ant." Spilotro hated the name as much as Bugsy Siegel hated his nickname: both men detested being identified with insects. And no one was foolish enough to use those sobriquets in their presence.

Spilotro could be as violent as an enraged attack dog. In the three years he was in Las Vegas, more gangland-style murders were committed than in the previous twenty-five years. His combination of unsanctioned violence and his notorious and well-publicized jewel heists infuriated his mob bosses. They had sent Spilotro to Vegas to make sure that their skim ran smoothly at the Stardust, the Hacienda, the Marina, and the Fremont. He was supposed to keep a low profile, not be the focus of media attention every time there was a major jewel robbery. His Hole-in-the-Wall Gang committed robberies that never failed to garner newspaper headlines and nightly TV news reports. This was not exactly what the mob bosses wanted. The bosses decided it was time to do away with Spilotro. He and his brother were nearly beaten to death and buried alive in a Midwestern cornfield.

Lefty Rosenthal, who also had been sent by the Outfit to Vegas, presented another kind of problem. It's not that he wasn't doing his job. In fact, he dramatically increased the skim. Though the Outfit initially saw Spilotro as Mr. Outside and Rosenthal as Mr. Inside, their roles detoured into a collision of interests. Spilotro was having an affair with Rosenthal's wife, and his crimes were so high profile that his name was placed in the Black Book, which was like putting his name on a wanted poster. And because Rosenthal couldn't get a casino license due to his criminal record, he filed suit against the Gaming Commission and hosted his own TV show where he could air his complaints. The show, which was broadcast irregularly, nevertheless attracted a sizable audience by booking celebrity guests, such as Sinatra and Don Rickles. The Outfit had initially thought that Spilotro and Rosenthal would positively complement each other; instead, they negatively complemented each other by drawing the fire of law enforcement. Investigations of the bosses went into high gear, and Rosenthal was suspected of being an FBI informant. Nothing can sink a ship of illegal enterprises more than a hidden spy. A death sentence was decreed. Rosenthal was supposed to meet a violent end, but one designed to end his life quickly. It was a consideration not applied to Spilotro's murder. Rosenthal was the victim of a failed car bombing. Such bombings were a favored means of execution ordered by Frank Balistrieri, head of the Milwaukee mob. Killing Mr. Outside and Mr. Inside did not solve the mob's problems. The bosses who ordered their deaths were indicted, convicted, and sent off to long prison terms.

New bosses replaced the imprisoned ones as efficiently as is in most corporations. The new bosses next attempted to regain their footing in Vegas by sending a man cut from a different pattern than Spilotro. He was Donald Angelini, known as the Wizard of Odds for his acute understanding of casino operations and how best to facilitate a skim that would go undetected by the prying eyes of government agents. In addition, he had the personality of a seasoned diplomat, whose smoothly congenial relations with customers, gaming officials, and law enforcement did not inspire anger, vengeance, or investigations. However, his self-confidence about keeping law enforcement at bay ultimately proved his undoing. He extended himself beyond his normal boundaries by participating in an attempted illegal takeover of a casino on the Rincon Indian Reservation. He was caught, indicted, tried, and sent to prison for thirty-seven months. The Outfit's last best hope for controlling Vegas was extinguished.

It was now time for a new breed of mogul: ambitious entrepreneurs who entertained visions of Vegas as a center for theme-park resorts and five-star luxury hotels. They were Jay Sarno, Kirk Kerkorian, Steve Wynn, and Sheldon Adelson.

Jay Sarno was a showman extraordinaire with a love of being on center stage. He could be seen waving to customers as he rode an elephant through the lobby of Circus Circus. At his other resort, Caesars Palace, he would be attired like an ancient Roman emperor. He didn't just dress the part, he turned Caesars Palace into a decadent Roman experience complete with sexy goddesses who seductively welcomed guests. There were tantalizing shows with stunningly sexy showgirls. There was an extravagant pool into which dove curvaceous topless beauties. The decadence was an all-encompassing experience that exemplified the motto, "What happens in Vegas stays in Vegas." Delighted male customers spread the word, and men from around the world made reservations months in advance of their visits.

Sarno's other venture was the less successful Circus Circus, a hotel-casino with all the conventional acts of a Ringling Bros. and Barnum & Bailey Circus. There were trapeze artists flying through the air above the gaming tables, distracting dealers, who could then be cheated by unscrupulous bettors. There was even an elephant in a harness circling above the tables. Since Circus Circus attracted so many families with children, the casino was not generating as much money as expected. Changes were made and Circus Circus soon became extremely profitable and a destination for family fun, including gambling. Its Carnival Midway; its indoor amusement park, Adventuredome; and its Slots-of-Fun casino drew in millions of eager tourists.

Kirk Kerkorian, who arose from dire poverty and left school in the eighth grade, proved to be not only one of the most brilliant dealmakers in Vegas, but in the United States. He built the magnificent MGM Grand and the stunning International (which in 1967 was the largest hotel in the world), where Elvis Presley performed for more than a million fans. In addition to building hotel-casinos, Kerkorian, a licensed pilot, started airlines and bought and sold movie studios. By the time of his death, he was one of the richest men in the United States and esteemed for his generosity. His foundation, during its existence, distributed more than $1 billion. When he died in 2015, his estate was valued at more than $4 billion.

Steve Wynn, after taking over his deceased father's bingo parlors, became the developer of some of the largest resorts in Vegas. His obsessive attention to every detail in the development of his mega resort made each one a breathtaking embodiment of luxury. His resorts, especially the Bellagio and the Wynn, offer wealthy guests the finest, most luxurious amenities available anywhere in the world. In addition to those two resorts, he took over the Golden Nugget and transformed it into a magnificent luxury hotel and casino. There was also his themed Treasure Island, which was a big hit with families. It was a combination of a Disney movie and a themed Disneyland. There was also the Mirage and Beau Rivage. With the acute eye of an aesthete and the discernment of a disciplined art collector, Wynn acquired some of the most magnificent works of art, which were subsequently displayed in the Bellagio and the Wynn. American public television broadcast a documentary that included his collection of Monet paintings. Fine art in Vegas resorts was about as far removed from the early days of mob-controlled casinos as one can get.

Finally, there was Sheldon Adelson. Born in poverty to immigrant parents, he started on the road to entrepreneurship at the age of twelve, when he borrowed money to open a newspaper distribution service. At age fifteen, he borrowed $10,000 from his uncle to start a candy vending machine business. Before becoming a billionaire, he started more than fifty businesses, some of which succeeded, some of which failed. In 1979, he had a brilliant idea that grew into a multimillion-dollar business. It was the Computer Dealers Exposition, which is better known as COMDEX. It became the largest computer trade show in the world when he and his partners sold it in 1995 for $862 million, of which $500 million was Adelson's share. He went on to purchase the Sands Hotel and Casino for $128 million and eventually built the magnificent Venetian, which incorporates the charms and beauty of Venice, Italy. It was followed by the Palazzo Hotel and Casino. To have a voice in how Vegas was run, he bought the *Las Vegas Review-Journal*, the largest and most influential daily newspaper in Vegas.

Adelson, Sarno, Kerkorian, and Wynn completely changed the architecture, landscape, and skyline of Vegas. They were the new faces who brought Vegas out of the era of mob control, making Vegas the gaudiest, most popular entertainment capital of the world.

I

DON'T EVER CALL HIM BUGSY

Life for the mob in New York was getting too hot. Prosecutors were turning over rocks. Big-time mobsters did not want to be seen crawling out from under those rocks. Lucky Luciano would soon be sentenced to fifty years in prison for pimping and procuring. The killers of Murder Inc. were in the sights of prosecutors and would eventually be strapped onto the electric chair (aka Old Sparky) in Sing Sing prison. Smart criminal bosses were departing for safer climes or moving their operations to states and cities where crime was an integral local business.

Two who decided to depart were Benjamin (aka Bugsy) Siegel and Meyer Lansky. They had been the founders of the Bugs and Meyer Gang, which evolved into Murder Inc., in which hit men were each paid a monthly stipend plus bonuses for each hit. The Murder Inc. bosses, who remained stalwart boosters of the Big Apple, were Louis (Lepke) Buchalter (the only mob boss to be fried in Old Sparky) and Albert (the Mad Hatter) Anastasia, also known as the Lord High Executioner.

While those two thumbed their noses at prosecutors, Lansky departed for Florida, where he could easily corrupt local officials and operate his gambling casinos undisturbed. His compatriot Frank Costello (Prime Minister of the Underworld) moved his slot machines to Louisiana, where he paid Governor Huey Long $1 million to be free of legal hassles. Siegel, a glamour guy of the mob, chose Hollywood, California, where one of his boyhood pals, the actor George Raft, would welcome him and act as his gofer. There, no one would call him Bugsy. He hated the name not only because it referred to an insect and was derived from the saying, "Crazy as a bed bug," but also because it was the kind of name one associated with low-life big-city gangsters, such as Buggsy Goldstein, Bugs Moran, and Benny the Bug. As Dean Jennings wrote in *We Only Kill Each Other*, "Going to California would slam the cover on the dirty sewer from which he crawled."[1]

Siegel loved Hollywood, loved the sunshine, loved the glamour and the movie stars, some of whom became his good friends, including Cary Grant, Jean Harlow, and Clark Gable among various others. He declared himself to be a wealthy sportsman and had business cards printed with the name Benjamin Siegel, Esq. He would plant his flag in Beverly Hills and take over the Los Angeles rackets with the aid of local mobster and former boxer Mickey Cohen. So much for "Esq."

Still, he needed an appropriate address for a man with a newly polished identity. It was the mid-1930s, and he arranged to rent the mansion of opera singer Lawrence Tibbett, which was impressively situated at 326 McCarty Drive. He paid a higher rent than anyone else would have. It didn't matter to Siegel. He had money pouring in from his enterprises with Lansky and Costello and would soon be running a racing wire and controlling bookie joints and several Hollywood unions, through which he accepted large pay-offs from movie studios to ensure labor peace.

He not only hobnobbed with famous movie stars but also with an heiress, Countess Dorothy DiFrasso, who had not long before been jilted by Gary Cooper. Her father was a wealthy manufacturer of leather goods and a board member of the New York Stock Exchange. Dorothy had married an Italian count, who had been on the lookout for a rich American heiress. She wore the title of countess as if it were a bejeweled tiara that would never slip off her luxuriant mane of dark hair.

Siegel soon invested his own and some of Lansky's money in a dog track and some small-time gambling dens. From there, he invested in a gambling ship that catered to celebrities, politicians, and business owners. Though an astute gambler, he managed to involve himself in a cockamamie expedition to discover buried treasure believed by him and his cohorts to be worth $90 million. They had obtained maps leading to a cave on the island of Cocos, hundreds of miles off the coast of Costa Rica. It was little more than a boy's comic book adventure. The trip turned out to be a treasure-island fantasy that swallowed up thousands of dollars and paid no dividends. There was no hidden treasure. Siegel was better suited to unearth millions from gambling in Las Vegas.

As his social circle became more exclusive as a result of his affair with the countess and his association with A-list Hollywood stars, he decided that the Tibbett home, though stately and luxurious, was not up to the standards of an independently wealthy sportsman. He decided to build his own mansion on Delfern Avenue in the tony Holmby Hills section of Los Angeles. It would make the Tibbett home look like a guesthouse by comparison. He would now be in the neighborhood that included the homes of Bing Crosby, Humphrey Bogart, Alan Ladd, and Judy Garland, among other luminous stars of Tinseltown. In addition to all of the accoutrements of a grand mansion, Siegel had two secret getaway passages built just in case he had to make a sudden rapid escape from either the law or murderous competitive mobsters.

When he wasn't overseeing the development of his new home, he was at the gym, not only exercising, but developing his skills as a pugilist. Mickey Cohen, who had been a professional boxer, said Siegel wasn't bad, but he could have taken him down in a couple of rounds, perhaps even the first one. Nevertheless, his pals George Raft and Champ Segal (whose brother invented the Segal lock) refused his challenges to get into the ring with him. While he maintained a strong, lean, physically fit body and a sunlamp-produced tan, he worried about losing his hair. Every morning he would notice the evidence of his hair loss in a brush; he felt he was shedding like an Afghan Hound. Had he lived into old age, his vanity would have had him sporting a toupee, an often-failed tribute to one's hirsute youth. So concerned was he about maintaining a handsome, youthful appearance that every night he slept with a strip of elastic tied behind his ears that supported the flesh beneath his chin and jaw.

One day, while sitting under a sunlamp at the local YMCA, Siegel asked Champ to bring Mickey Cohen over for a talk. The Mick, as he was known, did not usually respond to what he considered a summons to meet someone, unless he was about to collect on a debt. "If he wants to meet me, he knows where I live," he told Champ. But Champ explained that it would be worthwhile for him to go; so armed with a pair of pistols and a fierce gaze under a broad-brimmed cowboy hat, Cohen went to meet Siegel. He took one look at the handsome gangster stretched out on a lounge chair, eyes covered with dark plastic lenses and his face turned up to the rays of a sunlamp. Siegel was wearing blue boxer shorts and matching blue socks. Appraising the notorious gangster, Cohen decided that Siegel was some kind of Eastern dude, a guy probably more interested in self-beautification than in dames. (Years later, he said that Siegel was almost pretty. His eyelashes were as long and feathery as those on the lids of the beautiful actresses Cohen regularly seduced.) Cohen jumped to the erroneous conclusion that Siegel's reputation as an impetuous tough gunman with the Bugs and Meyer Gang was all tabloid bullshit. Nevertheless, Siegel was winning over the skeptic, complimenting him on his reputation for toughness and his skills as a former boxer. He seemed to know a lot about Cohen, who was impressed by Siegel's knowledge. Siegel offered Cohen a lucrative deal. Now believing he had finally succeeded in recruiting Cohen as an important member of his evolving gang, Siegel offered him a broad smile. Siegel's blue eyes beamed with pleasure at Cohen, whose fiery contempt had been fully extinguished. As Siegel laid out his plans for taking over bookies and a competitive racing wire, Cohen became enthusiastic, for Siegel's operations would mean increased income. Cohen, like most gangsters, was a sucker for schemes that would increase his wealth. If it meant serving as Siegel's junior partner, what the hell, it was worth it. For the remainder of his life, Siegel could depend on Cohen to be his muscle, ready to do battle with whoever threatened him or rebuked his demands.

Cohen's first job in Siegel's employ was to help his boss take over the local racing wire. Bookies relied on the racing wire for odds, results, and payoffs. They could no more operate without the racing wire than restaurants can operate without food delivery services. A racing wire, at that time, charged bookies anywhere from $200 to $1,200 a week. And with thousands of customers, the take was substantial. Siegel set up his own racing wire, the Trans-America Wire Service, and took in Jack Dragna (local Mafia boss) as his partner. He also brought along Moe Sedway, an early member of the Bugs and Meyer Gang in New York. Sedway had the mind and appearance of a bookkeeper and kept meticulous records. There was one problem, however, that prevented Siegel from scooping up all the bookies on the West Coast: a competitor, Continental Wire Service. Its manager was a brash tough guy named Russell Brophy, who believed that his payoffs to judges, cops, and prosecutors guaranteed him not only legal immunity but also provided him with the ability to operate as a monopoly, much like a local utility company. Siegel tried to buy Brophy's cooperation, even offering him a minority partnership in Trans-America. Nothing doing. Brophy believed himself invulnerable and wanted all profits for himself. He paid a lot of money for protection. And what Siegel offered was a small slice of a big pie that was already Brophy's. He told Siegel to take a hike. Back in New York, such a response would have gotten Brophy shot, but Siegel did not want to tarnish his reputation as a sportsman and friend of the stars.

Brophy would require an additional incentive to the one Siegel had offered. Siegel called on Mickey Cohen and another local tough guy named Joe Sica to pay a sales call on Brophy. The two men strode into the Continental wire room and began tearing out all the wires. Hearing the commotion from clerks, Brophy rushed out of his office and confronted Cohen and Sica, yelling at them to leave. He was about to call the cops when Cohen used the handgrip of his .38 caliber pistol to beat Brophy into submission. Again and again, the gun came down on Brophy's bloody head. As he slumped to the floor, Cohen and Sica continued beating him, kicking him in the gut and groin. Brophy's career was over. His wire service was swallowed into the maw of Trans-America. Though Cohen and Sica were arrested, their penalties amounted to nominal fines.

While Siegel preferred to polish his reputation as a sportsman among his Hollywood pals, he couldn't resist the temptation to be part of a major hit. It would be like the old days with Murder Inc. in Brooklyn. Frank Costello, Albert Anastasia, and Lepke Buchalter wanted to silence Harry "Big Greenie" Greenberg, a rat who was prepared to testify against them, which could result in the New York trio ending their lives in the electric chair. Siegel agreed to oversee the execution of Greenberg. It was an undertaking that called upon Siegel's well-honed skills. He didn't even mention the contract to Cohen, whom he considered a publicity hound who might drop hints about the hit. (Siegel was sagacious, for by the 1950s Cohen was often a guest on television talk shows, where his bluster and braggadocio knew no bounds.) Big Greenie had to be eliminated quietly and smoothly. The men Big Greenie had agreed to testify against were not only Buchalter, Anastasia, and Costello, but also the hitters of Murder Inc., who—if indicted— might try to cut deals for leniency with the prosecutor. The board of the National Crime Syndicate agreed with Siegel that out-of-town hit men should do the job, so Allie "Tick Tock" Tannenbaum and Frankie Carbo (the man who would assassinate Siegel in the home of Virginia Hill and who would corrupt professional boxing) were given the contract. Greenberg was temporarily residing in a boardinghouse located at 1804 Vista Del Mar in Hollywood. That was Siegel territory, and he knew the area as well as a tour guide. He gave detailed directions to Tannenbaum and Carbo about how the hit should be executed; Siegel would supply a stolen car for the hit men, a getaway car, and a crash car to block police, who might respond to shots fired. On the night of November 22, 1939, Greenberg emerged from his Ford convertible in front of the boardinghouse. Tannenbaum was waiting in the shadows and opened fire with two pistols, a .38 and a .45, hitting his target multiple times: toppling over, Greenberg was dead before he hit the pavement. Tannenbaum rushed into the stolen getaway car, which sped away to another stolen car. Tannenbaum quickly exited the first car and dashed into the second one. At the wheel of the car was Champ Segal, who drove Tannenbaum to San Francisco, where he boarded a plane to Philadelphia. Carbo, the backup shooter, boarded a plane in Burbank and flew home. Siegel returned to his life as a popular local sportsman, saying nothing about news stories of Big Greenie Greenberg's execution.

The threat to the bosses back East, though reduced, was not eliminated. Waiting in the wings to offer his testimony was Abe "Kid Twist" Reles, a vicious Murder Inc. killer who killed each of his many victims with an ice pick to the brain. Though he usually killed only when ordered to do so, his violence could be easily provoked. One day, a valet in a parking garage did not bring his car as quickly as Reles had wanted it, so he killed the valet. Other times, he was capable of biding his time like a tiger waiting to leap onto the neck of an unsuspecting victim: Reles invited an associate to his mother's house for dinner. It was a convivial meal, both men seeming to relax as they enjoyed the delicious dinner that Mrs. Reles had prepared. Following the dinner, Mrs. Reles retired to her bedroom. Reles joked with his guest and smoked a cigar. At the point when he believed his mother had fallen asleep, he leapt from his chair, grabbed his guest around the neck with a powerfully muscular arm, then with his free hand drove an ice pick into the man's brain. It was quick and efficient. Reles disposed of the body hours before his mother could have discovered it.

Though he killed dozens of people, Reles knew his own life could be as easily extinguished as those of his victims. If the prosecutor was going to save Reles long enough to have him testify against the bosses of Murder Inc., he would have to set up round-the-clock protection. And not in some jail cell where another inmate could knife the protected witness. Instead, he was being held in room 623 at the Half Moon Hotel in Coney Island, where he was guarded by five cops and periodically coached on his forthcoming testimony. His court date was November 12, 1941. On that day, instead of taking the witness stand, Reles was flung out the window of his hotel room by the cops who had been charged with guarding him. The defenestrated Reles landed on the roof of a second-floor outbuilding. For years afterward, he was known as the canary who could sing but couldn't fly. According to an attorney for Frank Costello, the cops who pitched Reles to his death equally split a $100,000 payoff. They uncomplainingly accepted their subsequent demotion but complained about the ridicule they received in newspapers throughout the city. Siegel never publicly commented on the death of Reles, but he serenely benefitted from his demise as he had from Greenberg's. The press speculated on the mob's involvement in the death of Kid Twist and Big Greenie, the names used by headline writers. Their speculations were soon replaced by a more immediate development: Tick Tock Tannenbaum made a deal for leniency and agreed to testify against Lepke for the death of Joe Rosen. Lepke was found guilty of murder and sentenced to death in the electric chair at Sing Sing. He remains the only mob boss executed in the twentieth century.

While Siegel continued to mix with the cream of Los Angeles society, he found the true love of his life, Virginia Hill, a beautiful, uneducated young woman from the Deep South who could have been cast in a Hollywood movie about hillbillies. Though not formally educated, she was wise in the ways of the mob, having been a bag woman and mistress for various mobsters, including Joe Adonis and Joe Epstein. She spoke the lingo of the mobsters she bedded and exhibited the cool adaptive wits of a scam artist. Her sexual energy was enticing and provocative. Its appeal for Siegel was instantaneous and irresistible. He found her unlike any mistress, high or low, that he had enjoyed. She was a world apart from Siegel's middle-class wife, Esta, the mother of his two daughters, Millicent and Barbara.

Hill was born in 1916 in Lipscomb, Alabama. She was number seven of a nine-sibling barefoot brood of children, who frolicked around their property like a pack of wild uninhibited dogs. They regularly got into trouble with neighbors but remained undisciplined by their parents, who seemed to believe that children needed no guidance and could be left to educate and entertain themselves. When she was eight years old, Virginia's parents separated. She, her siblings, and her mother moved to Marietta, Georgia. There, she attended school, but not for long. She dropped out after completing the eighth grade. Her real education was about to begin. In 1933, she shook off the dust of Marietta and prostituted herself to pay for a trip to Chicago, where she intended to break into show business or pornography. The sex trade proved more attainable to her ambitions than the dance hall. And waitressing proved a good way to meet johns; it was while working at a mob-run restaurant at the Chicago World's Fair that she attracted the attention of Joe Epstein, a bookmaker for the Chicago Outfit. Though some thought Epstein was gay, he and Hill became lovers. His love for her never dimmed; in fact, it turned into an obsession, and he remained ardent, even playing the cuckold as Hill took on one lover after another, including Joe Adonis, Gene Krupa, and Charles Fischetti, a member of the Capone mob. One night while attending a party as Fischetti's guest, Hill, after a few drinks, got down on her knees and fellated Fischetti in front of speechless guests that included Fischetti's wife. After the performance reached its expected conclusion, partygoers continued to chat and drink as if nothing unusual had happened. (Though she became a trusted bag woman for the

Fischetti brothers, they also used Frank Sinatra as a bag man to deliver $1 million in an attaché case to Lucky Luciano.)

Epstein never objected to Hill's affair with Fischetti. Indeed, nothing seemed to extinguish or even cool the relationship between Epstein and Hill. He would continue to support her for the rest of her life, sending her thick envelopes of cash whenever she said she was in need of money.

From Chicago, Hill moved on to New York City, where she began an affair with Joe Adonis. However, that didn't stop Siegel, who was in New York to discuss business with Lansky and Luciano, from spending a night at the Waldorf Astoria Hotel with Hill. The two would meet again in Los Angeles. But regardless of where she was, Hill was always Epstein's go-to bag woman, placing bets for the mob for fixed races and for fixed boxing bouts. Though the money had originated from various illegal enterprises, it could be declared winnings from sporting events and reported as legitimate income to the IRS. She would either hand-deliver the winnings or send it by courier to Epstein, who never failed to give her a 10 percent commission. Rather than just being a woman who profited from doing errands for mobsters, Hill was like a mobster herself, one of the few women to ever attain that status. In Chicago, New York, Miami, and Los Angeles, she was the mob's trusted bag woman, tough and reliable and always fun.

Siegel had not forgotten about his night at the Waldorf with the beautiful redhead and wanted to spend more time with her. And once in Los Angeles, Hill wanted to test-drive the handsome, dashing gangster who had given her a night of intense sexual pleasure. She claimed that it had been the best sex she ever had. Would Siegel be able to do it again, or was he just a onetime shot in the dark. At their first meeting in Los Angeles, the sparks flew. The sex, she said, was better than expected. They could not stay away from each other, but they also fought like wild animals. For them, sex and violence were concomitant.

Though Hill was a sexual magnet drawing Siegel to her, Las Vegas was another kind of magnet, one that compelled Siegel's greed. For a poor boy from the slums of New York, owning a Las Vegas casino was a greedy wet dream.

It began in Lansky's brilliant and opportunistic mind. He saw Las Vegas as the future of America's gambling playland. He explained it all to Siegel, who was soon on board. A situation arose that they would quickly take advantage of. Billy Wilkerson, owner of several celebrated Hollywood restaurants as well as the owner and publisher of the *Hollywood Reporter*, was building a casino/hotel in Vegas. He called it the Flamingo, but the project stalled because Wilkerson, a compulsive gambler in debt to the mob, had run out of money. It has erroneously been mythologized that the Flamingo Hotel and Casino was named for Virginia Hill; instead, it seems as if Siegel regarded Hill as a physical personification of all that the Flamingo represented for him: brashness, glamour, sexiness.

In December 1945, Siegel resumed construction of the Flamingo. That same month, his wife filed for divorce in Reno. Siegel agreed to pay her $600 a week for the rest of her life. It was a bad investment on her part, for Siegel would be dead in less than two years, and his estate had no obligation to continue the payments. The unfortunate Esta had also given her husband an unsecured loan of $45,000 to help finance the building of the Flamingo. Siegel's successors saw no reason to repay the loan.

Free from his marriage, Siegel found time to take Hill to Mexico for a quickie wedding ceremony. According to Dean Jennings,

> Siegel had bought a ruby and diamond ring, and he slipped it on her finger, and when the Spanish ceremony was over they left as man and wife. Siegel never mentioned this brief and hasty wedding and five years passed before Virginia even identified the ring she had. Then she showed it to a newspaperman, saying only: "Ben gave me this. It was to be our wedding ring."[2]

As Siegel wanted Hill for himself and no one else, so he wanted the Flamingo for himself. He intended to rid himself of Wilkerson, whom he not only disliked as a possible competitor, but also for his anti-Semitism and vicious red baiting. (In 1946, Wilkerson began writing a column, *Billy's List*, for the *Hollywood Reporter* that baited possible communists in the movie industry and published names of suspected communists and their sympathizers. His efforts led to the infamous Hollywood blacklist.)

The forced exit of Wilkerson from the Flamingo began on June 20, 1946, when Siegel formed the Nevada Project Corporation (NPC) with himself as president and major stockholder. Siegel issued stock to Wilkerson and then forced him at the point of a gun to sell back those shares. Once that transaction was completed, Siegel informed Wilkerson he was not only to leave Vegas, but also the United States. Not wishing to dawdle when his life was at stake, Wilkerson sailed for France, where he stayed for several months. With Wilkerson gone, the remaining shareholders were the board members of another company, the National Crime Syndicate (NCS). Of the NPC, Siegel owned 195 shares, Lansky got 100 shares, Frank Costello got 22.5 shares, and Luciano got shares issued to a holding company. Altogether, 1,075 shares were issued. Though Hill wanted some shares for herself, there is no record of her owning any. The total value of the shares was $1 million.

In addition, Siegel was able to borrow more than $1 million from two southwest banks for the ongoing construction of the Flamingo; yet, more money was needed and supplied by Lansky and associates.

As a savvy opportunist, Siegel had an ownership position not only in the Flamingo but also in the Northern Club, the Frontier Turf Club, the Las Vegas Club, the El Cortez Hotel, and the El Dorado Club. To front for him, he brought in Moe Sedway and Gus Greenbaum, a no-nonsense tough bookie from Phoenix, Arizona (whose good friend Senator Barry Goldwater would attend his funeral). In addition, he brought in his brother-in-law Sollie Soloway and hit man Dave Berman (whose daughter, Susan, would years later allegedly be killed by real estate heir Robert Durst).

During that time, Siegel was able to eliminate the Continental racing wire, the only national competition for his own racing wire. Its owner, James Ragan, received an offer from Jacob "Greasy Thumb" Guzik and Al Capone to buy him out for $100,000 and give him a small share of future profits. Ragan declined the offer, and several weeks later his body was sprayed with numerous shotgun shells. He spent six weeks in the hospital, and doctors assured him that he would survive. That was not good news for the Chicago Outfit, so a friend of the recovering patient was deputized to take him daily doses of mercury. The poison was given along with intravenous medication and nourishment. Ragan succumbed to the mercury poison, and Siegel's racing wire picked up all of Continental's bookie clients.

Though crafty and rapacious, Siegel was no businessman. He was not a real estate developer. He had neither the skills nor the experience to build a hotel/casino cost-effectively. On whims and daydreams, he altered architectural plans, incurring huge excess costs that angered his mob backers. He could not get additional bank loans to cover his costs, and the mob only reluctantly advanced him additional funds. Complaining to Meyer Lansky, Siegel said that Sicilians would rather eat their children than part with a dollar.

In addition, the contractors took advantage of Siegel's ignorance. In numerous cases, they double-billed him and/or charged him inordinately high prices. But Siegel was on a tear, a man with a mission to create the Taj Mahal of gambling, not as a mausoleum, but as a temple to lady luck. By the time of its grand opening on December 26, 1946, the unfinished Flamingo had cost $6 million. The opening was a flop. The mob was furious, and the banks were demanding their money. Before Siegel reopened the Flamingo in 1947, the casino had paid out $300,000 to lucky (and crooked) gamblers. Gus Greenbaum, one of Siegel's trusted lieutenants, took the house for tens of thousands of dollars. He had brought in several other sophisticated cheaters who robbed the house. Only Siegel's devoted pal, the actor George Raft, dropped a large sum of money at one of the card tables; he reportedly lost $67,000. The odds favor the house, declared the mob. There's no way the loss could have happened, unless Siegel was siphoning off money for a private offshore account, they complained. The mob is all about money and will go to extraordinary lengths to make sure that money always flows in, never out. Siegel seemed to have forgotten that basic rule of mob-run businesses.

Though Siegel was warned not to spend money the Flamingo didn't have, he spent oodles of it on advertising and publicity. He became such an honored customer that *Las Vegas Life* instructed its reporters and advertisers never to refer to Siegel as Bugsy. It was always to be either Benjamin Siegel or Mr. Siegel. He figured that the advertising would more than pay for itself by increasing the number of customers who would flock to the Flamingo. He worked desperately to salvage his situation. He figured he could restore the mob's money; get them even more money and then enjoy the benefits of being a casino baron.

Other than money, he found solace in another kind of pleasure: he had four beauties stashed away in different suites of the Flamingo. There was, of course, Virginia Hill, who despised Siegel's other mistresses. He tried to keep actress Wendy Barrie, singer and actress Marie MacDonald, and the Countess Dorothy DiFrasso away from one another. One night, however, Hill spotted Barrie in the casino, strode over to her, and without warning delivered a powerful clenched fist to Barrie's chin, nearly fracturing her jaw. Hill had heard a rumor that Barrie was Siegel's secret wife and that she bore his child, a girl name Caroline. Marie MacDonald did not have any run-ins with Hill. She remained coolly discreet. Siegel first heard of the leggy beauty when she gained fame as the beauty Queen of Coney Island. Sexy and alluring, she became known as "The Body" and was a favorite pinup for World War II soldiers. Siegel had offered to manage her singing and acting career, but she never consented. Their affair was short lived, a mere interlude in 1947 between two of her seven marriages. There had been one thing about MacDonald that Siegel could not tolerate: she was never on time. He was not the kind of guy to be kept waiting by a woman, no matter how gorgeous and sexy. Eleven years after her affair with Siegel, MacDonald had a three-month relationship with George Capri, one of the numerous later owners of the Flamingo.

But it was the Countess DiFrasso who was perhaps the most exotic of Siegel's mistresses. She was a multimillionaire, an heiress of Bertrand

Taylor, a manufacturer of leather goods. She married a poor Italian count named Count Carlo DiFrasso; he enjoyed her fortune, and she loved being a titled woman. She bought them a palace in Italy known as the Villa Madama and took Siegel for a vacation there. Following his return to the States, he told Mickey Cohen, "This joint was bigger than Grand Central Station (*sic*), and half the guys she had hanging around her were counts or dukes or kings out of a job."[3]

While a guest there, he briefly encountered two other guests, both of whom he told the countess he would kill. She warned him not to, because—if he did—her husband would be blamed, their lands confiscated, and they would probably spend years in jail, if not executed. The men Siegel wanted to kill were Hermann Goering and Joseph Goebbels. He referred to the former as an overstuffed couch and the other as a crippled runt. Had he killed them, one can only wonder about the course of World War II.

Though Siegel found fornicating solace with his various mistresses, the mob received neither solace nor money from the playboy gangster. A contract had been issued by Luciano and reluctantly approved by Lansky. Years earlier in New York, Lansky had said to Siegel, "This is the life we have chosen. It has consequences, good and bad."[4] Though an outlaw, Lansky lived by the rules of the mob, which may explain why he did not die as the recipient of a hit man's bullets. Siegel heard the rumors that there was a contract on his life, and so he went around with a pair of heavily armed bodyguards. When the Flamingo builder Del Webb asked about the rumor, Siegel told him that he had already killed sixteen people and if anyone tried to get him that person would be number seventeen. Somewhat nervously Webb asked Siegel if his own life was in danger. Not from me, said Siegel. "In the mob, we only kill each other."[5]

Seemingly unconcerned about his fate, Siegel continued to bet big on fixed races at Santa Anita and on fixed boxing matches. He would bet small amounts on events that weren't fixed, but when it came to cleaning up big, he placed bets only on preordained outcomes. All he needed were two or three fixed events a month to rake in large sums of money. In addition to Siegel putting down big bets, Hill was betting mob money. Joe Epstein would send her the money and tell her what to place bets on. For her efforts, Hill received her standard 10 percent commission. However, a new worry popped up: she was being investigated by the IRS and the FBI, both of which had uncovered information about her cash transactions on behalf of Epstein. Siegel warned her that any investigation of her could touch him, and she better be more cautious and discreet than she had been. Hill agreed but didn't alter her modus operandi, and Epstein continued to send her envelopes thick with $50 and $100 bills. Though rolling in cash, Hill would have problems other than those caused by the IRS.

Unknown to her, the death sentence on Siegel was a fait accompli; only the trigger remained to be pulled. On the night of June 20, 1947, as Siegel sat on a plush floral couch in Hill's Beverly Hills home, he chatted desultorily with Allen Smiley while dipping into stories in the *Los Angeles Times*. A man camouflaged in darkness crept up as silently as an Apache scout to a living room window. He cautiously placed the barrel of a .30-caliber military M1 carbine on the window ledge. A sudden barrage of bullets shattered the glass window and tore into Siegel. One of Siegel's eyes flew out of its socket and landed across the room on a carpet. The bridge of his nose was shattered. There were bloody holes in his cranium. His once-handsome face sagged onto the back of the couch.

Ralph Natale, onetime crime boss of Philadelphia, confirmed what the mob had long suspected: the shooter had been Frankie Carbo, Siegel's former partner in Murder Inc. and accessory in the murder of Big Greenie Greenberg. Lansky and Luciano had personally chosen Carbo, because in the mob, one is invariably killed by one's friends.

Though Siegel slept the infinite sleep of the great silent majority, his dream of Las Vegas as the capital of legal gambling would soon become a reality, whose profits would support mob heirs and political candidates throughout the nation. And what of the mob's investment in the Flamingo? Out of the count room, they made many millions of untaxed dollars.

Siegel's end meant Hill would no longer benefit from his protection. Her future became increasingly perilous. First, she learned that Moe Sedway, Gus Greenbaum, and former New York burglar Morris Rosen had taken over management of the Flamingo. They would make sure that only the mob skimmed profits and had exclusive access to the count room. No longer would an innocent child such as Siegel's daughter, Millicent, be permitted to wander into the count room. The Siegels were history.

And if you had a plan to cheat the casino, you better enact your plan someplace else. Cheaters were lucky if they weren't taken into a basement, killed, and their bodies buried in the desert. Dealers were also warned: when catching dealers who had attempted to cheat the casino, Greenbaum would take them into a back room and shatter the bones of their hands with a baseball bat. For good measure, he would also break their collarbones so they couldn't lift their arms. Word quickly got around. Nobody cheated the Flamingo.

However, there was a pair of punks who thought they could heist the casino and get away with their loot. Tony Trombino and Tony Broncato (aka the two Tonys) held up the sportsbook and took off to Los Angeles. Not long afterward, they were lured into a sleek black Cadillac limo in Hollywood. Their bodies were discovered days later; each had four bullet holes in his head.

The mob loved Greenbaum. He was the most successful manager on the Strip. And after his highly profitable management of the Flamingo, he decided to retire to his home in Phoenix, but the mob wanted him back. He was golden. Tony Accardo, of the Chicago Outfit, implored Greenbaum to return. Greenbaum refused. Accardo insisted. Greenbaum continued to refuse. Accardo told him he was very unhappy. The point was emphasized after Greenbaum's sister-in-law was murdered. Greenbaum got the message and returned to Vegas, this time to run the Riviera. However, he had become addicted to heroin and was gambling compulsively. Both habits took over his life. To support his addictions, he began skimming from the casino. He needed a break. He was a nervous wreck, frequently angry, lashing out at employees, ignoring the needs of customers. He decided to go home and celebrate Thanksgiving with his wife, Bess, in Phoenix. He never returned. While asleep in bed, his throat was sliced down to his vertebra. Police figured it had been done in one swift whack by a machete. Beside him lay his wife, whose head had been hammered and her throat slit. The Greenbaum funeral was attended by three hundred mourners, including Gus's good friend Senator Barry Goldwater. The Moe Sedway–Gus Greenbaum partnership, though dead in Vegas, lived on when their names were combined in *The Godfather* for the character named Moe Greene.

There were other loose ends that the mob had to tie up. Sedway informed Hill that Lansky wanted whatever money she had embezzled during the construction of the Flamingo. If she didn't give up the cash, she would wind up like her lover. As if that were not sufficiently nerve wracking, the IRS told Hill that they were investigating her for tax evasion. In 1951, she was subpoenaed to testify before the Kefauver Committee investigating organized crime. She sounded like a street-smart gun moll out of a 1930s gangster movie. She clammed up when asked about mob activities and expressed ignorance about money laundering. Finally fed up by the badgering questions of the Senate committee, Hill's wiseguy persona burst forth. The ears of puritans were about to be assaulted. Here is the exchange that drew gasps and disbelieving grunts from senators and a sanitized version in newspapers and magazines:

Senator Tobey: "But why would Joe Epstein give you all that money, Miss Hill?"

Virginia Hill: "You really want to know?"

Senator Tobey: "Yes, I really want to know."

Virginia Hill: "Then I'll tell you why. Because I'm the best cocksucker in town!"

Senator Kefauver, banging his gavel, shouted: "Order! I demand order!"[6]

Outside the hearing room, Hill punched a female reporter whose questions she found impolite. Her ordeal was not over. In 1954, she was indicted for income tax evasion, the government's usual charge aimed at members of organized crime. The government sold most of her possessions and froze whatever bank accounts it could locate. Hill didn't hang around long. She and her ski instructor husband, Hans Hauser, departed for Europe with their son, Peter. On March 24, 1966, after several failed suicide attempts, Hill swallowed a handful of sleeping pills and died. She was forty-nine years old. She was buried in Aigen Cemetery in Salzburg, Austria, far from Siegel, who is interred in the Hollywood Forever Cemetery in Hollywood, California. The two had sworn to each other that they would lie together through eternity.

Siegel may have a better shot at immortality in the Vegas he envisioned than in the flickering reality of Hollywood, where stars flame out like meteors. Outside the wedding chapel on the grounds of the Flamingo is a memorial garden with a plaque honoring Siegel. It is regularly visited by gamblers who honor Siegel as a Vegas visionary.

NOTES

1. Dean Jennings, *We Only Kill Each Other* (New York: Fawcett World Library, 1968), 39.

2. Jennings, *We Only Kill Each Other*, 156.

3. Jennings, *We Only Kill Each Other*, 41.

4. This is said by Hyman Roth, a character based on Meyer Lansky, in the movie *Godfather II*.

5. Steven Otfinoski, *Bugsy Siegel and the Postwar Boom* (Farmington Hills, MI: Blackbirch Press, 2000), 32.

6. https://noirsville.blogspot.com/2019/06/npirsville-bonus-virginia-hill-femme .html, https://www.tumblr.com/tagged/virginia-hill?sort=top (accessed December 21, 2020).

2

MOE SEDWAY AND GUS GREENBAUM

Before Bugsy Siegel's body could be shipped to the county morgue, Moe Sedway and Gus Greenbaum arrived at the Flamingo as if shot out of a cannon. They announced to the managers that "Siegel is dead, and we are the new owners."[1] They said it with such firm authority that no one objected. Not one person so much as asked a single question. They all attended to their responsibilities as if nothing had changed.

Sedway and Greenbaum were treated by the mob as if they were a pair of wizards who could transmute lead into gold. They set to work, not turning lead to gold, but red ink to black. In their first week as managers, they began producing profits as quickly as bettors put down their foregone cash. No longer would the casino be a palace for just the rich and well-dressed, a Monte Carlo in the desert for high society; instead, it was open to anyone with cash and a yen to bet. Cowboys in shit-kicker boots and dirt under their fingernails found a new home for their money. Games of chance, which gave them little chance of winning, voraciously consumed their cash. When they weren't betting, they were paying prostitutes who operated as if they had taxi meters on their thighs.

For the mob, money is all that counts, and count it they did as they skimmed pre-tax profits from the count room and used call girls, such as Virginia Hill, to launder the money and ferry it back to her mentor Joe Epstein in Chicago, who invested it in offshore banks. Sedway and Greenbaum were heroes to the boys in New York and Chicago. They referred to their two operatives as MoeandGus, a single word that Mario Puzo altered to Moe Green, the character killed by the Corleones for not selling them his casino. Within months, Moe and Gus had turned a white elephant into a golden goose, posting a profit of $4 million. As long as the river of cash flowed, no one was going to kill the wizards of profitability.

So impressed were mobsters, not only in New York and Chicago with the success of the Flamingo, but also in Cleveland and Kansas City, that they also invested in the Flamingo and any other casinos that Moe and Gus would manage. Even banks that had turned down Siegel's requests for second or third loans were suddenly eager to part with their money. As Robert Lacey reports in his biography of Meyer Lansky: "With Benny dead, Greenbaum and Sedway were able to go back to the Valley National Bank in Phoenix and get a loan of $1.4 million—half a million dollars more, in one shot, than the hotel had managed to collect when Benny was in charge. The bank evidently considered that the Flamingo was now a good risk."[2]

Who were these two astute casino operators?

Moe Sedway (né Morris Sidwirtz) was born in 1894 in Poland. His family moved to the United States in 1901 and settled on the Lower East Side of Manhattan. As a teenager, Sedway found his path in life after joining the Bugs and Meyer Gang, where he committed thefts and helped his pals with their protection and extortion rackets, which targeted a number of small, local businesses:

- Newsstands run by men with little capital were easily intimidated by the gang, whose members would demand protection money to prevent arson from obliterating their stands. If a payoff was not forthcoming, an owner's stand would be set on fire. Since most of the owners of newsstands did not have fire insurance, those who didn't pay protection were put out of business. Other newsstand operators who witnessed what happened to their brethren quickly paid for protection.
- Peddlers who hawked their wares from horse-drawn wagons often had their nags stolen if they didn't pay off the gang. The stolen horses were tied to trees in distant parks and not returned until the peddlers agreed to weekly payoffs. If a peddler could not or would not make the required payments, his horse was sold to another peddler. Occasionally horses, old and hobbled, were sold to slaughterhouses. For the gang, the outcome was always profitable.
- Owners of such small stores as lingerie stores, candy stores, hardware stores, and diners were more profitable targets than peddlers and newsstand operators. When they refused to meet the demands of

the gang, they had their merchandise stolen or ruined in the dead of night; if the merchants were steadfastly recalcitrant, their stores were firebombed. Many such victims were left bereft of their livelihoods; as with the owners of newsstands, many did not carry fire or theft insurance.

For Sedway, his participation in the gang filled his pockets with plenty of cash, enough to make him feel superior to the poor guys who worked for what he called "slave wages." Though making more money than anyone else in his family, Sedway nevertheless suffered the embarrassing indignity of being arrested numerous times, serving his first prison sentence in the early 1920s. Following his multiple releases, he was anything but reformed. As a newly minted associate of Lucky Luciano, he ventured into more sophisticated rackets. His life as a criminal was set; yet in his later years, he would emerge as a major philanthropist for Jewish charities. As with many men who had led less than honorable lives, he had attempted to whitewash his past through philanthropy, accepting numerous awards for his good works. Had his immigrant family been told that Moe would be an honored member of his Las Vegas community, they would have been stunned.

The transit from the Lower East Side via Chicago to Las Vegas was the great journey of Sedway's life. His boyhood pal Meyer Lansky had invested in the development of Vegas as a gambling playground for those eager to part with their money on games with little chance of winning. Sedway was sent to the burgeoning gambling mecca and invested mob money in various land deals and casinos. By 1945, he and Gus Greenbaum were not only put in charge of running the El Cortez Hotel/Casino, but they were also made shareholders in the enterprise. In addition, Sedway's responsibilities extended to acting as Bugsy Siegel's representative in dealing with the customers of the Trans-America Wire Service. Sedway was regarded as Siegel's Vegas lieutenant, a loyal employee carrying out whatever his boss demanded. And as in many similar relationships, the boss had a low opinion of his second-in-charge. In fact, on several occasions, Siegel considered killing Sedway, who was lucky to escape Siegel's murderous wrath with a non-homicidal tongue-lashing.

Presenting an image of an upper-middle-class businessman in his customary blue conservative suit, Moe was often accompanied by his young wife, Bea, a former vaudeville dancer and singer. He had first seen her perform in 1935 at the Paradise Cabaret in Manhattan. They had a son, but rumors swirled like a Nevada dust storm that the boy was not Moe's son. Gossipers speculated that a man named Matthew "Moose" Pandza was the father. And Bea did not dissuade friends from learning that she and the Moose were lovers. She prided herself on being a minor femme fatale, dangling two men on the prongs of her ego. In the 1980s and 1990s, she was often interviewed about the relationship between Moe and Siegel. Though she lovingly talked about Benny's seductive bedroom blue eyes, she was never his lover, though she would have jumped at the opportunity. Siegel did not think of her as a glamour girl, certainly not in class with the many Hollywood stars and starlets that he had seduced. He even poked fun at the hairline space between Bea's two front teeth. Yet, her adoration of the handsome gangster was evidenced when she noted that such a commanding celebrity as Frank Sinatra would stand up when Siegel entered Chasen's restaurant in Hollywood. Benny was the man they all wanted to be, she said. By the 1990s, Bea was considered such an authority on the life, loves, and businesses of Siegel that she was hired as a consultant for the movie *Bugsy*, starring Warren Beatty and Annette Bening. In addition to being a consultant, she operated an exclusive women's shop, Beatrice Sedway Originals, on North Beverly Drive in Beverly Hills, where she sold handmade handbags and a variety of other expensive fashion accessories and gifts.

Though Bea's reputation was free of any mob taint, her husband was not so fortunate. His reputation as a mobster had reached investigators in Washington, D.C., who called him to testify to the Kefauver Committee about organized crime in Vegas. Sedway had hoped that his many good works would stand him in good stead with the committee members. It was noted that he served on the board of directors of the Clark County Library, was a Clark County alderman, and headed the United Jewish Appeal of Las Vegas. The committee members were not fooled by the veneer that Sedway had used as camouflage for his criminality.

On November 15, 1950, his life as a mobster would be examined by the committee. In addition to being a man of good works, he attempted to make himself sympathetic by letting the committee members know that he had suffered three coronary thromboses and was currently suffering from an ulcer, an intestinal abscess, six months of diarrhea, and hemorrhoids. It's amazing that the committee did not call for a nurse. Sad eyed, fidgety as a jumping bean, abjectly accepting the grilling of his tormentors, Moe went on to claim he had not made much money from the casinos, had no associations with organized criminals, and was just a Vegas businessman and real estate developer. In addition, he offered the preposterous opinion that none of the mob-run casinos were involved in illegal activities. Skimming? What skimming? He further claimed that if he had his life to live over, he would get a good education and perhaps become a US senator. When told by Senator Tobey that gangster gamblers were the scum of the earth, Moe said that being a gambler was not as much fun as people often assumed and that the stress of running a casino had gotten him three heart attacks. It was an earnest performance by an unconvincing actor. He was so tense and nervous during his interrogation that an FBI agent noted that Moe "wrings his hands, becomes wild eyed and resembles a small dog about to be subjected to the distasteful procedure of being bathed."[3] Following up on the testimony of Sedway and others, Hank Greenspun, the editor of the *Las Vegas Sun*, opined that a young boy could have decided that crime and politics in Nevada went hand in glove.

When it was all over, the sad little Moe looked as sick as he claimed to be. He died in 1952. Long after the deaths of Sedway and Greenbaum were given immortality of sorts in *The Godfather*, in which their names were conjoined to form Moe Greene, a character based not on them, but on Bugsy Siegel, who would have been appalled that he was put in the same class as his two Flamingo successors. Even worse, Siegel would be spinning in his grave if he knew that he and Moe are buried not far from each other in the Hollywood Forever Cemetery.

Though Moe Sedway was not bold and loud, in fact was even cautious, his partner Gus Greenbaum came on like a Sherman tank bursting through enemy lines. He was a big man, full of bluster and high self-regard. He had shown his toughness and resourcefulness as a young man on the Lower East Side of Manhattan, where he became an associate of Meyer Lansky. After honing his criminal skills with the Bugs and Meyer Gang, he moved to Chicago, where he went to work for Al Capone's Outfit. Capone and others were soon impressed by Greenbaum's take-no-prisoner toughness and bottom-line financial wizardry: he proved exceptionally adept at squeezing money out of mob-backed operations as easily as one might squeeze water out of a sponge. He was just the kind of big earner that the mob loved. They figured he could do in Phoenix what he had done in Chicago, so with Meyer Lansky's concurrence, the Outfit sent Greenbaum west to add to their coffers. There, he managed the mob's racing wire and bullied its subscribers. He made sure that all the bookie joints paid top dollar for their subscriptions to the racing wire or they would be cut off from the up-to-the-minute horse racing results. Though tough and greedy, Greenbaum was not just a mobster on the make; he could also be a charming diplomat who valued the friendships of influential politicians as well as members of the judiciary and police departments. It was not surprising that he developed a long-term friendship with Senator Barry Goldwater.

Greenbaum loved Phoenix; it was a city that offered no resistance to an influx of mobsters. He was only thirty-four years old when he arrived, and he wanted to make the city his home and the seat of his operations. Though it had only forty-eight thousand residents at the time, it was much more attractive than the Windy City with its stinking slaughterhouses and brutal winter weather and stifling summer heat. Phoenix seemed to have extended a welcoming hand to Greenbaum. It was a wide-open city: Gambling went on night and day, seven days a week. Prostitutes, loan sharks, and book-makers did a thriving business. Everyone seemed on the make, everyone seemed on the take. City commissioners and detectives lived on bribes, under-the-table commissions from their criminal cohorts, and a plethora mob-generated freebies. So profitable and corrupt was the police depart-ment that young men paid to join it. Mobsters and their associates arrived weekly on the Santa Fe and Southern Pacific Railroads. To welcome the mob as possible business associates, there were entrepreneurs eager to par-take of the profits from mob-run enterprises. And there were the politicians who not only greased the skids for the mob but also benefitted handsomely from generous campaign contributions.

In this milieu of corruption Greenbaum thrived. He was a man with unabashed exuberance, a man with a voracious taste for fun and money. When necessary, his impatience as a collector of debts would reveal a take-no-prisoners tough guy with a hair-trigger temper. Running bookie joints and the Trans-America Race Wire of Arizona, he did not suffer deadbeats or cheats. The Outfit and the Syndicate in New York regarded Greenbaum as a wholly owned and highly profitable subsidiary. Based on his golden touch, he was evaluated as the perfect candidate to take over the Flamingo following the murder of Bugsy Siegel. He was not going to be another free-spending gangster, suspected of skimming the skim. Under the watchful eyes of Greenbaum, every skimmed dollar would be accounted for and shipped via courier to the Outfit and the Syndicate.

When Greenbaum received orders to take over the Flamingo posthaste, he was eager to get his hands on greater wealth but also reluctant to leave the comforts and privileges of Phoenix. His reluctance to leave was quickly overtaken by the mob's insistence. Saying no to the mob is akin to a death wish. Though he loved his plush office on the ninth floor of the Luhrs Tower and enjoyed every amenity available to a successful corporate CEO, he knew he had to obey. The bosses were like generals, and those who refused to abide by an order were not court-martialed and stood in front of a firing squad, but were simply eliminated by two bullets to the back of the head. Driven by intense pressure, Greenbaum packed a couple of suitcases,

filled his pockets with a few rolls of $100 bills, strapped on a shoulder hol-
ster, and departed, leaving his wife with access to whatever she might need:
money, safe-deposit box keys, phone numbers, a loaded .32, and a list of
politicians and cops who could smooth out whatever rough spots she might
encounter.

Greenbaum brought the same anger and impatience to produce profits in Vegas that he had demonstrated in Phoenix. If a drunk was being
disruptive, causing a commotion, and distracting bettors in the Flamingo,
Greenbaum would grab the guy by the seat of his pants, kick his ass, and
toss him out onto the street as if the drunk were no more important than a
bag of garbage. If a dealer was conniving with a card cheater, Greenbaum
would take the dealer into a back room and beat him senseless, often breaking the dealer's hands so that he couldn't deal for months. To say that Gus
had a short fuse would be an understatement, but there were times when
he seemed to have no fuse. He was both the thunder and the lightning in
a storm of anger.

One day, two brazen thieves, Tony Broncato and Tony Trombino, with
guns drawn, held up the Flamingo. They escaped as far as Los Angeles.
They would not get any farther. Greenbaum was infuriated that such a heist
could occur on his watch. It would not only be an invitation to other heist
men, but an extreme annoyance to the bosses in Chicago and New York.
Greenbaum needed to reassure the bosses that no further heists would
occur, and he also intended to warn other wiseguys that the Flamingo
was a death trap for thieves. Once the two Tonys were located, Greenbaum issued a contract on their lives. They were murdered by Jimmy "the
Weasel" Fratianno, onetime boss of the Los Angeles Mafia and subject of
The Last Mafioso, a man who became (prior to the confessions of Sammy
Gravano) the highest-ranking mobster to inform against his fellow mobsters
and go into the Witness Protection Program. Frank Sinatra called him a rat.

In Vegas Greenbaum quickly discovered that the skim from casinos
dwarfed the take from bookmaking in Arizona. The Flamingo seemed to
be printing money: more than $100,000 a month was skimmed from its
counting room. Greenbaum was pleased, because he owned a percentage of the casino. In fact, he not only owned shares in the Flamingo, but
along with Sedway, he had shares in the El Cortez, the Tropicana, and
other casinos. For a pair of poor Jewish boys, the sons of impoverished
European immigrants, "Moe and Gus" (which is how they were often
referred to by the mob, as they had melded them into a single corporate
entity) had turned their American dreams into a reality that made them
multimillionaires.

Though seen as a unit, it was Greenbaum who was regarded by the mob as the more brilliant manager. Indeed, the mob was so impressed by his Midas touch that they wanted him to increase the profits of other casinos. He was offered the job of running the Riviera for Anthony "Big Tuna" Accardo and Sam "Mooney" Giancana, both bosses of the Chicago Outfit. Greenbaum was especially esteemed as an expert at managing the mob's skim; he was like a plumber who arranged for casino cash to flow from a private pipeline into mob coffers in Chicago, New York, and Kansas City. And the flow was a torrent of millions of dollars in untaxed cash.

And unlike Bugsy Siegel, Greenbaum was a man who could be trusted and depended on. There was no bullshit. According to the bosses, Greenbaum simply told you the facts, not what he thought you wanted to hear. And he delivered. He was all business. The bosses didn't worry that Greenbaum would skim the skim.

Yet, this much sought-after casino wizard did not want to run the Riviera. He thought he would return to his life in Phoenix, where he hobnobbed with local pols and mobsters. Accardo and Giancana were disappointed. Greenbaum rejected several more of their entreaties and so the bosses decided that Greenbaum needed additional convincing. Money alone, apparently, was an insufficient lure. It took one event for Greenbaum to have a mob-inspired epiphany that would change his mind: the mob murdered his sister-in-law, slitting her throat from earlobe to earlobe, leaving her to bleed out Gus's resistance. Upon learning of her grisly murder, Greenbaum phoned Accardo, letting him know he would take the job, plus a 27 percent interest in the Riviera. Accardo congratulated Greenbaum on his decision and agreed to the 27 percent share in the casino. Neither man mentioned the death that had inspired Greenbaum's change of mind.

Prior to taking over the management of the Riviera, Greenbaum had enjoyed the services of the prostitutes who worked the casino at the Flamingo. He had also become addicted to heroin. In his new position at the Riviera, he soon began partying every afternoon and night with chorus girls and hookers. His passion for heroin became an uncontrollable addiction. He became one of the Riviera's most spendthrift gamblers, losing thousands of dollars a day. He paid his gambling debts with Riviera markers. He was spending the casino's money to satisfy his voracious appetites and was not repaying so much as a dime. In addition to his growing pile of markers, he was skimming the skim to pay for hookers and drugs. He was committing the crime that the mob had not anticipated, but would soon notice. For a man who had been associated with mobsters since his teenage years, he knew that stealing from the mob was not a pathway to riches. Greenbaum had seen numerous men killed for stealing from the mob, but his heroin-induced daze clouded reality. He had anesthetized himself to danger.

As Greenbaum partied on, the flow of skimmed cash to the bosses diminished week by week. Word finally got back to them that Greenbaum was the problem. He had to be disciplined and deprived of his position. The mob could accept that some of its employees might pocket some money. That was a cost of doing business. But Greenbaum's appetite for cash had become ravenous. Though Greenbaum was writing his own suicide note and sending it the mob, the bosses uncharacteristically respected him as the man who had turned on the spigots that resulted in millions of dollars in untaxed cash that flowed to them. Word was sent to Greenbaum that if he repaid a good deal of the money he had stolen and agreed to retire, the mob would be lenient and let him live. Greenbaum said no and then decided he needed a vacation to clear his head. He would return to his home in Phoenix.

The mob wanted to make sure that Greenbaum would depart from Vegas and never return. They sent the very intimidating Marshall Caifano to let Greenbaum know that he better put in his retirement papers. "Marshall Caifano made another trip to the Riviera. He told Gus the Chicago bosses wanted Gus out of the Riviera that very day.

"Gus said no, he wasn't goin' anywhere. He knew that he was safe in Las Vegas because no one gets hit in Vegas, although he hired a squad of bodyguards 'just in case.' He then went about his gambling and heroin and whoring until the next morning."[4] Caifano further warned Greenbaum that he should sell his 27 percent interest in the casino and get out. Greenbaum said that Vegas was in his blood. He couldn't leave.

His stance was either courageous or foolhardy, given not only Greenbaum's current troubles with the Outfit, but also that he still had not repaid them the $1 million he had borrowed for the Flamingo Hotel improvements after Bugsy's death. What happened next may have been the result of a Thanksgiving 1958 meeting of the "the four Joes" (Joe Accardo, Joe Bonanno, Joe Magliocco, and Joe Profacci) 124 miles south of Phoenix. The site was the Grace Ranch, owned by Detroit gangster Pete "Horse Face" Licavoli.

In the late morning of December 3, less than a week after the Grace Ranch summit, Gus Greenbaum's housekeeper happened upon a grisly scene in the Greenbaum bedroom. Still in his silk pajamas, Gus Greenbaum's corpse lay across his bed, his head nearly severed by a vicious swipe from a butcher knife.

On a sofa in the den fifty feet away was found the body of Gus's wife, Bess, also the victim of a slashed throat.[5]

Her face had been beaten bloody with a heavy bottle that police found on the floor. She lay facedown on pillows that prevented her blood from flowing onto a carpet. The steaks, which Gus had been cooking when attacked, were eaten by the killers. One of the cops said the hard work of murder had given the killers a good appetite.

> The gory murders were said to have upset Lansky. Not that he had not authorized the Greenbaums' assassination[s], but he had undoubtedly let the contract go to the Chicago Outfit, known to prefer brutal murders to simple kills. The dispatching of Mrs. Greenbaum, Chicago felt, would be an added inducement to other employees to play fair with the mob.[6]

Jimmy "the Weasel" Fratianno confirmed to John "Johnny Handsome" Rosselli (whose birth name was Filippo Sacco) that Meyer Lansky and other casino investors had ordered the hit, though it was unusual that Greenbaum's wife was also killed. The FBI surmised that she was killed so that she would be unable to identify the killers. The FBI assumed that two killers were involved, because two gangsters had arrived from Miami the day before the murders and left soon after. They were never identified.

More than three hundred people, including Senator Barry Goldwater, attended the Greenbaums' funeral. The event received wide coverage in Phoenix and Las Vegas media. Reporters compared the murder to that of Greenbaum's gangster friend Willie Bioff, who was also killed in Phoenix, though he met his end by a bomb blast. Bosses who had ordered Greenbaum's hit were surprised that he had resisted their warnings and did not regard the fate of Willie Bioff as an example of what might happen to him. They subsequently surmised that Greenbaum had sunk so deep into the well of heroin that he was drowning in darkness.

Who was Willie Bioff, and why did the mob have him murdered? He started out as a pimp in Chicago and then went to Hollywood, where he extorted movie studios to ensure labor peace. He did so as a member of the Chicago Outfit. While Bioff extorted millions of dollars from the studios, he pocketed hundreds of thousands of dollars for himself. In effect, he was doing what his pal Greenbaum was doing: stealing from the mob. Eventually the government caught up with Bioff and indicted him for tax evasion. Looking at a long prison sentence, he negotiated a plea deal with prosecutors. He agreed to inform on his compatriots in the Outfit. His targets were Paul "The Waiter" Ricca, Philip D'Andrea, Charlie "Cherry Nose" Gioe,

Johnny Rosselli, Lou Kaufman, and Frank "The Enforcer" Nitti. While his targets received ten-year sentences, Bioff got off with a significantly reduced one. Theft and then treason doomed Bioff. Greenbaum even warned him that being a rat would lead to his death. But Bioff had decided to take his chances rather than suffer through a long prison sentence. Following his release, Bioff moved to Arizona, not far from Greenbaum, and changed his name to Willie Nelson (Nelson being his wife's maiden name). Through Greenbaum, Bioff developed a friendship with Senator Goldwater and went into business with one of the senator's nephews. The Outfit, as Greenbaum had warned, would neither forget nor forgive Bioff's treachery. If located, he would surely be killed. One sunny Arizona morning, an unworried Bioff kissed his wife good-bye at the front door of their house, walked to the driveway, and got into his truck. He turned the ignition key and was immediately blown into countless bits and pieces. Parts of his arms and legs were found hundreds of feet from the explosion. As in the murder of the Greenbaums, the killer or killers were never identified.

Though the murders of Greenbaum and Bioff reduced the number of mobsters in Phoenix, the FBI calculated that by 1950 Phoenix had more mobsters per capita than any other city in the United States, even more than Vegas, though Vegas remained the mob's playground and continued to generate millions of skimmed dollars.

NOTES

1. Michael Shnayerson, *Bugsy Siegel: The Dark Side of the American Dream* (New Haven, CT: Yale University Press, 2021), 172.

2. Robert Lacey, *Little Man: Meyer Lansky and the Gangster Life* (Boston: Little, Brown and Company, 1991), 158.

3. Doug J. Swanson, *Blood Aces, The Wild Ride of Benny Binion* (New York: Viking, 2014), 103.

4. Steve Fischer, *When the Mob Ran Vegas* (New York: MJF Books, 2007), 121.

5. Gus Russo, *The Outfit* (New York: Bloomsbury, 2001), 331.

6. Carl Sifakis, *The Mafia Encyclopedia* (New York: Checkmark Books, 1999), 168.

3

MEYER LANSKY

Godfather of the Skim

Though Moe Sedway and Gus Greenbaum were out front contributing substantially to the success of the Flamingo, it was Meyer Lansky who was the power behind the curtain: investor, general of an army of mobsters, and master of the skim. Having operated carpet joints (as opposed to clip joints with sawdust on the floors) in Saratoga, New York; and plush casinos in Hallandale, Florida; and luxurious hotel/casinos in Havana, Cuba; Lansky was one of the underworld's most knowledgeable casino operators. He regarded the fortunes that could be made in Vegas the way an agricultural farmer regards his crops just before the harvest season. The pickings were that plentiful. Though a casino has a substantial advantage over bettors and so rakes in profits from every game of chance (actually games of little chance for bettors), Lansky and his partners were never satisfied with just the profits from gaming; they wanted millions more in untaxed dollars that could be obtained only by skimming money out of casino count rooms. Being a math wiz and possessing an unconventionally creative mind for a gangster, Lansky designed ingenious maneuvers for breaching the security of the count rooms so that the skim turned into a torrent of cash as if released from a dam.

Having been cheated in a dice game when he was a boy, Lansky learned at an early age that the only way to make money gambling was to control the game. And not some penny-ante back-alley craps game, but all the games in a completely outfitted casino. To own such casinos became an ambition so intense it was as if it were implanted in his mind. There, it grew until he finally had achieved his goals.

He had been taught a great deal by his mentor, Arnold Rothstein (fixer of the 1919 World Series), about the intricacies of running a casino, for Rothstein ran some of the most profitable and luxurious casinos in the Tenderloin section of Manhattan. Lansky had also learned from Rothstein that if one paid off cops and local politicians, one could operate casinos with impunity. The money would pour in at such great quantities that it would—at times—be difficult to find places in which to hide it.

Lansky opened his first casinos in Saratoga, New York, followed by one in Hallandale, Florida. There, he put into practice the bribery of politicians, cops, and do-gooders, all of whom let him operate without harassment and arrest. When he decided to operate the biggest and most luxurious hotel/casinos in Cuba (the Riviera and the Nacional), he paid the island's dictator, Fulgencio Batista, $3 million. Batista, as Lansky's partner, was happy to accept the money, which he deposited in his Swiss bank account. He made sure that Lansky could operate as he saw fit with no interference from police and possible competitors.

Vegas, even before Castro cast out the mob, was by comparison an ideal location for Lansky's mob-run casinos, for gambling had been made legal in 1931 and no one would have to be paid off. In addition, as an American town, it offered mobsters a place to conduct their gambling businesses without fear of being indicted. It would be a totally legal adult playground, where hordes of people would come to lose their money. And it was a wide-open town: there were no territories that were the exclusive domain of any one mob organization. Mobsters from New York, Chicago, Miami, Los Angeles, Detroit, Cleveland, and Milwaukee could all plant their flags in Vegas.

At the time the mob arrived, Vegas was a visual smorgasbord of different style casinos, ranging from nondescript stores to old-style Western saloons with sawdust on the floors that operated amid the tinkling keys of cheap upright pianos. The saloons were the most prominent. Along Fremont Street, the main drag in the 1930s and 1940s, one could see gambling saloons with hitching posts, dilapidated paint-chipped stagecoaches parked out front, and signs promising true Old West experiences. The Old West was emphasized on those signs by images of lassos and smoking six-shooters. The entire Western ambience seemed more a reflection of Hollywood than of Dodge City. The only thing lacking was real shoot-outs at high noon.

In any of those Old West saloons, seated at round tables that were spur-scarred, were men in cowboy hats and cowboy boots; they played Down the River, Acey Deucey, One-eyed Jacks, Roll Your Own, and other poker variations. At a rectangular table, a dealer would deal blackjack. Another man with garters on his sleeves and perhaps an eyeshade would spin a roulette wheel. An ingratiating prostitute in a low-cut dress with a perfumed bosom, bloodred lips, and hair piled high would bring drinks to the gamblers and encourage them with softly purred words that the prospect of winning a boodle of cash could be theirs. If the bettor was an out-of-town rube, expecting to get laid in an upstairs room, he would most likely just get screwed out of whatever money he hadn't lost in the casino.

Though those Old West saloons were not what Lansky, Siegel, Costello, and Luciano had in mind, the very existence of those gambling saloons was the inspiration for the luxurious, elegant casinos that would be the hallmarks of post-war Vegas. Siegel loved the idea of creating another Monte Carlo in Vegas. To own a modern hotel/casino, similar in style to the modernist and art deco hotels in Miami Beach, was as much the focus of his ambition as was his lust for Hollywood beauties. Nothing would stand in his way.

Though Siegel has been mythologized as the first visionary who saw the possibilities of Vegas as a gambling destination for high rollers from all over the United States, he was preceded by other lesser-known figures: the men who owned the El Rancho, which was built in 1941, and the Last Frontier, which was built in 1942. Yet, it was Siegel and his mob partners who quickly realized that the end of World War II would mean an influx of vets with money to burn from their new jobs. Industries were popping up all over Los Angeles that would pay ex-servicemen generous wages. With plenty of cash to spare and a yen to gamble, many of them would make the drive through the desert to a weekend of fun in Vegas. With Lansky and his partners providing much of the necessary funding, Siegel would build the kind of hotel and casino that would be a magnet not only for those ex-servicemen, but also for Hollywood celebrities. It would be no mirage in the desert. It would be a real pleasure palace like nothing that Vegas had ever seen.

The pleasure palace would be the Flamingo Hotel and Casino. Though originally conceived by Billy Wilkerson, proprietor of the *Hollywood Reporter* and several celebrity restaurants in Los Angeles, he ran out of money before he could see his dream become a reality. He had envisioned the Flamingo as an elegant, stylish attraction for movie stars, directors, and producers. He figured they would love it, come in droves, and gamble away large sums of money. But Wilkerson was stumbling before he could reach the finish line; the mob was set to take up his torch and run with it. Before doing so, however, they lent Wilkerson the money he needed, but then they pushed him off the track with a death threat. Believing that he should make

himself absent not only from Vegas but from the state of Nevada, Wilkerson initially considered returning to Los Angeles, but then he decided
that Europe would be an even safer bet. Vegas would remain a dangerous,
foreign land with borders he should not cross.

The East Coast mobsters believed as Wilkerson had that the elegant
Flamingo would be patronized by Hollywood high rollers. They thought
the casino would generate cash faster than the US Treasury Department.
Unfortunately, Siegel was not the man to manage it. He was neither a
builder nor a businessman. Del Webb, the builder whom Siegel had hired
to construct the Flamingo, overbilled him on everything, beginning with
screws and nails. As the cost of the construction mounted, Siegel was seen
less as a visionary and more like a sponge soaking up the mob's money. The
syndicate, which was run by Luciano, Costello, and Lansky, was quickly
losing its patience. The mob, after all, operates to make money, not to lose
it. In that respect, Siegel was an un-mobster. The syndicate's hierarchy
voted twice to kill Siegel, but Lansky withheld his vote, which in effect was
a veto. However, he could not do so forever. He had been able to engineer
a pair of stays of execution, but three strikes and Siegel was out. The assas-
sinated Siegel passed into legend; and in death—as so often happens with
mobsters—he became a tourist attraction, one that brought thousands of
gamblers and millions of dollars to the Flamingo.

Lansky was now like the general of an army, issuing orders, moving men
around like soldiers on a battlefield. One of his early moves was to put Sanford Adler, one of the owners of El Rancho Vegas, in charge of the skim
at the Flamingo. It turned out to be a bad choice. Adler proved unreliable
and lacking sufficient control of his responsibilities. Money wasn't being
skimmed to the extent that Lansky had anticipated. In fact, the casino's
profits were so low that no serious gambling auditor, such as Lansky, could
believe it. Lansky told his brother Jake to call Adler and get rid of him.
According to Steve Fischer, as reported in his book, *When the Mob Ran
Vegas*, the following telephone conversation occurred between Adler and
Jake Lansky:

Sandy: "Hello?"

Jake: "Sandy? This is Jake. Meyer sends his regards and says he wants for you
to sell your interest in the Flamingo back to him. Okay, Sandy?"

Sandy: "What? No way am I gonna sell out of the Flamingo. You tell Meyer
that our luck's been running a little cold, but it's about to turn around."

Jake: "Oh! And Sandy? I was told to tell you that you and your partners are going to have your throats cut and be buried out in the desert if you don't sell out right now. And Sandy? Give my best to your wife and kids."[1]

A few days later, Adler was beaten into unconsciousness and hospitalized; upon reviving, he wisely decided that neither living with brain damage nor dying at the hands of the mob was preferable to selling his shares to Lansky. Easy come, easy go. It was a wise decision, one that Siegel never could have made.

Jake Lansky did more than threaten unprofitable operators on behalf of his brother. He was his brother's adjutant, often told to travel to Vegas to make sure that the skimming from various casinos was running smoothly, bring back suitcases of money, and make sure that no one was stealing. Lansky's grandson, Meyer Lansky II, told the author that Jake often traveled to Vegas to make sure that the skimming was being handled appropriately. Lansky, however, did not particularly like Vegas and visited the city as infrequently as possible. From his home in Florida, he divided up the skim and distributed it proportionately to each of the mob investors who had points, not only in the Flamingo, but also in numerous other mob-controlled casinos. While government officials were never able to unravel the snarl of shell companies whose owners and fronts had points in the casinos, Lansky was able to keep all the information in his head. He knew who owned which shell companies, and he knew which men were fronting for those companies. He was so brilliant that an FBI agent commented: "He could have been the chairman of General Motors if he'd gone into legitimate business."[2] The mob respected his brilliance, knowing that his mind was like a computer full of essential information and that he was as savvy and discreet as an accountant. He was not only a brilliant and strategic businessman, but he was also that rare gangster: a person whom the mob trusted. His compatriots knew that they could always depend on him. He was a man of his word. Ralph Salerno, famed organized crime investigator for the New York City Police Department, told the author that "a handshake with Meyer Lansky was better than any written contract."[3] He would never be placed on the mob hit list. He was golden.

Lansky had come a long way from his days on the Lower East Side of Manhattan with his boyhood pals, Siegel, Luciano, and Costello. In those days, he and Siegel had run one of the most violent gangs in New York, the Bugs and Meyer Gang. It hijacked liquor trucks, provided protection at high prices to bootleggers, burnt down buildings, and carried out murders, all for a price. It extorted businesses and blackmailed politicians. By the time Lansky had graduated to running sophisticated gambling joints, the gang had evolved into Murder Inc. Lansky was no longer involved in the crass, violent side of the gangster life, but Siegel thrived on it and loved taking on hits, often with Murder Inc. colleague Frankie Carbo, the man suspected of being Siegel's assassin. Though Lansky would not be known for murdering anyone, he could always call upon others to carry out hits or beatings. For those not deemed targets for murder, Lansky's reputation might cause a belligerent to infer that his life would be in danger if he defied Lansky. While Lansky would not hesitate to use his reputation as a gangster to achieve his goals, he mostly wanted to present himself as a conservative businessman in a blue, pin-striped suit, the picture of well-groomed decorum. He didn't need to be seen on the floor of a casino. He much preferred being the behind-the-scenes manipulator.

The man who matched Lansky's image of himself as a soft-spoken, unflappable businessman was another gangster named Vincent Alo (aka Jimmy Blue Eyes), who had also given up a life of violence. The two had met in the early 1930s and found that they approached the gangster life similarly. Each was low-key, never wanted to be in the spotlight, and aspired to be a legitimate businessman. In addition, each was a voracious reader and had a love of knowledge that was unusual in the world in which he operated. Integral to Lansky's low-key attitude, he never let anyone photograph him with another gangster; the only exception: a photo of Meyer with Alo, both of whom are in their late seventies in the photo. (There is an early photo of Lansky in a police lineup that includes Luciano; but, of course, Lansky had no control of that.) Alo was born in 1904 in Harlem and grew up to be a captain in the Genovese crime family. As a young man, he served five years in Dannemora Prison for bank robbery. He never denied his youthful past, but he preferred to focus on the present. He was charming, courteous, and well-spoken, hardly the image of a gun-toting stickup man.

He and Lansky, more interested in gambling than in murder, operated a casino (with Meyer as senior partner and majority stockholder) in Hallandale, Florida, the success of which had been guaranteed by their payoffs to local politicians, cops, and fraternal organizations. They also distributed modest sums to the town's residents so that they wouldn't complain about the casino. That first casino was so successful that Lansky invited Alo to be a minority partner in a second casino. However, it all came to an end in 1947, when politicians believed that the presence of casinos would turn off prospective businesses, such as real estate developers who wanted the town to have a wholesome reputation that would attract young families. Lansky and Alo, who had lucrative investments in Cuba and who had points in the

El Cortez and the Flamingo in Vegas, were on the lookout to make up for their Florida losses. They found numerous casinos whose bosses welcomed their investments. For those casinos, Lansky engineered a number of successful schemes for carrying out skims that would go undiscovered by the Justice Department and the IRS.

Unfortunately, as low-key as Alo intended to be, he was convicted in New York on an obstruction of justice charge in 1970 and served three years in prison. Alo's sangfroid, however, did not fail him as commented on by New York District Attorney Robert Morgenthau, who said that Alo was "charming, intelligent, and well-liked by his associates." The DA's estimate did not end there, for Morgenthau went on to acidly note that Alo was a partner of Meyer Lansky, whom he placed at the "apex of organized crime." Morgenthau either did not know or chose not to say that Alo was also a partner of Moe Dalitz in Wilbur Clark's Desert Inn. In 1985, after Lansky's death, Wilbur Clark would often introduce Alo to his friends and business associates as his "uncle Jimmy" or as his "Goomba."

Unlike many of the other original casino owners, Clark led a charmed life. In the history of Vegas casinos, Clark is best known for having built the Desert Inn in 1947. As Billy Wilkerson had run out of money while building the Flamingo, Clark ran out of money while building the Desert Inn. To his rescue came Moe Dalitz and his mob partners from Cleveland (for more about Dalitz, see chapter 4). Unlike Siegel, Dalitz was a calm, rational boss, and he let Clark keep a small percentage of the Inn, estimated to be 17.5 percent. Dalitz was not just being kind to Clark, he also used him to publicize the Inn by serving as its public face: a big, illuminated sign proclaimed the casino as Wilbur Clark's Desert Inn. Clark was the perfect front for Dalitz, who—like his partner Lansky—always wanted to keep a low profile; he was pleased to have Clark step into the limelight. In time, Clark became more than the public face of just the casino. He was also the moving force behind the Tournament of Champions that was televised by NBC from the Desert Inn Golf Course. Other well-publicized events followed. Clark, never shy about seeing his name in lights, also organized Wilbur Clark's Cavalcade of Charities. Articles about his philanthropy regularly appeared in print. Alo, like Dalitz, was happy to let Clark brightly reflect the (illusory) golden opportunities that awaited bettors at the Desert Inn.

A typical glad-hander, Clark not only introduced his uncle Jimmy to business newcomers in Vegas, but he also would add—with a wink and a smile—that the two men could arrange certain benefits, could open doors to the offices of people of power and influence.

Though Alo enjoyed Clark's company, he was happier to be with his old, retired gambling buddies back in Hollywood, Florida. There, he continued his self-education, reading biographies and books of history, economics, and science. There were few things as enjoyable for Alo as discussing the subjects of books with his friends at the regular meetings of their book club, though he also enjoyed whatever income came his way from the casinos.

Before Alo and Lansky retired to Florida, money from skimming casinos was their primary occupation. And the number of mobsters who received shares of the skim was more than the FBI could keep track of. In the Fremont Hotel and Casino alone, there were forty-two individuals who had points in the casino, and each regularly received his dividend. Lansky and Alo used unlikely looking individuals, such as poor, badly dressed Mexicans, to carry suitcases of money back to Miami. (Who would suspect them of being members of the silk-suited syndicate?) Other than poor Mexicans, there was the fashionable and elegant Ida Devine (who had replaced Virginia Hill, who in contrast to Devine was a flashy mob moll). Devine was elegant, well-dressed, and the picture of affluent respectability; she was the wife of Irving "Niggy" Devine, a supplier of meat to the Fremont Hotel. He was heard to refer to his wife as Ida the Divine. Though she was completely reliable, she presented one annoying problem for the mob: she was frightened of flying and so refused to get on a plane. Carrying the mob's skim money in expensive suitcases, she took trains from Vegas to Miami, to Chicago, to Kansas City, to New York, to Milwaukee and any other destinations to which the mob sent her. Eventually the FBI, through bugs placed in the executive offices of the Fremont, learned of her role as a mob courier and began referring to her not as Ida the Divine, but as the "Lady in Mink," which sounds as respectable as the name of a character portrayed by Doris Day in a romantic Hollywood daydream. Devine's career was longer than a ninety-minute Hollywood movie, but it was—nevertheless—shortlived, not because she refused to fly, but because the mob learned that the FBI had fingered her. A series of nondescript replacements would have to be found and greater discretion would require that they remain anonymous. Cheaply attired Mexicans returned. And without interruption, the skim continued, but so did the FBI bugs. Based on those bugs, the FBI estimated that Lansky was taking in $1 million a year from the Fremont and did so for a period of five years.

One person who helped the mob continue with its skimming was Nevada's lieutenant governor, Clifford Jones (aka "the Big Juice"). An investigation revealed that he had points in several Vegas casinos: the Thunderbird, El Cortez, the Dunes, the Pioneer, and the Golden Nugget. From the last two casinos, he received a total of $26,000 in 1948. When asked about criminals controlling the casinos by the Kefauver Committee, which was investigating the mob in Vegas, Jones said he didn't see it as a problem if owners had criminal records as long as they behaved legally and did not injure residents and visitors. The committee members did not hide their expressions of disbelief.

By 1955, government officials could no longer avoid the problem of mob-run casinos. The *Las Vegas Sun* had reported that Jake Lansky had taken part in counting the gambling proceeds at the Thunderbird. Nervous politicos, fearing negative publicity about their cozy relationships with mobsters, acted with unaccustomed celerity and revoked the Thunderbird's license. Such actions threatened the smooth flow of the skim out of one casino and into the offshore bank accounts of numerous mobsters. Governor Charles Russell, sensing the community's appetite for reform and a clear opportunity to burnish his reputation, asked members of the legislature to create the Nevada State Control Board, which was charged with investigating all applicants who applied for gaming licenses. The board came into being in 1955, and numerous licenses were suddenly revoked. The establishment of the Control Board gave impetus to the mob to hire squeaky-clean front men who would have no trouble being licensed to run casinos. Once men with clean records were put in place, the skimming continued as it had before the board was established. And though the Thunderbird had temporarily closed its doors, those doors were soon flung wide open, and gambling profits soared.

Years later, the Fremont presented a new problem for Lansky and his partners. The FBI had illegally bugged the Fremont's offices. It picked up a great deal of information about the skim, about Lansky, Alo, and Devine. The FBI believed that the Fremont was a clearing center into which flowed the skim from the Sands, the Horseshoe, and the Flamingo. The agency soon added two additional casinos whose skim came into the Fremont: the Stardust and the Desert Inn. The evidence that the agency's bugs picked up may have been useful for investigations, but it could not be used in court in 1963. At that time, such bugs were considered illegal. Lansky and Alo must have smiled at their victory, for they knew that they had escaped indictment, and not through their own cleverness. Having escaped from the predations of a mighty government, they decided they should take their money and ease their way into safe havens of ostensible legitimacy. They wanted quiet and comfortable lives, though they would never be free from government prying.

When it came to Nevada, it was clear to both Meyer and Jimmy that the glory days were over. The two decades of expansion that Las Vegas had enjoyed since World War II had been a period of transition in which illegally acquired expertise—and illegally acquired capital—had constituted the main engine of development. Nevada was the biggest enclave of them all. It could hardly have been built without the outlaws of the carpet-joint fraternity, and Las Vegas's network of hidden points holders was reflection of that.[4]

The Flamingo, in which Lansky and his fellow East Coast mobsters had heavily invested, was sold in 1960 for $10.6 million. Those who fronted for the mobster owners were the actor George Raft and the singer Tony Martin. Albert Parvin was one of the owners, and he had told Lansky that he wanted to sell the hotel/casino. Lansky agreed to act as an agent who would find the right buyer. He found a pair of Miami hoteliers who purchased it, and Lansky received a $200,000 finder's fee. He would use the money, paid out over a period of years, as legitimate income to prove to the IRS that he was no longer living on the skim.

However, the Justice Department didn't buy it. Lansky's partners Sam Cohen and Morris Landsburgh had admitted to skimming and distributing $10 million of untaxed money. Having pled guilty, they each received twelve months in prison. The government hoped that the two jailed conspirators would flip and provide evidence against Lansky. The only evidence that the government thought they could use against Lansky was the fact that he received a $200,000 finder's fee for the sale of the Flamingo. However, he had paid all the necessary taxes on the fee. When the government brought the case to court, Lansky's lawyer requested that the case be tried in Nevada, not Miami. The government agreed, but then Lansky—in his seventies—proved too ill to travel to Nevada. The government then tried to have the case brought back to Miami, but once the case was transferred, it could not be transferred back to the original jurisdiction. The judge listened to what seemed interminable testimony about Lansky's health. It went on for more than four years. And though the government wanted to maintain its indictment against Lansky until he died, the judge thought that was unreasonable and cruel. On November 3, 1976, he dismissed the case. As one FBI agent commented: "He was able to go to his grave laughing that he whipped us all."[5]

Lansky and Alo had not only divested themselves of their interests in the Fremont and the Flamingo, but other casinos as well. It could not be done overnight, but the divestments went on steadily through 1967, when they sold their interest in the Sands.

Prior to the sale of the Sands, the mob had brought in Jack Entratter to run it. He had started as a bouncer-doorman at the famed Stork Club in Manhattan, and then he moved to the Copacabana (owned secretly by Frank Costello), where he served as maître d'. There, he hired big-name entertainers, such as Frank Sinatra, Dean Martin, and Jerry Lewis. He would be an ideal manager for the Sands, hiring many of the same entertainers he had hired in New York. Entratter was given twelve points in the Sands but actually owned only two: he held the others as a front for mobsters who didn't want their names on the casino's books. The FBI later concluded that Alo, Lansky, and Doc Stacher (a member of the Bugs and Meyer Gang) were among those for whom Entratter was fronting. Many anonymous holders of points would fly to Vegas to collect their money. Some of them were gamblers, and they were permitted to gamble on credit up to the value of their points. As the FBI made life increasingly uncomfortable for Lansky, he decided to sell. Though one of the sellers of record was Jack Entratter, it was Lansky and Alo who encouraged and executed the sale. From the Sands alone, Lansky walked away with $1 million, which seemed like a large sum at the time. But years later, when publicly held corporations started buying and selling casinos for hundreds of millions of dollars, Lansky's take seemed like a pittance by comparison. After Howard Hughes bought the Sands for $14.6 million in 1967, the casino lost a great deal of money and became a shadow of its former self. The reason was that the mob was still able to continue the skim under Hughes' ownership without the proprietor being aware of what the mobsters were doing. They nearly turned the place into a corpse. Others came along and restored it to good health.

To this day, no one knows how many casinos Lansky had an interest in. He was clever and never put his name on anything that could get him in trouble. If he owned property, it was held in the name of a front man or a shell company that was a subsidiary of another shell company that was owned by a front man. Lansky kept his well-hidden liquid fortune in Swiss bank accounts and offshore banks. His brother, Jake, was not only his bag man, traveling to and from Vegas carrying bags of cash, but he was also his brother's keeper. And he made sure that Meyer could always maintain distance between himself and what he owned. Though Lansky was as elusive as a jaguar in a nocturnal jungle, his reputation among mob bosses across the country was that of a wise godfather. So much so that when the Chicago Outfit (Al Capone's old gang) decided to put down roots in Vegas, one of its leaders, Tony Accardo, called upon Lansky for advice. According to Mafia lore, Lucky Luciano allegedly stated, "Listen to Meyer and you'll never lose money." Instead, the Outfit made the fatal mistake of sending hit man Tony Spilotro to Vegas, and his murderous deeds and attacks on police lit a fuse that led to an explosion of the mob's edifice of investments in Vegas.

Lansky, by contrast, quietly lived out his last days in an elegant, fifteen-story, blue-and-white Miami Beach apartment building, The Imperial House, located at 5255 Collins Avenue. He and his wife occupied a modest one-bedroom apartment near the beach. Lansky died of lung cancer at age eighty in 1983. His home was just down the coast from Hallandale, the town in which he had once operated his own gambling casinos. He was a rich man (though he claimed he was nearly broke) who lived modestly, out of the spotlight that the IRS shined on the lives of other mobsters. He had created a structure in which organized crime operated for many years. "Lansky in large measure created the American Mafia and was its real godfather."[6] His contributions to the early days of Vegas were more valuable to the mob than those of the legendary Bugsy Siegel, yet it is Siegel who has been mythologized as the man who invented Vegas.

NOTES

1. Steve Fischer, *When the Mob Ran Vegas* (Las Vegas: Berkline Press, 2005), 26.
2. Carl Sifakis, *The Mafia Encyclopedia* (New York: Checkmark Books, 1999), 202.
3. Interview with author, 1992.
4. Robert Lacey, *Little Man: Meyer Lansky and the Gangster Life* (Boston: Little, Brown and Company, 1991), 300–301.
5. Lacey, *Little Man: Meyer Lansky and the Gangster Life*, 382.
6. Sifakis, *The Mafia Encyclopedia*, 205.

4

MOE DALITZ

Mr. Las Vegas

Though Meyer Lansky is considered one of the brainiest bosses of organized crime, Moe Dalitz was—at least—his equal, if not in some cases his
superior. Lansky held on to his Havana casinos at the outset of the Castro
revolution, but Dalitz perceived the likelihood of a communist takeover and
got out. In the autumn of 1958, Dalitz and his partners had sold their interests in their Cuban casinos and left the island. Lansky, however, remained
behind and continued to operate the Riviera and Nacional. On January
1, 1959, Fidel Castro's revolution had succeeded. Lansky's protector and
partner, Fulgencio Batista, was no longer the island's dictator. Lansky had
stuck around too long. As he later said, "I crapped out."[1] Las Vegas was the
safer bet for those who operated casinos. And there was no more successful
mobster in Vegas than Moe Dalitz, often referred to as Mr. Las Vegas (or
by some others as Mr. Mobster).

Morris Barney Dalitz was born on Christmas Eve, 1899, in Boston to
Jewish parents, Barnet and Anna. His father moved the family to Michigan,
where he opened Varsity Laundry in Ann Arbor. Young Moe grew up learning the business from his dad and operated laundry service businesses for
the rest of his life. In addition to Varsity, Dalitz had interests in the Pioneer
Linen Supply Company in Cleveland and the Michigan Industrial Laundry
in Detroit. Like many other small businesses, the laundries were targeted
by union organizers. And as unions are anathema to the owners of most
businesses, young Dalitz took whatever actions were necessary to disrupt

and defeat the union. One such tactic included hiring mob thugs, including members of the infamous Jewish Purple Gang, to beat up picketers. Few laundry workers were willing to trade fractured skulls for increased wages and job security. During this time, Dalitz befriended Jimmy Hoffa, future mob-supported boss of the Teamsters Union, and the two would do business until Hoffa's murder. In addition, Dalitz worked with the Mayfield Road Gang, based in Cleveland. He did not act alone but had formed partnerships with Morris Kleinman, Sam Tucker, Louis Rothkopf, and Ruby Kolod, men who would remain partners through the development of Vegas casinos.

When Prohibition became the law of the land, Dalitz—through his recently formed friendships with mobsters—ventured into the bootlegging business. He became a seasoned sailor, transporting liquor from Canada into the United States via Lake Erie. He spent so much time on the lake that numerous of his colleagues referred to it as the Jewish Lake.

An ambitious entrepreneur who took advantage of new opportunities, whether legal or illegal, Dalitz invested some of the millions he acquired from bootlegging into building casinos in the Midwest. Adept at staying beyond the clutches of the law (he never spent one night in jail), he was known to pay off cops, prosecutors, and judges, many of whom were patrons of his gambling joints. Years later, when asked if his casinos were illegal, Dalitz disingenuously commented with a smile that "there were so many judges and politicians in them, I figured that they had to be all right."[2]

Following the repeal of Prohibition, Dalitz took profits from his bootlegging businesses and opened more casinos. According to John L. Smith in a *Las Vegas Review-Journal* article, Dalitz had "opened a series of illegal casinos with names like the Mound Club, Pettibone Club, the Jungle Inn, and the Beverly Hills Club and the Lookout House."[3] Each of those casinos generated millions of dollars, which Dalitz invested in legitimate businesses. He not only knew how to launder his profits into legitimate businesses, but he also was clever enough to avoid the snares of the IRS. In addition to avoiding problems with the taxmen, he was smart enough to keep a low profile. Only a fool would broadcast his illegal activities, thus extending an invitation to law enforcement.

By the time the Second World War erupted, Dalitz was a multimillionaire. He was grateful to the country that provided him with the numerous opportunities to acquire so much wealth. Like many Americans, Dalitz was incensed by the Japanese attack on Pearl Harbor and Germany's treatment of Jews. Though deferred from the military draft because of his age, Dalitz enlisted in the army. Perhaps because he was forty-two years old, the military brass did not perceive him as a formidable infantry soldier, so they assigned him to exercise his expertise in the crafts of laundering. In that job, he was such a conscientious soldier that he was promoted to the rank of second lieutenant. By war's end, he felt satisfied that he had made a contribution to the war effort, but the army was no place for a risk-taking adventurer. He had enough of military service; he needed to break free from its dull routines and devotion to conformity. Having run illegal casinos during the 1930s, Dalitz took that knowledge and headed for Las Vegas. There, he and his partners would flourish. He was in the perfect milieu for his tastes and abilities. There he was—drink in one hand, a cigarette in the other, dressed in a natty sport jacket and tailored slacks, smiling for a camera: the picture of a happy and successful sportsman.

Though Dalitz had invested in Cuban casinos with his friend Meyer Lansky, he rightly believed that democratically elected officials who oversaw a state and city where gambling was legal would provide the necessary protection for his business ventures. He was a realistic cynic who proved that every politician he dealt with had a price. And, of course, he was right. In Vegas (as in many other cities), the mob could influence the politicians by generously supporting their candidacies. And once elected, those politicians would repay the mob's generosity by making sure neither rules nor regulations would hamper the profitability of their casinos. Dalitz wined and dined those politicians, contributed generously to their campaigns, and invited them to go sailing on his yacht and accompany him on hunting trips. All their expenses were paid.

With the behind-the-scenes help of politicians, casino owners became rich power brokers. For them, Vegas was better than the federal mint. Though banks in the 1950s and 1960s regarded casinos as pariah enterprises run by unreliable gamblers, the mob was able to finance their casinos from loans handed out by the Teamsters Central States Pension Fund (CSPF). With money from CSPF, Dalitz and his partners bought acres of land, built numerous casinos, and attracted hordes of bettors to their gaming tables, slot machines, and roulette wheels. As the money poured into the count rooms, millions were whisked out as skim in suitcases, enriching each investor who had points in a casino.

And it was in that monetary paradise that an irresistibly man-made opportunity presented itself to Dalitz and his partners. It was the Desert Inn. Wilbur Clark had borrowed $250,000 to build the Desert Inn; like Bugsy Siegel, he ran short of money to build his dream of a luxurious hotel and casino. And unlike Siegel, he chose not to borrow from the East Coast gangsters who would kill you if you spent too much of their money, not to mention if you stole additional sums and shipped the loot overseas to Swiss banks. In addition to not being a spendthrift, Clark knew the risks of skimming money from his lenders. He asked Dalitz and his partners for the money he needed to finish the building of the Desert Inn. They gave Clark all the money he requested, and then they took a 75 percent ownership stake. Clark was happy to be left with the remainder. The Desert Inn would be built. Clark was thrilled. Dalitz and his partners, always intent on avoiding scrutinizing searchlights on their various activities, decided that the public should perceive the Desert Inn as Clark's own. And the big outdoor sign boldly declared, "Wilbur Clark's Desert Inn." Dalitz, Kleinman, Tucker, and the other mob investors knew the tax-free skim from the Inn's count room would be millions of dollars, and they didn't want anyone looking over their shoulders. Wilbur Clark's perpetually smiling face was both a distraction and camouflage. It was part of the Inn's brand, like a happy face on a box of cereal.

Restless, always on the move, Dalitz didn't stop with the Desert Inn. He had a jeweler's eye for spotting profitable opportunities. When Tony Cornero (born Anthony Cornero Stralla) came to Dalitz in 1955, he needed money to complete the building of the Stardust Casino. Dalitz conferred with Meyer Lansky, and Cornero was subsequently loaned $1.25 million to complete the building. Two additional loans were made to Cornero. Dalitz and Lansky knew that betting on Cornero would not be much of a risk. If he failed to pay back the loans, he would forfeit ownership of the Stardust to his lenders. If he paid back the loans in full, he could still be forced out by other means. During Prohibition, Cornero had succeeded as a bootlegger, but he later failed as an operator of offshore gambling boats. He would serve as the mob's temporary front, the alleged owner of the Stardust.

Cornero was no exception to the men with checkered careers who sought to own casinos in mid-twentieth-century Vegas. He had used the millions he made as a bootlegger to venture into Vegas gambling. Fifteen years before Siegel opened the Flamingo, Cornero had opened the Meadows Casino and Hotel in Vegas. He was initially riding a wave of success, but then Lucky Luciano and Meyer Lansky heard about all the money Cornero was taking in. They wanted a piece of the action. Cornero made the mistake of denying their request; and not ones to take no for an answer, the aggrieved partners-to-be torched the Meadows. Cornero, not waiting to clean away the ashes, embers, and blackened burnt timbers, headed back to Los Angeles, where his bootlegging career had thrived. He figured that Lansky and Luciano would move on to other targets of opportunity. Cornero decided that he would take his gambling smarts to sea. Beyond the three-mile limit, he figured his boats would be free of legal harassment and perhaps not be of interest to the East Coast mobsters. He purchased two large ships, the SS *Rex* and the SS *Tango*, for $300,000 and converted them to luxurious gambling casinos. The *Rex*, the more luxurious of the two ships, regularly accommodated two thousand bettors, who were served by a crew of 350, some of whom were gunmen on the lookout for cheaters. In addition to serving fine French food prepared in the ship's kitchen by a first-class chef, Cornero made sure his guests were entertained by a full orchestra and popular singers. When his guests weren't gambling, they were dining and dancing, putting themselves in happy, optimistic moods about their chances for beating the house.

To an outraged state Attorney General Earl Warren (later governor of California and Chief Justice of the US Supreme Court), the gambling off the coast of California was as offensive as a floating version of Sodom and Gomorrah. Warren threatened to send the navy and coast guard to tow the casinos to shore and then arrest Cornero and his crew of gangsters. That was followed by rumors that the navy might try to sink the ships after all the passengers had disembarked. Cornero seemed to thumb his nose at Warren's threats, and so the frustrated Warren finally ordered the police to close down the two gambling ships. When a small armada of police boats surrounded the floating casinos, Cornero had his crew turn the ships' fire hoses on the invading cops. The drenched cops withdrew. An eight-week standoff ensued, during which Cornero was charged with piracy on the high seas. Seeing the instruments of his defeat finally sailing to his destruction, Cornero capitulated and decided to return to Vegas. On the dry land of Vegas, gambling was legal. There, Cornero would have to deal with gangsters and appease them by cutting them into the action. It was better than being put out of business. Cornero applied for a gaming license and was turned down because of his criminal record. Smarter men with criminal records simply hired front men to run their casinos. Why Cornero didn't immediately employ such a tactic remains a mystery. A disappointed and frustrated Cornero returned to his palatial home in Beverly Hills. He weighed his options. Should he return to Vegas and make a deal with the mob? Was it worth it? What would they expect from him? Would he owe his life to them?

He was annoyed when his doorbell rang unexpectedly. He opened the door and facing him was a grim-faced stranger with fiery eyes. Before Cornero could speak, the stranger shot four bullets into Cornero's gut. He collapsed and was rushed by ambulance to a local hospital; he underwent several surgeries, after which he was delivered back home by private ambulance. Not one to give up, he was determined to go to Vegas.

Back in Vegas, a resiliently ambitious Cornero bought forty acres of land. To fund his new casino, the Stardust, he issued unregistered stock for $10 a share; however, he purchased 51 percent of the stock for himself at $.10 a share, for a total of $6,500. And again, he applied to the Nevada Gaming Commission for a license. As a former bootlegger who had served time in prison, he was again turned down. He was not surprised and referred to the commission as a quiver of straight arrows. He would not accept defeat. Though he wanted the world to know he was the boss and owner of the Stardust, he decided to get a front man. It was his only option. He contacted his pal Milton Page and set him up as the ostensible owner and operator of the casino. Though having sold all the unregistered shares to investors, Cornero was still short of cash to build the Stardust. That's when he turned to Dalitz, asking for a loan of $1.25 million. It was granted.

Demands for the loan's repayment quickly followed. Dalitz and his partners were eager to get their hands on another casino. They knew that Cornero would have a difficult time repaying the loan on time. Dalitz, though often generous, could be a hardheaded businessman for whom empathy was a weak spot in the armor of a tough man's dealmaking abilities. He daily pressured and threatened Cornero for the repayment of the loan. Dalitz knew that Cornero had a heart condition. Stress and anxiety only made it worse. Cornero sought refuge in alcohol. He ignored his doctor's warning not to drink too much. But he couldn't stop; alcohol temporarily doused his flaming anxieties. But after a few drinks and time spent worrying about repaying his loan, the alcohol had become an accelerant that caused Cornero's anxieties to flare up and nearly consume him. On July 31, 1955, following another heated meeting with Dalitz, Cornero made his way to a craps table, intent on proving that he was no loser, that fate was his friend. Each throw of the dice only proved that he was a loser. Rather than stare fate in the face, he imbibed drink after drink. He was down more than $37,000. His losses fed his desperation, which fed his anxieties. He could find no relief. Then to make matters worse, a waitress presented him with a bill for all the drinks he had consumed. He screamed at her that he was the casino's president! But before another angry protest could explode from his mouth, Cornero fell onto the craps table then rolled off onto the floor. Many, though not the medical examiner, attributed Cornero's death to a poisoned drink. Immediately following his death, the glass from which he had been drinking was carried into the kitchen and briskly washed. The police were called two hours after Cornero's death. They couldn't identify the glass from which Cornero had taken his last drink.

Steve Fischer writes in *When the Mob Ran Vegas*, "More than 1,000 mourners attended Cornero's funeral, including nearly all the casino owners from the Strip."[4] He had often told friends that at his funeral, he would like his favorite song, "The Wabash Cannonball," to be sung. Fischer goes on to report that though Cornero had raised nearly $10 million for the Stardust, "his bank account, which had turned out to be all of [his] assets had only $800 in it the day he died."[5] He did receive immortality of sorts when Cary Grant played a character based on Cornero (Joe Bascopolous, aka Joe "the Greek" Adams) in the movie *Mr. Lucky*.

Following Cornero's death, Dalitz offered the position of running the Stardust to the dead man's brother, Louis Stralla, but—as was predicted by many of the casino's employees—Stralla didn't last long. It would have been an untenable position for him if he suspected Dalitz and his partners were responsible for his brother's death. However, it initially appeared as a thoughtful and generous gesture, for Dalitz was, in addition to his other talents, a superb public relations man. And he may have genuinely regretted hounding Cornero to the point of uncontrollable anxiety. Dalitz, after all, proved to be man of unpredictable contradictions: one moment a hard-edged and pitiless casino owner, another moment a caring and generous employer.

The death of Cornero left the mob with another Bugsy Siegel–like opportunity. After the departure of Stralla, the mob moved in quickly, and they installed Jake "the Barber" Factor as front man and head of operations. Jake was the brother of famed cosmetic tycoon Max Factor. In an earlier career, Jake, after abandoning his vocation as a barber, had sailed to England. There, he presented himself as an astute investor with a Midas touch. His astuteness, however, was of the Ponzi variety. He managed to swindle his clients out of $7 to $8 million. Back in Chicago, he faced the inevitability of extradition to England. Not sitting around waiting for government agents to clasp handcuffs on his wrists, he arranged with the assistance of Murray "the Camel" Humphreys, a consigliere to the Chicago Outfit, to have himself kidnapped. Nothing quite takes one out of circulation like a good kidnapping, and Humphreys was the man to make an ersatz crime look genuine. (Humphreys was a well-known criminal mastermind whose name eventually appeared in the Nevada Black Book and so was never permitted to visit Vegas.) When the likelihood of extradition had passed and a ransom paid, a freed Jake made a surprise public appearance. He expressed gratitude for being alive. His face was that of a man who had just been released from a horrible ordeal: he was unshaven, his hair was uncombed. However, below his grungy chin, he was nattily dressed in a clean, well-ironed white suit and polished shoes, not exactly the attire of one who has been bound, gagged, and nearly starved. Though looking as if attired for a Palm Beach cocktail party, he told police he had not yet recovered from the harrowing experience of being kidnapped by desperate men. A few cynical crime reporters noted that by the time of the release, the statute of limitations had run its course on Jake's swindle. He was now free to become a Las Vegas hotshot. The mob toasted Humphreys' successful maneuver in the art of outwitting the law. However, the scenario needed a fall guy, a bad guy who could be blamed for the wicked act of kidnapping. So the crime was pinned on not-too-bright Roger Touhy, a rival Chicago gangster, who was sent to prison on the trumped-up kidnapping charge. He was so cleverly framed that neither the police nor the district attorney believed that Touhy had been set up. However, following a series of clever maneuvers by his lawyers, Touhy was finally released from prison on November 24, 1959. Unfortunately, his freedom was shortlived: it came to a bloody end on December 16, 1959. While standing on the front steps leading up to his sister's house, he was shot multiple times by three gunmen, who made a quick getaway. Poor Touhy, not able to rat on the men who framed him, died an hour after being blasted.

With Jake fronting as boss of the Stardust, the casino proved to be one of the most popular casinos in Nevada. "Its one thousand rooms rented for $6 a night; its Lido de Paris can-can show, with French showgirls and elaborate sets, revolutionized Las Vegas entertainment. 'We planned a variety-type show where we could have ice skating one moment and a full production number in another,' Dalitz said in 1983."[6]

Money poured into the casino and out of the count room into the hands of Dalitz and his partners. If money is your god, then the Stardust was not merely a place of worship, it was heaven on earth.

However, not all was good. There were annoying threats blowing across the desert like a hot desert wind from just over the horizon: Senator Estes Kefauver was gunning for Vegas mobsters, and Dalitz was looked upon as a leading target of opportunity. The committee thought he was an ideal prey for its mob-hunting party. Dalitz, however, was warned, and he proved as elusive as a desert fox, escaping baying hounds.

The determined Kefauver, who would campaign for the presidency in 1952 while wearing a Davy Crockett coonskin hat, complete with raccoon tail, was not a man who gave up easily. (Though he repeatedly sought higher office, he was not above lamenting that it was too bad Davy Crockett's young fans weren't old enough to vote. The coonskin cap would be a campaign artifact.) Not like a backwoodsman Crockett, but with the bloodhound zeal of a Javert, Kefauver pursued Dalitz. For the rest of his life, Dalitz was the subject of FBI surveillance, even when on vacation with his wife and daughter.

When subpoenaed to appear before Kefauver's committee (i.e., the Senate Special Committee to Investigate Crime in Interstate Commerce), Dalitz vanished as if he could smell that a subpoena was near. From city to city, subpoenas went unserved. While the most likely place to bag Dalitz should have been Vegas, the committee finally caught up to him in Los Angeles. Facing the grim and stern faces of the men of the committee looking like a Daumier etching of a panel of hanging judges, Dalitz appeared with his lawyer, Charles Carr. The choice of lawyer was a brilliant maneuver, for Carr was a good friend and Yale Law School classmate of Kefauver. Dalitz anticipated the questions he would be asked; each one arrived like gentle tosses of a foam-rubber ball to be batted back by a plastic bat. There were no strikes, no errors, just foam balls gently batted back to the committee.

> Kefauver: "Efforts were made to serve a subpoena on you at various and different places but without any success. You were aware of that; were you not?"
>
> Dalitz: "I assumed that there was a subpoena for me from what I read in the papers."
>
> Kefauver: "The marshals at Cleveland, Detroit, and other places had a subpoena for you but could not locate you."
>
> Dalitz: "Nobody came to my home with a subpoena . . ."
>
> Kefauver: "You were not there; you left."
>
> Dalitz: "I have been back and forth a few times, yes . . ."
>
> Kefauver: "Why didn't you let us know where you were so we could have you come in and testify at Cleveland or Detroit?"
>
> Dalitz: "Well, Senator, I frankly was just alarmed at the whole thing and all the publicity. I have never had any publicity in the past."

Dalitz left the hearing like a multiple home run hitter.[7]

Dalitz's new Desert Inn front man, Wilbur Clark, was also called to testify before the committee. His testimony was as unrevealing as Dalitz's.

> Q. "What is your function at the hotel? What do you do there?"
>
> A. "Well, I am supposed to be the general manager."

Q. "Are you?"

A. "I think so."

Q. "You have the most nebulous idea of your business I ever saw. You have a smile on your face but I don't know how the devil you do it."

A. "I have done it all my life."[8]

Free from having to testify, Dalitz refocused his attention on the Desert Inn. He decided it needed attractions other than just gambling to draw in out-of-town bettors. He built a magnificent 18-hole golf course, which he named the Desert Inn Country Club. And to attract top-flight golfers, he started the Tournament of Champions, with cash prizes and a large donation to charity. Among the celebrities who Dalitz befriended and who regularly played at the club were Bing Crosby and Bob Hope. Though they benefitted from their association with the club, they were not the only entertainers who experienced Dalitz's largess: Frank Sinatra's career had spiraled down in the early 1950s. He could barely make a living. His records weren't selling and his club dates had withered. After receiving calls for help from a couple of Sinatra's Mafia protectors in New Jersey, Dalitz hired the forlorn singer to perform at the Desert Inn. Sinatra, a mob wannabe, would remain a friend of Dalitz and perform whatever favors Dalitz asked of him.

In addition to polishing his image by his sponsorship of golf tournaments and his friendships with beloved celebrities, Dalitz became a primary sponsor and big fund-raiser for Senator Pat McCarran. From his earliest days in Vegas, Dalitz had come to rely on McCarran, who had demonstrated his early support of mobsters running casinos when he removed obstacles facing Bugsy Siegel's development of the Flamingo. As Steve Fischer noted in *When the Mob Ran Vegas*, "McCarran repriortized (*sic*) the building needs list for projects going on in southern Nevada. They were repriortized so that Ben and the Nevada Projects Corporation could receive the copper fixtures and tilings they needed to get the Flamingo up and running by Christmas 1946."[9]

And when the Kefauver Committee had nettled Dalitz, co-chairman of the Judiciary Committee McCarran had worked behind the scenes to make sure that the committee's questions were nonincriminatory. He had also sought to reduce the budget for Kefauver's Committee.

"Nevada politics represented a classic old boys' club, and the biggest old boy on the block was Senator Patrick McCarran, a Reno native born in

1876. . . . He opposed any federal moves against gambling and organized crime, a side effect of his friendship with sundry notorious mobsters."[10]

Dalitz so relied on McCarran's friendship that he would not tolerate anyone attempting to belittle or diminish the senator. Hank Greenspun, the publisher of the *Las Vegas Sun* newspaper, presented a problem that had to be quickly solved. Greenspun had written a series of devastating articles attacking McCarran. Dalitz was furious. He and other casino owners sought to censor Greenspun by cancelling their advertising in the *Sun*. A furious Greenspun confronted Dalitz at the Desert Inn.

"What's behind all these ad cancellations?" Greenspun demanded.

"You should know," Moe replied. "Why did you have to attack the Old Man?"

"What business is it of the Desert Inn, or any other hotel, what I print in my paper?" Greenspun challenged.

"You've put us all in a terrible position," Moe said. "You know as well as I that we do what he tells us. You know he got us our licenses. If we don't go along, you know what will happen to us."[11]

Greenspun sued McCarran and the casino owners. The trial dragged on, and finally the casino owners paid Greenspun $85,500, which was considerably less than the $1 million he had demanded. The casino owners also agreed to continue their advertising and refrain from trying to influence the paper's editorial policy. McCarran, much to his chagrin, had to sit through a deposition, during which he denied any conspiracy on his part to affect the editorials in the *Sun*.

That Moe Dalitz and many other Jewish casino owners had befriended McCarran demonstrated their need for a strong lobbying presence in Washington; it was so essential to their success that they were willing to overlook McCarran's anti-Semitic and racist opinions. And it wasn't only his opinions that were offensive: McCarran had worked zealously to limit the number of Jewish refugees from Nazism who were seeking asylum in the United States. If it hadn't been for McCarran's usefulness, none of the owners would have associated with him. In fact, they probably would have supported an opposition candidate for the Senate, but if their candidate had lost, the mob would have risked sacrificing its financial interests. Better to stick with the bigot you know. Though McCarran expressed his noxious opinions in private, he never did so in the company of Dalitz and his partners. He knew when to censor himself.

Senator Harry Reid said McCarran was "one of the most prejudiced people who has ever served in the Senate."[12] Following his death, McCarran's reputation as a bigot became well known. On February 16, 2021, the Clark County commissioners voted unanimously to officially change the name of McCarran International Airport to Harry Reid International Airport. McCarran had served the interests of the mob, and he took his prejudices to the grave. He would be replaced not only by other Nevada politicians who would benefit Dalitz, but also by Richard Nixon, who invited Dalitz to his presidential inauguration.

Following his uneventful Senate testimony, Dalitz had a clear road ahead to expand his interests. He purchased property adjacent to the Stardust so that the hotel would have thirteen hundred rooms. In addition, he brought over the *Lido de Paris* show and offered an audience the most beautiful topless showgirls. To say the show was a hit would be an understatement. He next got a $1.2 million loan through the efforts of his pal Jimmy Hoffa, president of the Teamsters Union, which was used to build the Stardust Golf Course and Country Club. (The relationship of Hoffa and Dalitz continued until Hoffa's death.)

Though Dalitz is primarily known for his ownership positions in the Desert Inn and the Stardust, he had additional positions in several other casinos. His partners were not only Jewish mobsters but also Italian ones. Each group played a different role. As Suzanne Dalitz (the daughter of Moe Dalitz) explained to the author: "The Italians resorted to the threat of violence to achieve their ends, while the Jews used their brains."[13] The relationship of Italian and Jewish mobsters worked well because they had goals in common: to make as much money as possible. However, there were some Italian mobsters who resented the largely Jewish control of the casinos. They often referred disparagingly to Vegas as "Jew Town." One such resentful gangster was Jimmy "the Weasel" Fratianno, who claimed that Dalitz was in thrall to Tony Accardo and Sam Giancana of the Chicago Outfit. If anything, those Chicago mobsters were often dependent on Dalitz for his knowledge about how to execute the skim. When they ventured into Vegas, it was Dalitz whom they called on for advice. Other times, it was Meyer Lansky whom they also relied on. It is not surprising then that Angelo "Gyp" DeCarlo, of the New Jersey mob, was reported in an FBI memo to have "complained the fact that the Jews wield so much influence in Las Vegas, giving the Italians only a few crumbs."[14]

Sam Giancana also expressed his anger at the Jews of Las Vegas: "A January 1962 [FBI] memo reports Sam Giancana speaking very derogatively of

Jews who were 'taking advantage in Las Vegas that barred Mafiosi from legal gaming.'"[15]

Some of the Italian mobsters felt that they were more important than their Jewish brethren and so attempted to demean and/or diminish them—usually when just talking among themselves, but while being taped by the FBI. It was commonplace, for example, to state that Meyer Lansky was nothing more than the mob's accountant, when in fact he was as powerful as Lucky Luciano, both of whom ruled from their prominent positions on the National Crime Syndicate's board of directors.

Perhaps as a rebuke to the Outfit, Dalitz demonstrated his power while having lunch with the Outfit's man in Vegas, Johnny Rosselli. Dalitz, Rosselli, and another man were seated in a booth about to partake of their lunch when a sheriff's deputy came to their table. He asked Rosselli to step outside for a moment. Rosselli rudely refused and berated the deputy for his intrusion. The deputy left and was soon replaced by the sheriff, who grabbed Rosselli by his collar, jerked him to an upright position, and warned him never to refuse an order from one of his deputies. He then marched Rosselli out of the restaurant and put him in a jail cell for twenty-four hours. Dalitz and the other man went right on eating. Neither one commented that the sheriff was a benefactor of Dalitz's largess and was doing a favor. The message was relayed to Chicago and that was the end of it. As everyone knew: Moe Dalitz was Mr. Las Vegas. He was even thought of that highly out of Vegas, though some attempted to show he was not as tough as his reputation. One such person was heavyweight boxer Sonny Liston, who even scared Muhammad Ali before their first fight in Florida.

The following encounter was described in Michael Newton's book *Mr. Mob*:

> On October 25, 1963, while Moe and a companion lunched at Hollywood's Beverly Rodeo Hotel, Liston rolled in looking for trouble. He approached Moe's table with the comment that Dalitz "ain't such a tough guy away from Las Vegas." Moe's unknown response made Liston raise his fist as if to strike. Author Don Remnick claims it was "a joke," but Moe replied in deadly earnest. "If you hit me nigger," he declared, "you'd better kill me. Because if you don't, I'll make one phone call and you'll be dead in twenty-four hours." Liston gasped, then turned and fled—not only the hotel, but California, hurrying home to Las Vegas.[16]

Though Dalitz wanted to be respected and feared as a tough guy, he also wanted to be accepted into a cosmopolitan society of philanthropists, tycoons, and the socially elite. He had an exquisite instinct for public relations and used it to create an image of himself that no other mobster would have considered. Dalitz and his partners borrowed $1 million in 1959 from Jimmy Hoffa's Teamsters Pension Fund to build Sunrise Hospital (now Sunrise Hospital and Medical Center). It opened with great fanfare, covered by all local media. Dalitz was lauded by the governor and the senators of Nevada and the mayor of Vegas. Tributes poured in from business leaders and celebrities. It was the community's first children's hospital, and its pediatric care was honored with numerous awards. The institution quickly grew and became a prominent teaching hospital that is affiliated with the University of Las Vegas School of Medicine. All credit was given to a proud Morris Barney Dalitz. He next moved on to developing the Las Vegas Convention Center, for which he was lauded for helping to make Vegas a top destination for trade shows and conventions. In addition, his company, the Paradise Development Company, built the first shopping mall in Vegas, hundreds of houses and apartments, golf courses, synagogues and churches. The new housing and religious structures attracted thousands of new residents to the city. As Dalitz's accomplishments generated more and more media coverage and a cornucopia of awards, he became less known as a gambler and casino owner and more as a builder of the modern Vegas. So impressive were his contributions that the media could barely catch its breath when congratulating him. He had become Mr. Las Vegas, a far cry from the bootlegger of the 1920s and associate of Detroit's Purple Gang and Cleveland's Mayfield Road Gang. Men and women who had personal and professional relationships with him were often quoted in the *Las Vegas Review-Journal* as if commenting on a one-man endowment fund.

Marydean Martin, a Vegas advertising executive, said of Dalitz: "He gave back to the community. When the Maude Frazier Building (at UNLV) was built, it had no furniture. He bought all the furniture and didn't want anybody to know about it. He was that kind of person."[17]

And Stardust manager Herb Tobman commented: "He never turned me down for anything charitable. I was in awe of meeting him. As far as I'm concerned he was a great man. . . . Moe's charity is legendary around this town. There has never been a greater influence on this city."[18]

Dalitz was named Humanitarian of the Year by the American Cancer Society and presented with the Torch of Liberty Award by the Anti-Defamation League of B'nai B'rith: a plaque was lovingly presented by Joan Rivers at a special Torch of Liberty gala ceremony. And the awards just kept coming. Dalitz was honored and decorated like a conquering general. And his philanthropy did not cease with his death. Fourteen charities were happy to receive Dalitz's posthumous gifts of more than $1 million from his estate. The charities included the United Way, the City of Hope, the Salvation Army, St. Jude's Children's Research Hospital, the National Parkinson's Foundation, and a number of local charities. Had he been alive, he surely would have received even more awards. Instead, numerous personages acclaimed the wonder of Dalitz's generosity to a media that was hungry to gobble up the encomiums.

Senator Paul Laxalt said of Dalitz: "My general opinion of him, as a citizen of Nevada, is favorable. He's been a good citizen, and his dealings with gaming authorities over the years, they too have been favorable."[19]

Allard Roen, a partner in the Paradise Development Company, added his encomium: "[Dalitz] was always in the forefront of charitable and civic drives. I, to this day, do not remember him ever turning a charity down. It was always his contention Las Vegas has been good to us, we want to give something back to Las Vegas."[20]

Suzanne Dalitz told the author that her father was so much more than just a bootlegger and a gambler (though liquor and gambling became legal), he was a true benefactor of society. You cannot say that of someone who is just defined as a mobster.

Nearly to the end of his days, in addition to being a philanthropist, Dalitz had never ceased being an entrepreneur, investing in projects that he thought would be highly profitable for himself and his partners. One venture led to Carlsbad, California, where he helped Mervyn Adelson and Irwin Molasky develop La Costa Resort and Spa. Unfortunately, it turned out not to be a media-friendly venture. No crowning act of philanthropy was celebrated. The media already had its knives out for the Teamsters Pension Fund for having funded mob-run casinos in Vegas. Now there was evidence that the Teamsters Pension Fund had also loaned the money for the building of La Costa.

Combine the Teamsters, the legacy of Jimmy Hoffa, and endless fascination with the mob, and you have the makings of an irresistible scandal and a hot-off-the-presses story. It was a bonanza for the media. It salivated for a good mob story, especially during the decade when *The Godfather* was a whirlwind in the Zeitgeist. In 1975, *Penthouse* magazine, known for its frontal nude photos of luscious babes, was about to make journalistic history. It published an article titled "La Costa: The Hundred Million Dollar Resort with Criminal Clientele." The article wove together the Teamsters Pension Fund and La Costa, citing the resort as a mob playground. Rare for *Penthouse* to write an exposé, but the article generated news. It pointed out that the resort was developed by Dalitz, Adelson, Molasky, and Roen, all of whom had questionable backgrounds. And to connect the dots, the article emphasized that the money to build the spa came from the Teamsters Central States Pension Fund, which had assets of more than $1.5 billion. The money was used to create a playground for mobsters and their friends and business associates. The article could have turned the sweet tributes to Dalitz's philanthropy into sour ironies. His carefully veneered image could have cracked if enough people accepted the article as true. Almost as if to make sure that readers knew who Dalitz was, the writers gave his full name, Morris B. "Moe" Dalitz, and noted that he and Roen were officials of the resort. The four subjects of the article were not about to let a slick nudie magazine besmirch their reputations and so they filed a libel suit asking for $522 million. In 1982, a jury absolved *Penthouse* of any liability and the plaintiffs, as expected, appealed the decision. In 1985, just prior to the commencement of another trial, the two sides agreed to settle. *Penthouse* issued a statement that the plaintiffs were not members of organized crime and did not imply that they were. In addition, it issued a statement commending Dalitz and Roen for their philanthropic activities. Furthermore, *Penthouse* acknowledged that among the plaintiffs' successful business activities is La Costa resort itself, "one of the outstanding resort complexes of the world." In return, the plaintiffs issued encomiums for Bob Guccione, publisher of *Penthouse*, for his magnanimous contributions that were honored by numerous awards attesting to his personal and professional accomplishments. And so the case came to an end, following millions of dollars spent on legal fees and three days that Dalitz had spent giving testimony. As a footnote to the matter, in March 2013, Merv Adelson confessed to a *Vanity Fair* writer that he once had ties to organized crime. Very few people were surprised by his confession. But perhaps some would have been surprised to know that beginning in 1963 Dalitz generously paid $5,000 a month to the wife of imprisoned loan shark and hit man Harold Konigsberg, who had been indicted, convicted, and sentenced to life in prison for the murder of a New Jersey Teamsters official on orders from Anthony "Tony Pro" Provenzano, a capo in the Genovese crime family and a vice president of the Teamsters Union. The monthly payments to Konigsberg's wife continued until Dalitz's death. For Dalitz, perhaps it was just another act of charity.

One person who did not know of Dalitz's reputation for charity and for being a tough guy was Judith Campbell, the mistress shared by President Kennedy and Chicago Outfit boss, Sam Giancana. At one of Dalitz's New Year's Eve parties,

Campbell got drunk and quarreled with [her date, Johnny] Rosselli, where-upon Moe kissed her cheek and said, "Come on, now, don't get so mad." Campbell slapped Moe's face, prompting a stunned Rosselli to remark, "You must be crazy." Next morning, Rosselli told Campbell, "Nobody smacks Moe Dalitz across the face. Christ, don't you know anything yet? Haven't you learned anything?"[21]

Dalitz let it go.

Everyone else in Vegas knew the name of Moe Dalitz. Outside of Vegas, however, most people only learned the name of Moe Dalitz either because of the *Penthouse* article or because of Howard Hughes, whose every move seemed to have generated headlines. Hughes had moved into the Desert Inn, taking over the two top floors, which were usually reserved for high rollers only. However, Hughes and his army of Mormon attendants neither gambled nor drank liquor. Dalitz and his partners were losing a fortune because of Hughes. They wanted him out. Hughes was told he either had to buy the Inn or move out.

In the late 1970s, my then wife and I were spending the Christmas holidays at La Costa. There, we met a friendly couple from Shreveport, Louisiana. They invited us to a New Year's Eve party at their home on the grounds of the resort. I found myself sitting next to a kind-looking grand-fatherly man and got talking with him about the resort and other topics. After complaining of a lower backache, he brought up the name of Howard Hughes, and he said to me,

> You know, my partners and I used to own the Desert Inn. Hughes moved in and wouldn't leave. He took over the penthouse, which was usually reserved for high rollers. He had dozens of his guys with him. None of them drank or gambled. We couldn't make any money. We told him to leave. We got a mes-sage back that he wanted to buy the place. How much did we want? We came up with a figure that we thought he would find too high. We figured he would reject it and move out. Instead, he agreed to our price.[22]

I was astounded to hear such inside information from someone whom I had just met and asked him his name: Morris Kleinman. He had been Dalitz's partner since their early days in Detroit and Cleveland. I never saw him again, but I later checked out what he had told me. It was true. (Chapter 6 is about Howard Hughes and his Vegas casinos.)

As he was nearing the end of his transit through an exciting life, Dalitz was listed in *Forbes* magazine as one of the four hundred richest men in America. The year was 1981, and the magazine listed Dalitz having $110 million. It was unusual (an understatement) for a mobster to be listed on the magazine's list of the richest Americans, but Dalitz had already proven to the world that he was no ordinary mobster. He had become one of the most esteemed and honored citizens of Las Vegas, a man seemingly venerated by the news media, a man who could do no wrong.

On August 31, 1989, Dalitz died of heart and kidney disease. His death defied the accepted fate of so many mobsters who died violently. Dalitz had lived a charmed life, and he left behind monuments to his generosity. At his funeral, 350 mourners, including politicians and celebrities, attended. Former governor Grant Sawyer delivered one of several eulogies.

Speaking at the Mob Museum, Suzanne Dalitz stated: "In growing up, I began to realize what an amazing person and what an amazing journey he had, and I was incredibly proud of him."[23]

In one of our conversations, she said that her father "was a gambler, not a mobster, and he should be remembered for all the good works he did. He gave millions to charity. How many mobsters do that?"[24] She was, of course, correct. He was a tough guy, who never denied his past, but he also took pride in his many acts of benevolence. He had enjoyed being a bootlegger, but he also enjoyed being honored for being a good citizen of Vegas. Yes, he was a tough guy, for whom Judaism was an important part of his life. And as a Jew he performed many mitzvahs (i.e., individual acts of kindness and generosity). It is not surprising that at his funeral he was eulogized as a mensch.

Several months before writing this chapter, I was having lunch with a lawyer who had worked for prominent lawyer Roy Cohn. The subject of Moe Dalitz came up, and the lawyer told me that "Roy had been handling a divorce case for Dalitz's wife, Averill Knigge. Roy called Dalitz a punk. His client responded: 'He's no punk. Believe me, he's no punk.'"[25] Indeed, he was not.

NOTES

1. Robert Lacey, *Little Man: Meyer Lansky and the Gangster Life* (Boston: Little, Brown and Company, 1991), 258.

2. John L. Smith, *Las Vegas Review-Journal*, February 7, 1999, p. 3, www .reviewjournal.com/news/moe-dalitz/ (accessed May 15, 2021).

3. Smith, *Las Vegas Review-Journal*, p. 3.

4. Steve Fischer, *When the Mob Ran Vegas* (Las Vegas: Berkline Press, 2005), 96.

5. Fischer, *When the Mob Ran Vegas*, 96.

6. John L. Smith, "Moe Dalitz and the Desert," in *The Players: The Men Who Made Las Vegas*, ed. Jack Sheehan (Reno: University of Nevada Press, 1997), 41.

7. Michael Newton, *Mr. Mob: The Life and Crimes of Moe Dalitz* (Jefferson, NC: McFarland and Company, Inc., 2007) 143.

8. Newton, *Mr. Mob*, 143.

9. Fischer, *When the Mob Ran Vegas*, 14.

10. Newton, *Mr. Mob*, 120.

11. Newton, *Mr. Mob*, 152.

12. Richard N. Velotta, *Las Vegas Sun*, August 25, 2012, https://lasvegassun.com/news/2012/aug/25/harry-reid-pat-mccarrans-name-shouldnt-be-anything/ (accessed May 4, 2021).

13. Conversation with Suzanne Dalitz, February 14, 2022.

14. Newton, *Mr. Mob*, 196.

15. Newton, *Mr. Mob*, 197.

16. Newton, *Mr. Mob*, 199.

17. Smith, "Moe Dalitz and the Desert," 44.

18. https://www.reviewjournal.com/new/moe-dalitz/ (accessed May 5, 2021).

19. Smith, "Moe Dalitz and the Desert," 43–44.

20. Smith, "Moe Dalitz and the Desert," 43–44.

21. Newton, *Mr. Mob*, 218.

22. Morris Kleinman, conversation with author.

23. The Mob Museum, https://vimeo.com/289784892 (accessed May 17, 2021).

24. Suzanne Dalitz, interview with author.

25. Conversation with author, November 2020.

5

JIMMY HOFFA
Las Vegas Financier

When it came to investing in Las Vegas, Moe Dalitz could not have found a more agreeable banker than Jimmy Hoffa and his Teamsters Central States Pension Fund (CSPF). Hoffa and Dalitz had met as young men in Detroit when Hoffa was beginning his career as a union organizer and Dalitz was trying to keep his laundries free of unionization. The two had come to a mutually beneficial agreement at that time; it was a presage of mutuality that would sustain their relationship years later in Vegas. It was not only Dalitz's Desert Inn that benefitted from the CSPF, but so did Caesars Palace, Circus Circus, the Sands, the Dunes, and the Stardust. Hoffa allegedly took a fee for each loan and received 1 percent of the skim from each casino to which he had lent money. He became the most powerful financier of Vegas casinos.

From where did this powerful corrupt union boss emerge? James Riddle Hoffa was born on February 14, 1913, in Brazil, Indiana. He was the son of John Hoffa and Viola (née, Riddle) Hoffa. His father worked as a coal driller, and the coal dust would invade his lungs, eventually causing lung cancer. When Jimmy was seven years old, his father succumbed to the disease, leaving a family struck by the devastations of poverty. Though Viola had taken in wash to supplement the family's income, it was not sufficient to feed and clothe them following the death of her husband. She moved the family to Detroit, where she hoped to earn enough to keep food on the table and a roof over the heads of herself, her two sons and two daughters.

She worked as a cook in a restaurant, worked as a maid, and took in washing. Her older daughter, Jennetta, helped her wash and iron clothes, and the younger daughter, Nancy, helped whenever her mother needed assistance. Her sons, Jimmy and Billy, delivered the cleaned clothes to customers. The two boys also "helped the family finances in other ways: to augment the food supply at the Hoffa table, the two typically barefooted small-town boys stole apples and pears, shot rabbits and trapped birds, and strung clam lines in the local river."[1]

Viola eventually found more profitable work in an automotive factory, where she polished radiator caps. The repetitive work was exceedingly boring, but at least it meant a regular paycheck that was more than she had earned as a cook, maid, and laundress. Nevertheless, she was an understandably bitter woman whose kindness had been worn away by the acid of economic deprivation. Jimmy felt that his mother's hardships should be alleviated to the extent he was able to offer some relief. He needed to contribute to his family's welfare. He quit school after completing the ninth grade and got a job as a stock boy in a department store. Unfortunately, the Depression soon spread like a disease across the country, driving businesses into bankruptcy and their employees onto the dole. Yet, Hoffa was determined not to be victim of an economy infected by the greed of Wall Street manipulators. He spent days looking for work and was finally given a job at the Kroger Grocery and Baking Company. In order to get the job, he had to lie about his age. He said he was eighteen, though his true age was sixteen. Though only 5'5" (which would be his ultimate height, seven inches shorter than his father had been), he was powerfully built with bulging biceps and thickly muscled forearms. He was an ideal specimen of physical strength for unloading railroad cars that were packed with lettuce, strawberries, carrots, and various seasonal fruits and vegetables. The pay was a meager thirty-two cents an hour, but the warehouse workers were paid only for the time they were actually unloading produce. Much of the time they simply sat around waiting for the next shipment to arrive. They were often in the warehouse for sixty hours a week but usually paid for only about forty-eight hours of work. A good weekly wage would amount to $15. The $60 a month that Hoffa could bring home made a significant difference in the daily diet of the Hoffa family. They would not have to survive on noodles and spam. Among poorly paid warehouse workers, it was not unusual for each of them to stuff a few leaves of lettuce, stalks of carrots, and a handful of strawberries deep into their pockets. Had their thefts been discovered, they would have been immediately fired. The more cautious ones, however, refrained from minor thefts.

Nevertheless, there was much grumbling and resentment from most of the men about their working conditions and low pay. But they felt helpless to effect any changes. If they complained directly to a supervisor, they were told that if they were unhappy, they could quit. There were many others who would be eager to take their places. So their complaints remained muffled, shared only among themselves. They were all poor young men who could not live without their weekly salaries.

Hoffa saw a future that was not shared by his fellow workers. He saw a time when they could develop leverage and make demands that management would have to accept. He believed that he and perhaps a handful of like-minded workers could eventually inspire all the workers to rebel. He bided his time, waiting for an opportunity to strike successfully. He knew the workers would need time to overcome their fears of retribution and their anxieties about being unemployed. Hoffa worked diligently to fire up the courage of his fellow workers, telling them that if they stuck together and struck as a single unifying force, they would win concessions from management. He succeeded. The workers were becoming a simmering revolutionary force, fired up with anger and determined to make management bend to their demands. There would be no turning back. And then it finally happened: the workers refused to unload a truckload of fresh strawberries that needed to be quickly refrigerated. Management was furious and threatened to fire all the rebellious workers. Still the workers refused to obey management's demands to get back to work; they stood firm against threats to their livelihoods. Management had impotently threatened to bring in strikebreakers, but it was nighttime and no scabs could be rounded up. Management was so frustrated that they agreed to meet the following morning with Hoffa and four other leaders of the work stoppage: James Langley, Bobby Holmes, Frank Collins, and Sam Calhoun. But first the workers would have to unload and refrigerate the strawberries. The freshness of the fruit was management's top initial concern. If the fruit were to become moldy, the company would not only lose money on its shipment, but the company's reputation for reliability would be tarnished and there might be fewer shipments at a higher cost in the future. Trusting management's commitment to negotiate, the workers followed Hoffa's lead and agreed to unload the strawberries.

The next day, the five leaders of the work stoppage met with management and began negotiations that lasted for several days. Negotiations waxed and waned, tempers flared and cooled. In the end, both sides agreed that the workers would be guaranteed a raise to forty-five cents an hour and a minimum of a half day's pay. The workers were pleased and looked upon

Hoffa as their advocate, who had won for them their increased salaries and some minor benefits. For Hoffa, his accomplishments gave him a new sense of power. He not only commanded respect from his fellow workers, but also a grudging respect from management, though his immediate supervisor despised him and sought ways to make his life difficult. Hoffa was too tough and determined to continue unpacking boxes of fruits and vegetables. Losing his temper with his provocative supervisor caused him to break out of the prison of his limited existence and seek a greater role for himself. He decided to become a union organizer and a negotiator on behalf of working men and women. It was a more consequential role than being a forty-five-cents-an-hour warehouse worker.

After several attempts, he finally succeeded in being hired as an organizer for the International Brotherhood of Teamsters. He believed that he had found his calling. He was an inspired organizer and natural leader. His ability to vividly express the concerns and grievances of working-class people attracted truck drivers to the ranks of the Teamsters. Once drivers heard Hoffa's appeals, they believed that he could win them increased pay and benefits from fleet owners. And he did not disappoint them. He was indeed a fierce advocate who would fight for his members, getting them the results that they couldn't get for themselves. As an extremely productive organizer and brilliant negotiator, his status in the union increased. Where others had failed, Hoffa pulled concessions out of stubborn fleet owners.

His techniques were not the ones of the boardroom: if he had to use his fists, he used his fists. He got into brawls with strikebreakers and was arrested numerous times. But neither billy clubs nor brass knuckles dissuaded him from carrying on the fight for unionization. He was exactly what the Teamsters needed and what put-upon drivers wanted. He was a force that was detested by fleet owners, who tried to castrate Hoffa's efforts by hiring goons who fought with lead pipes, brass knuckles, wooden clubs, and chains.

Though Hoffa was a fighter who went toe-to-toe with strikebreaking goons, he knew that because he was outnumbered, he needed to have his own army of goons. Hoffa, however, did not have the resources to recruit enough brawlers to match those of the union's enemies. He would have to make deals with organizations that could supply the number of fighters he needed. A tough, pragmatic realist, Hoffa started making deals with mobsters. He believed it was worth it. Without their aid, strikes could go on for weeks and perhaps months, resulting in drivers being unable to pay for food and rent. With mob muscle, however, he could end strikes quickly and bring opponents to the negotiating tables. So he made a pact with the mob: he not only used mob muscle to combat the strikebreakers, but he also used the mob's goons to intimidate independent truck drivers into joining the Teamsters.

> From then on, Hoffa's relationship with the underworld was to be an ongoing one. From his liaison with the Detroit gangsters came introductions and often strong social ties to mobsters around the country—in Cleveland, New York, Chicago (where many of Hoffa's allies had close connections to the old Capone organization) and ultimately in every major city.[2]

Among the prominent mobsters with whom Hoffa had dealings were Anthony "Tony Jack" Giacalone; Anthony "Tony Pro" Provenzano; Salvatore "Sally Bugs" Briguglio and his brother, Gabriel; John "Johnny Dio" Dioguardi; Allen Dorfman; and, of course, Moe Dalitz and his partners.

Anthony Giacalone had been Hoffa's main contact with the Detroit mob and was later thought to have set up Hoffa to be murdered. (Why was Hoffa murdered? Following his release from prison in 1971, Hoffa wanted to run the Teamsters again, but President Nixon had made it a condition of Hoffa's release that he could not run for president of the union. Yet, Hoffa was so determined to regain the presidency of the union that he became a threat to the mob, who benefitted from the union's new president, Frank Fitzsimmons, a man whom Hoffa regarded as a corrupt patsy and mob stooge. Giacalone rightly regarded Hoffa as a threat to the mob's control of the Teamsters Central States Pension Fund [CSPF], which was in effect the mob's bank. When Hoffa let them know he was not only determined to regain the presidency, but that he would end the mob's influence with the union, his doom was ordained. Careful to avoid incrimination, Giacalone arranged an alibi for his whereabouts at the time that Hoffa was supposedly killed. Giacalone was at the Southfield Athletic Club.)

Loyalty was obviously not a principal ingredient in Giacalone's character. It made no difference to him that Hoffa had arranged for him to get a $500,000 loan from the Central States Pension Fund. Though enriched by the loan, he nevertheless attempted to steal $500,000 from Hoffa's safe. Giacalone believed the 10 percent cash kickbacks that Hoffa took from each of his Vegas casino loans was placed in a bedroom safe. He was unable to gain access to the money and gave up. Though Hoffa didn't know about Giacalone's attempted safecracking venture, he certainly knew of Giacalone's gangster instincts and the numerous jail sentences that he had served, yet when reporters asked him why he associated with such a noxious character, he said that he was his friend and a great guy.

Seen together they were an odd pair and not only because of the difference in their heights: Hoffa was 5'5" and Giacalone was 6'. It was the way they presented themselves to the public. While Hoffa dressed in inexpensive off-the-rack suits, his mob pal was a comparative Beau Brummel. A stylish dresser, Giacalone was often pictured in a flashy sport jacket, elegantly tailored trousers, a custom-made shirt decorated by a colorful silk tie, imported Italian shoes, and tinted aviator glasses. A man so meticulously devoted to the highest standards of gangster fashion, Giacalone couldn't bear the fact that Hoffa always wore a pair of white socks with one of his inexpensive dark suits; he did so because his feet had an allergic reaction to dyes. Jack Goldsmith quotes his stepfather, Chuckie O'Brien, stating that Giacalone "has his guy in New York make socks with black, blue, and brown tops and the bottoms were white, which ended all that bullshit."[3]

Giacalone and Hoffa had met when they were in their twenties and forged a friendship that benefitted their overlapping interests in the labor movement. Giacalone wanted to keep his various front businesses free of unionization, and Hoffa needed Giacalone's mob contacts to beat up strikebreakers and intimidate independent truckers into joining the Teamsters. Giacalone's primary legitimate business was the Home Juice Company, a business that he and his brother had won in a dice game. Gambling was more than a sideline for Giacalone: he and his brother operated numerous illegal casinos.

Giacalone was known not only for his numerous gambling operations and for his larcenous ventures, but also for the ferocity of his temper; his cold, hard stare and clenched fists would often be the first signs of explosive violence. However, he was careful to control his temper in public, for he did not want more battery convictions. His lawyer warned him that further convictions might result in damage to his ability to continue earning large sums of money. Nevertheless, his hard, threatening stare and the angry set of his mouth did not intimidate a persistent reporter from bombarding Giacalone with questions about being a mobster. The reporter followed Giacalone into a building's revolving door. Once they were each enclosed in the turning glass sections of the door, Giacalone suddenly pulled back on the glass panel in front of him. The sudden halt resulted in the reporter's nose and forehead smacking into a glass panel. Blood poured from his nose. Giacalone turned to look at the stunned reporter and let out with a withering laugh. It was the only time anyone saw Giacalone laugh.

FBI agents who were watching were not amused by Giacalone's actions. They wanted to nail him, but not for silly stunts. Their ambition was to have him indicted for Hoffa's murder, but they were not able to garner sufficient evidence that Giacalone planned the murder. However, the government managed to convict him of income tax evasion (the old standby for nailing mobsters). He was sentenced to ten years in prison in 1976. He died of heart disease on February 23, 2001, at age eighty-two.

Another of Hoffa's prominent mob cohorts was Anthony "Tony Pro" Provenzano, who was so quick to anger and take offense at someone's lack of respect for him that one day he attempted to throw his lawyer's fresh associate out of an office window. Provenzano had many enemies, but only those who in some way went against him were known to perish violently. Those who hid their feelings and remained deferential tended to die of natural causes.

From the age of fifteen, when he quit school and got a job as a trucker's assistant, he developed a reputation for having a hair-trigger temper that often exploded in violence. He was initially guided in his career by Anthony Strollo (aka Tony Bender), a boss of several Teamsters locals and a capo in the Genovese crime family. He was impressed by Provenzano's drive and easy resort to violence. He arranged for Provenzano to be appointed business agent for Teamster Local 560, then president of the local. Provenzano eventually became Hoffa's man in New Jersey and rose in the ranks of the Genovese crime family. With Hoffa's encouragement, Provenzano became a vice president of the International Teamsters and formed a number of Teamster locals that existed only on paper. Such locals were known as paper locals because they had no members. Yet, Provenzano could vote those locals to determine Teamster leadership positions.

Once in power, Provenzano would not brook any challenges to his position. He was furious that in 1961 Anthony Castellitto, the secretary-treasurer of Local 560, had decided to run against him for the position of president of the local. To settle the matter, Castellitto, like Hoffa after him, was invited to a fateful meeting. There, as the FBI ascertained, Castellitto was knocked unconscious and strangled. (The agency also believes that Hoffa was similarly murdered.) To no one's surprise, the body of Castellitto was never found (a presage of the missing Hoffa corpse). At the time of Castellitto's murder, Provenzano was in Florida, getting married. Though years would pass during which Provenzano successfully relied on his solid alibi, the feds nevertheless succeeded in indicting him for murder. Others had talked in exchange for leniency.

Before that, however, Provenzano was serving a four-year term in Lewisburg prison for extortion. Hoffa was his prison mate, having been sentenced to a thirteen-year prison term for jury tampering, attempted bribery, conspiracy, and mail and wire fraud. When Provenzano asked that

Hoffa permit him to receive his Teamsters pension, Hoffa told him that under union law Provenzano was no longer eligible for a pension since he had been convicted of extortion. Provenzano was furious. He screamed and cursed at Hoffa, who spat out expletive for expletive. As their tempers grew hotter and hotter, their curses erupted into ferocious punches and kicks. To say that their friendship was ruptured would be an understatement. Provenzano said he would not only kill Hoffa, but he would also tear out the guts of each member of Hoffa's family. They managed to stay clear of each other during the remainder of their prison stay.

Yet, a connection remained. And after both were released from prison and wintering in their Florida abodes, Provenzano acted as if their friendship was intact. On several occasions, he phoned Hoffa, asking him to reconsider his pension request. Many times Hoffa would not take Provenzano's calls; but when he did, he would tell Provenzano there was no pension for him. Provenzano's volcanic temper would erupt and out would fly a hot assortment of expletives. Hoffa then would slam down the phone. Angry and frustrated, Provenzano told one of Hoffa's friends that he would pluck out Hoffa's granddaughter's eyes. He later reiterated that he would rip out Hoffa's guts.

Hoffa decided to ignore Provenzano's threats. Maybe it was all just bluster. He thought he could work around Provenzano's anger. After all, the two men still had union and Central States Pension Fund interests that coincided, all of which were mutually beneficial. Hoffa figured that Provenzano, even minus his pension, would see the value of Hoffa regaining the presidency of the union. Hoffa was fooling himself. Provenzano, Giacalone, Russell Bufalino, and other Mafioso told Hoffa that they preferred dealing with the malleably complaisant Frank Fitzsimmons, who never had the nerve to refuse a favor or a loan. Hoffa was told that he should enjoy his retirement from the union and live off his generous pension. Hotheaded Hoffa shouted, "Fuck no!" It was as good as yelling, "Kill me." On July 30, 1975, Hoffa got into a car in front of the Machus Red Fox restaurant in Bloomfield Township, Michigan. Why he agreed to meet with Provenzano and Giacalone remains a mystery, and neither one was in the car that drove Hoffa to his death. They made sure to have reliable alibis to July 30.

Two men who were thought to accompany Hoffa on his last ride were the Briguglio brothers who worked for Provenzano and Giacalone. Salvatore (aka "Sally Bugs," "Sally Dogs," "The Torturer") Briguglio and his brother Gabriel were members of Provenzano's Local 560. Sally Bugs was a notorious hit man who enjoyed torturing his victims. Though a bespectacled, 5'2", slender, professorial-looking gentleman, his reputation put the fear of a violent death in all those whom Sally Dogs threatened. He was known as Provenzano's pit bull and executioner. Gabriel was in a less violent line of work: he was a loan shark. Of course, his line of work was only less violent if debtors paid back their loans and the exorbitant interest (aka the vig) on time. Otherwise, Gabriel might call on the services of his diligent brother.

The FBI put tremendous pressure on Sally to tell them what he knew about the deaths of Hoffa and Castellitto. The agency believed that Sally was involved in the Castellitto hit, and in 1976 he was indicted for that murder. It turned out that Briguglio had tortured and murdered Anthony Castellitto and then transported the body back to New Jersey. Castellitto's corpse was never found due to Briguglio dismembering the dead man's body and then putting the body parts into a wood chipper. As reward for his services, Provenzano appointed Sally to Castellitto's former position as secretary-treasurer of Local 560.

However, Provenzano soon heard rumors that Sally's silence had not been guaranteed. He became worried that Sally would make a deal with the government. Sally had been talking with prosecutors and was indeed ready to make a deal for leniency in exchange for his testimony against Provenzano in the Castellitto hit. He was scheduled to appear with Provenzano and hit man Harold (Kayo) Konigsberg in court for the murder of Castellitto. Konigsberg (who remained true to the mob rule about never squealing to the cops) had reportedly been paid $15,000 to carry out the murder of Castellitto with Sally's assistance. Though silent about the murder, Kayo complained to mob bosses that Provenzano had short-changed him. He was not permitted to kill Provenzano, but beating him up would be acceptable.

On March 21, 1978, having finished dinner at an Italian restaurant on Mulberry Street in New York's Little Italy, Sally strolled outside and was slammed to the ground by two gunmen who blasted Sally's chest and face with a barrage of bullets. The gunmen then sprinted to a waiting car that carried them to safety and anonymity. Though the murder was allegedly witnessed by two NYPD Intelligence cops who were tailing Genovese capo Matthew Ianniello, Sally's dinner guest, they made no attempt to arrest the killers. The murder was a warning to others to remain silent. Though Sally had been silenced, neither Provenzano nor Kayo would be spared life in prison.

Though he resented Provenzano and could have made a deal for his testimony, Konigsberg accepted a life sentence in prison. Eric Konigsberg, grandnephew of Kayo, writes,

After his well ran dry, he said that as a favor to him, Moe Dalitz, a gambler and hotel tycoon in Cleveland, furnished them [Kayo and his wife, Catie] with five thousand dollars a month. When Dalitz died in 1989, Catie went to Boca Raton to see Gerry Catena, another aging gangster. He gave her ten thousand dollars but asked that she not come to him again.[4]

Konigsberg was spared the indignity of dying in prison. In 2012, at age eighty-six, he was paroled from prison. He died on November 23, 2014, in a Florida nursing home. He is buried at the Star of David Memorial Gardens Cemetery in Fort Lauderdale.

Provenzano was not as fortunate as Konigsberg. He would not enjoy spending his last years outside of prison. On June 14, 1978, he had been convicted of the Castellitto murder and sentenced to life in prison. As if that was not sufficient, on July 10, 1979, he was sentenced to twenty years in prison for a labor peace payoff; in other words, extortion. To his dying day on December 12, 1988, the seventy-one-year-old Provenzano claimed he had no idea what had happened to Hoffa or Castellitto. He died of a heart attack in Lompoc Prison and is buried in St. Joseph's Cemetery in Hackensack, New Jersey.

John Dioguardi (aka Johnny Dio) was another mobster who worked closely with Hoffa. He was a vicious labor racketeer who responded to a bad press by arranging to have a thug throw sulfuric acid onto the face and eyes of nationally syndicated labor reporter Victor Riesel. Though blinded by the attack, Riesel was not intimidated and continued to write muckraking articles about gangster-driven union activity. When Riesel's attacker asked Dio for more money, Dio had the man killed. Dio was arrested and tried for the Riesel attack, but he wasn't convicted. Others took the fall.

As with Provenzano, Dio established numerous paper locals for the Teamsters. He had conspired with Hoffa to oust Teamster president, Dave Beck. And one way to do that was to have all the paper locals in New York and New Jersey vote for Hoffa. In 1957, following his testimony before the Senate Select Committee on Improper Activities in Labor and Management and undergoing an inquisition conducted by Robert Kennedy, Beck was forced to resign as president of the Teamsters, but the locals continued to exist for several years, and Dio staffed them with mobster allies. He also used his position to extort dress and other garment manufacturers. Extortion was not all that was on Dio's agenda. With Hoffa's compliance, he attempted to organize thirty thousand New York City taxi cab drivers and extort payments from fleet owners.

But it was from the dress and garment manufacturers that Dio drew the lion's share of his income. He either extorted them to remain union free or threatened to make sure that their employees voted to join the Teamsters. In either case, he demanded that they use trucking companies in which he had an interest.

I saw firsthand how Dio operated: As I wrote in *Big Apple Gangsters*:

When I was a teenager I worked for my father on Saturday mornings. He owned and operated two dress manufacturing companies, one in Queens, one in Brooklyn. One day while carrying a bolt of cloth up from the basement to the cutter's table, I heard my father and another man yelling at each other. At the top of the stairs I was able to see both men, who looked as they would come to blows. Spittle sprung from my father's mouth, and his fists were clenched as if ready to throw punches. When he was a young man, he had been an amateur boxer, so an exchange of fists would not have been surprising. My father's antagonist called him a Jew bastard, and I thought for sure that would lead to violence. Instead, my father told him to "get the fuck out!" His antagonist didn't budge, but pointed his index finger at him and said, "We'll get you! You son of a bitch!" With that the stranger made the symbol of a pistol with his right hand, flexed his right index finger as if pulling a trigger and left.[5]

My father told me that the man was Johnny Dio, a notorious gangster who preyed upon garment manufacturers, not only in Manhattan's garment center but throughout the entire city, in each of its boroughs. My father said that Dio "wanted to unionize my employees, who voted down unionization because they would have been paid less than I am paying them." My father also provided his employees with limited medical insurance. In addition to wanting to unionize my father's workers, Dio wanted my father to use his trucking company. My father went to the president of the trucking company he retained and was told that he better go along with Dio, otherwise the mob would kill not only him but his family as well. Eventually, with the aid of a mob-connected cousin, a deal was negotiated whereby my father had to hire the trucking company at an initially low rate but wouldn't have to accede to the unionization of his workers. Several years later, my father died, and the mob began increasing the cost of trucking. It reached a point that went from onerous to outrageous, and so my father's former partner accepted a partnership with the mob. It was a deal with the devil. The mob muscled its way into the company, buying cotton, wool, and silk, buttons, zippers, and belts, then selling finished garments at steep discounts to retailers. While collecting money on sales, the mob ignored bills that continued to pile up in the bookkeeper's office. When the mob could no longer buy on credit, it increased the amount of fire and theft insurance it had taken through a corrupt broker. A few weeks after the last dresses, blouses, housedresses, and bathrobes had been sold to a retailer in Brooklyn, the mob burnt down the two factories that my father had operated.

By 1959, Dio expanded his activities. His Teamster locals were dismantled, and he was fighting off numerous investigations into his corrupt union activities. He spent some time in prison then found new ways of making an illegal buck. He turned to penny stock manipulations, bucket shop scams, and pump-and-dump practices. Though he was initially raking in large sums of money, he was less fortunate than he had been in operating illegal unions. He was investigated, indicted, tried, and found guilty. He was sentenced to fifteen years in Lewisburg Federal Penitentiary, where he was a member in good standing of what was known as "mobsters' row" in the prison. On the prison wing where Dio was tenanted, numerous of his colleagues in organized crime were in adjacent prison cells. They were represented in the movie *Goodfellas*. There was Henry Hill, Paul Vario, and Anthony Loria, among various others. Dio, in addition to cooking steaks for his mobster cohorts, was an effective jobs counselor. He got all of his pals easy jobs where they could either nap or spend hours playing cards or reading in the prison library. Though only briefly portrayed in *Goodfellas*, he made a far more lasting cinematic impression as the corrupt and violent union boss Johnny Friendly in the movie *On the Waterfront*. He and Friendly had nearly identical snarls. There is a famous photograph of Dio, mouth set in a snarl as a cigarette dangles between his angry lips. He had just finished testifying before a Senate committee and had exited a chamber when he was surrounded by a flock of clamoring news photographers. Dio attempted to push his way through when an International News photographer named Jim Mahan raised his camera and snapped a photo of a furious Dio. The belligerent gangster's anger erupted and he bellowed, "You sons of bitches, I got a family!"[6]

While serving a prison sentence in the 1970s for stock fraud, Dio became seriously ill and was denied compassionate release. He was transferred from prison to a hospital, where he died in 1979.

Though Dio was integral in helping Hoffa attain and keep the office of the presidency of the Teamsters, it was Allen Dorfman, a key advisor to Hoffa, who played a role that was essential to all the casino bosses in Las Vegas. Dorfman's rise to power and wealth would have been a surprise to those who knew the young man as an affable $4,000-a-year-salary gym teacher. Yet, from that modest position, he rose like a rocket to being the multimillionaire gatekeeper of the Teamsters Central States Pension Fund. In that role, he loaned millions of dollars to casino owners.

Nepotism has long been the means by which many men of modest accomplishments reach levels of success that would have been beyond their strivings if they had been born to others of modest accomplishments. Dorfman was a direct beneficiary of nepotism. His lineage was that to a notorious member of the Chicago Outfit. He was the stepson of Paul "Red" Dorfman, a gangster and lieutenant to mob boss Tony Accardo. Red, as head of the Chicago Waste Handler's Union, brooked no disagreements with his decrees and demands. His blunt threats and reputation for violence invariably terrified his victims, all of whom agreed to do what Red demanded of them. According to Steven Brill in his book *The Teamsters*, "[Red] was the kind of guy who would walk in, throw two bullets on a guy's desk and tell him, 'The next goes in your fuckn' head.'"[7]

Red had helped Hoffa organize locals for the Teamsters and used his mob connections to force others to support Hoffa's ambitions. He also worked with Dio in setting up paper locals in New York. A reward for his help included the hiring of twenty-three-year-old Allen Dorfman to run the Central States' health and welfare business. By the time Dorfman had been given control of the CSPF, his biggest Vegas customer was Moe Dalitz. As Suzanne Dalitz told the author: Banks wouldn't lend money for the construction of casinos, so her father and others had no choice but to borrow funds from the CSPF. And all the loans, plus interest, were paid back.

Arthur A. Sloane, in his biography of Hoffa, writes:

> Many of the loan recipients were something less than model citizens . . . and a variety of people whose names were linked to Midwestern organized [crime] received financing for the Las Vegas activities. Hoffa made it clear that business was business and that anyway, some of these people (like the hugely successful Las Vegas hotelier Morris Dalitz, a former bootlegger whom Hoffa had known since his early days in Detroit . . .) were close friends. He made no apologies.[8]

Among the casino/hotels controlled by Dalitz and funded by CSPF were the Desert Inn, the Stardust, and the Fremont. Other non-Dalitz loans were given to the owners of the Dunes, the Landmark, the Four Queens, Circus Circus, Caesars Palace, and the Aladdin. Without the CSPF, the development of Vegas in the 1950s, 1960s, and 1970s would have been modest at best. One of CSPF's more notorious loans, given with mob approval and with numerous strings attached, was $160 million to the Argent Corporation, which owned the Stardust Casino (subject of the book and movie *Casino*). Hoffa completely trusted Dorfman to make such loans that benefitted Hoffa's mob associates. In fact, so essential was Dorfman to the running of the CSPF that when Hoffa was sent to prison, he told his successor, Frank Fitzsimmons, that "Allen speaks for me on all pension fund questions. He's the guy in charge while I'm gone."[9]

Although dozens of mobsters benefitted from the loans granted by the CSPF, there were others who were left with empty hands. Some mobsters from New York and New Jersey were not happy that Dorfman provided loans primarily to the Outfit, former Cleveland mobsters, and Detroit mobsters. One day, as Dorfman was driving to his country club, a couple of shotgun blasts dotted the side of his Cadillac. Dorfman sped away and was unhurt, but he rightly interpreted the blasts as a warning to extend loans to formerly excluded Eastern mobsters. Dorfman took the message to heart and complied.

Such compliance didn't diminish Dorfman's reputation as a fearless tough guy who inspired stomach-churning fear in those who stood in his way. He could call a recalcitrant mob soldier or casino manager and tell him that if he didn't do as he was told, he could expect to be killed in twenty-four hours. When his temper flared, his targets of anger invariably acquiesced to his demands. His reputation for ruthlessness would have been further enhanced had people known that one of his close friends was Outfit hit man Tony Spilotro. They often dined together and were guests in each other's homes. Spilotro's name alone could inspire so much fear that no one who enjoyed living would rebel against his demands. Dorfman would use Spilotro's name only when his own threats went unheeded.

Yet, to corporate Las Vegas, Dorfman presented himself as a legitimate businessman. He was well spoken, knowledgeable, and wore expensive bespoke suits. He was a cool representation of smooth success. As a well-respected executive in charge of making enormous loans, he was as respected in Vegas as any bank president. He also numbered among his friends senators, congressional representatives, judges, and law enforcement officials. He regularly played golf with Vegas VIPs and was a member of exclusive country clubs. When hobnobbing with the elite of Vegas or Detroit or Chicago, Dorfman never mentioned Spilotro. In fact, he was never seen in the company of Spilotro, who was too much of a street thug. Even without the aid of Spilotro, if someone owed him money or had betrayed him, Dorfman would pick up a phone and threaten to kill the offender. His bespoke suits and presence as a buttoned-up successful businessman did not mean that violence wasn't second nature to him. It was his nature, for he was the son of Red Dorfman.

As cool and as discreet as Dorfman's operations were, he nevertheless became a target for the FBI. In 1979, the bureau launched "Operation Pendorf" (Penetrate Dorfman). From hidden microphones in Dorfman's offices and taps on his phones, the bureau obtained sufficient evidence for a prosecutor to go before a grand jury and ask for an indictment. Following a trial, Dorfman, Teamster president Roy Williams, and Joseph "Joey the Clown" Lombardo, of the Chicago Outfit, were convicted of attempting to bribe Democratic Nevada Senator Howard Cannon to kill a bill to deregulate the trucking industry. On January 20, 1983, three days before he was to be sentenced and while free on a $5 million bond, Allen Dorfman, accompanied by his friend Irwin Weiner, an associate of Chicago mobsters, went to a local bank. There, Weiner gave Dorfman a check for $7,500, which was partial repayment for a loan. As they walked through the parking lot of the Lincolnwood Hyatt in Lincolnwood, Illinois, two gunmen rushed up behind Dorfman and shot him six times in the head with a pair of .22 caliber pistols. Weiner was unharmed. Dorfman fell to the ground, where blood pooled around his head. The blood froze before police arrived on the scene. Law enforcement officials announced that the Outfit had been worried that Dorfman would make a deal to avoid a fifty-five-year prison sentence.

Though Dorfman was in charge of handing out loans to the mob, he nevertheless reported all his activities to Hoffa, for he had the ultimate control of the CSPF. According to Jack Goldsmith, author of *In Hoffa's Shadow*,

> During the twelve years that he ran the fund, Hoffa made hundreds of loans to finance projects from all over the country, but nowhere more so than in Las Vegas. "There would not be a Vegas today if it weren't for the Old Man," Chuckie [O'Brien] says correctly. "These stuffed-shirt asshole bankers, because of their reputation of being so legitimate, they couldn't give money to a gambling person, so we started loaning them money." Hoffa gave out Teamsters' loans for casinos and resorts through front groups run by Dalitz and Sarno [founder of Circus Circus and Caesars Palace] and others, but organized crime families around the country had hidden interests that allowed them to skim untold millions.[10]

Goldsmith goes on to quote his stepfather, Chuckie O'Brien, who claimed that Hoffa got a 10 percent fee of each casino loan and the money had to be paid before the loan was made. In addition, Hoffa had at least one point with each of the following eight casinos: the Desert Inn, Caesars Palace, Circus Circus, the Fremont, the Stardust, the Dunes, the Aladdin, and the Sands. "Chuckie speculates that Hoffa accumulated many tens of millions of dollars from his various loans and side deals. He spent money freely to win friends and buy influence."[11]

Though Hoffa operated with seeming independence, he was nevertheless beholden to mobsters, for they had to vote their approval of each casino loan. To pay the necessary consideration for each loan, each casino had to make sure that a portion of the skim went to the mobsters who voted approval of the loans. It worked well for the mob, providing them with a means for bypassing the Gaming Control Board, which would not license any mobster to run a casino.

Though Hoffa was without a doubt as mobbed up as a union leader could possibly be, he was nevertheless one of the most effective union leaders in the United States. Arthur Sloane, in his biography of Hoffa, writes:

> He was, after all, more than anything else a labor leader. If it is fair to judge him on criminological grounds, it is justifiable to measure him on labor relations ones, in the performance of his chosen profession. And here a very different and vastly superior Hoffa must by any objective standard be said to have existed. It is no exaggeration to say that no major union leader has ever enjoyed the combination of popularity with his own rank and file and respect from the employers with whom he dealt than did the school dropout from Brazil, Indiana.[12]

Sloane writes that Hoffa's appeal was in no small part based upon his down-to-earth persona. He came from dire poverty and never flaunted his wealth; he spoke like a truck driver; he wore inexpensive suits that looked as if they came off a rack at Sears; he lived in a modest house, owned an unimposing vacation cottage, and drove an inexpensive American-made car. His devotion to his clean-cut family and abstention from liquor and gambling were unusual qualities for a mobster. At mob banquets in Vegas, he was never accompanied by a showgirl or prostitute and never could be seen with a glass of liquor. Some even referred to him as a puritan.

Was he a puritanical mobster? Perhaps. Was he an opportunist with antennae for making deals and increasing his power? Certainly. More than anything, his life was devoted to being a great union boss and doing all that he could for the benefit of the Teamsters and its members. He cut corners, took payoffs, and was always available to help his members. And each of those members knew they could depend on him. Each one carried a card with Hoffa's direct phone number, and he took their calls often without the assistance of a secretary. Hoffa was their go-to man, and even from prison, he felt a responsibility to the welfare of his union's members. He also took pride that he was the one whose CSFP made the early days of Las Vegas a glittering reality. If Moe Dalitz was Mr. Las Vegas, then Jimmy Hoffa was the city's de facto Secretary of the Treasury, assisted by his able second-in-command, Allen Dorfman. Some Teamsters said that there should be a monument to Hoffa in Vegas, the man whose body has never been found and who has no grave to contain his remains. The FBI has never been able to prove who killed Hoffa, but it is irrelevant to all those in Vegas who benefitted from his financial acumen. The original casinos he supported are all part of the history of Las Vegas and so is Jimmy Hoffa.

NOTES

1. Arthur A. Sloane, *Hoffa* (Cambridge, MA: MIT Press, 1991), 4.
2. Sloane, *Hoffa*, 33.
3. Jack Goldsmith, *In Hoffa's Shadow* (New York: Farrar, Straus and Giroux, 2019), 136.
4. Eric Konigsberg, *Blood Relation* (New York: Harper Collins Publishers, 2005), 85.
5. Jeffrey Sussman, *Big Apple Gangsters* (Lanham, MD: Rowman & Littlefield, 2020), xiii.
6. *Life* magazine, "Strong Arm Dio Doing What Comes Naturally," August 19, 1957, p. 36.
7. Steven Brill, *The Teamsters* (New York: Simon and Schuster, 1978), 202.
8. Sloane, *Hoffa*, 274–75.
9. Brill, *The Teamsters*, 214.
10. Goldsmith, *In Hoffa's Shadow*, 90.
11. Goldsmith, *In Hoffa's Shadow*, 91–92.
12. Sloane, *Hoffa*, 404–5.

Moe Dalitz, with daughter Suzanne and wife, Averill. New Year's Eve, 1962. Suzanne is dressed as the "new year's baby" for the big bash at the Desert Inn Hotel, Las Vegas, Nevada.

Jay Sarno, with daughter September and son Freddie. The day of the Miss Nevada Universe Pageant, 1980. September made it into the top 10.

Richard M. Nixon and Elvis Presley at the White House, 1970. Credit National Archives (photo no. 1634221)

Meyer Lansky, half-length portrait, facing slightly right, being led by detective for booking on vagrancy charge at 54th Street police station, New York City. Credit Library of Congress, Prints & Photographs Division, N.Y. World Telegram & Sun photo by Orlando Fernandez, 1958, Reproduction number LC-USZ62-120717 (b&w film copy neg.)

From left to right: S. M. Chris Franzblau, counsel to New Jersey Joint Counsel of Teamsters; Michael Calabrese, president of Joint Counsel of Teamsters; Henry Garrod, president of Local 97 of Teamsters; and James R. Hoffa, international president of Teamsters.

Siegel associate Moe Sedway, who took over the operation of the Flamingo Hotel in Las Vegas on the very night Siegel was murdered. Credit Jay Robert Nash Collection

Sinatra at a party, 1982. Credit Library of Congress, Prints & Photographs Division, photograph by Bernard Gotfryd, Reproduction number LC-DIG-gtfy-03728 (digital file from original)

New York Jewish gangsters caught at a 1933 crime conference at the Franconia Hotel: left to right, Joseph Rosen (aka Doc Harris, who was later murdered on Lepke's orders); Benjamin "Bugsy" Siegel; Harry Teitlebaum; Louis "Lepke" Buchalter, wearing eye patch; Harry Greenberg (aka Big Greenie, later murdered by Siegel); Louis Kravitz; Jacob "Gurrah" Shapiro; Philip "Little Farvel" Kovolik; and Hyman "Curly" Holtz. Credit Jay Robert Nash Collection

Mug shot of Frank "Lefty" Rosenthal, Clark County, Nevada.

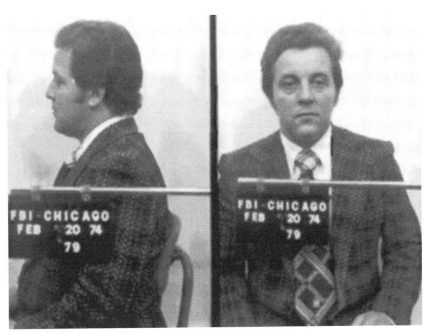

Mug shot of Anthony Spilotro, FBI, 1974. Credit FBI

6

THE MAN WHO BOUGHT LAS VEGAS

Howard Hughes may have been one of the most eccentric billionaires that America produced. He was an innovative aviator, the owner of airlines and airports, a TV station, a major movie company, and hotel/casinos. He was a producer and director of popular movies. He was a political fixer who manipulated senators and presidents of the United States. He was a frequent subject for gossip scribes because of the numerous Hollywood stars and starlets he seduced. His handsome face appeared on covers of slick magazines. His business deals were written about in major daily, weekly, and monthly business publications. Before the public eventually came to perceive Hughes as a cranky nut, they regarded him with admiration as an original American hero honored for his numerous feats of aviation and his sagacious dealmaking. However, a once fascinated public eventually came to learn that Hughes was paranoid, secretive, bigoted, and a germaphobe, who went to extreme lengths to protect himself from bacteria, viruses, and radiation. They learned that the man who had seduced some of the most beautiful women in Hollywood had become an intolerant puritan, made impotent by the excessive injection of drugs. He trusted no one, and no one was permitted to enter the inner sanctum of his fears and ambitions. His life was governed by his obsessive-compulsive behavior and a maddening desire to control everyone and everything.

That such a man would decide that Las Vegas was the best place to build an empire was as surprising to the mob as if Bobby Kennedy had decided to join the Mafia. When Moe Dalitz learned that Hughes wanted to buy the Desert Inn, he envisioned a transformation that would not only benefit him, but all of Vegas too.

For Hughes, the idea of buying up Vegas began on May 3, 1966, shortly after he sold TWA for $546,549,771.00. The interest on his payday bonanza was $85,000 a day. The tax bite would be enormous, and Hughes hated paying taxes. He imagined the IRS salivating in anticipation of gobbling up his fortune. Hughes was a buccaneer and believed no one and no institution should have the right to impinge on his freedom. And by freedom, he meant the freedom to be free of government rules and regulations. His decision to buy into Las Vegas was similar to that of Bugsy Siegel, who saw in the dusty city a gambling Eldorado free from all government restraints.

Before the IRS could pounce and get its claws into his fortune, Hughes departed California by rail (the great aviator had developed a fear of flying). He would settle in a low-tax or no-tax state and reduce his tax liability. After a brief visit to Boston, Hughes set Vegas as his no-state-tax destination. His body, covered with sores and boils, was gently placed on a stretcher and he was carried to a private railway car. It was one of two cars that Hughes had obtained for his journey westward. There would be no other passenger cars attached. His exclusive railroad car had been antiseptically cleaned, and the windows were sealed to prevent the entrance of germs.

On Thanksgiving day the Hughes train arrived in Vegas, and Hughes was carried off his car on a stretcher. He was met at the station by mobster Johnny Rosselli, Vegas fixer and an emissary of the Chicago Outfit, who made sure that the mob got its share of the Vegas skim. In an ambulance, Hughes was spirited to the Desert Inn, where he was carried up nine flights of stairs to the penthouse. His lieutenant, Bob Maheu, had rented the two top floors for Hughes. While Hughes occupied a 250-square-foot bedroom on the ninth floor, his staff—known as the Mormon Mafia—occupied the eighth floor. The staircase was sealed above the eighth floor, and if the curious attempted to ascend to that floor they were turned back by a pair of armed burly bodyguards. The elevator was also off bounds. The button for the ninth floor was removed. The eighth floor was not only a buffer zone to protect Hughes from ambitious entrepreneurs, con artists, and his enemies (real and imagined), but it was also antiseptically cleaned to prevent noxious, germ-infested air from drifting upward into Hughes' bedroom.

Though Hughes was paying $26,000 a day to rent the top two floors of the Desert Inn, it was still less than Dalitz and his partners could make from the high rollers who would fly in for the Christmas holidays and drop hundreds of thousands of dollars in the casino. Big bettors were often given free (aka comped) meals, rooms, and suites, and they expected it as a courtesy. Dalitz had been out of town when the rental agreement with Hughes had been signed by Desert Inn partner Ruby Kolod. Dalitz was furious. He wanted Hughes out, but the secretive billionaire refused to leave. Maheu, who was being paid more than $500,000 a year by Hughes, was eager to do his boss's bidding. When not stalling Dalitz, he made himself as elusive as a bat in daylight.

As a former FBI agent and private detective, Maheu had mastered the arts of secrecy and indirection. Hughes was convinced that Maheu would be a reliable and trustworthy second-in-command. And so he hired him for $500,000 a year (a tantalizing sum, which was more than Maheu had ever previously made), yet Maheu never had a face-to-face meeting with his boss. Hughes sent instructions to Maheu either by phone or by memo. Hughes eventually soured on Maheu and fired him in 1970. In a conference call on January 7, 1972, during which Hughes slammed Clifford Irving's bogus Hughes autobiography as a hoax, he also poured out his wrath about Maheu.

Hughes said of Maheu, "He's a no-good, dishonest son of a bitch, and he stole me blind. . . . You wouldn't think it could be possible with modern methods of bookkeeping and accounting and so forth for a thing like the Maheu theft to have occurred, but believe me, it did, because the money's gone and he's got it."[1] Hughes continued:

> Bitterly is a mild way of putting it. Note, everything [Maheu] has done, everything short of murder, as a result of being discharged. I don't suppose any disgruntled employee who was discharged has even come close to Mr. Maheu's conduct. . . . In light of that litigation and the struggle and harassment he has embarked upon, it's very, very difficult for me to tell you precisely the motives that led to [my leaving Las Vegas] without having some effect on the devastating, horrifying program of harassment that Maheu and his associates have launched against me.[2]

Maheu sued Hughes for $50 million for defamation of character. He was awarded $2.8 million, but the settlement was overturned on appeal.

But that was years after Hughes relied on Maheu to buy and keep him tenanted in the Desert Inn, and years after Hughes had Maheu buy the Stardust and the Sands for him. Maheu was his man, the most trusted individual in the Hughes organization. The casino owners saw Maheu as the king's prime minister. If you wanted to deal with Hughes, you had to deal with Maheu. His power was enormous.

When Dalitz insisted that Hughes depart the Desert Inn, Maheu first asked Rosselli to convince Dalitz to let Hughes stay. But Dalitz could not be moved, and Hughes would not move. About letting Hughes linger, the punning Dalitz said, "No dice. He's gotta go."[3] He had told Kolod that the Mormons would rather throw a punch to defend their boss than roll the ivories. How could you make money with them around? It was impossible.

Quick to find a more powerful influencer than Rosselli, Maheu called Jimmy Hoffa. He knew that Hoffa, through the Central States Pension Fund, had lent money to help Dalitz buy the Desert Inn. Not wishing to upset the reclusive billionaire, whose political connections might prove useful, Hoffa agreed to call Dalitz. The result was that Hughes would be able to extend his lease for the eighth and ninth floors of the Desert Inn for an additional two weeks. That's as far as Dalitz was willing to cooperate. After that, Hughes would have to go. No more delays. The only option for Hughes to extend his tenancy would be to buy the Desert Inn. It was an option that Maheu, via a memo, presented to Hughes.

After three months of often petty negotiations initiated by Hughes, the parties agreed to a deal. Hughes would pay $6.2 million in cash and assume $7 million worth of liabilities. For that price, Hughes did not get to own the Desert Inn or the ground on which it sat; instead, he bought a lease to operate it until 2022. As Morris Kleinman, one of Dalitz's partners in the Desert Inn, told the author: Hughes paid more than the place was worth.

Having closed the deal after months of prolonged nitpicking, Hughes was like a sweet-deprived kid with an unlimited budget who was suddenly unleashed in a candy store. Tasting one sweet, he wanted another and then another. He went on the biggest buying spree Vegas had ever seen. It was a spree that would make him the biggest employer in Vegas. In a memo to Maheu, Hughes had written: "I have decided this once and for all. I want to acquire even more hotels and to build this operation to be the greatest thing in the U.S. This is a business that appeals to me."[4]

Hughes not only bought the Desert Inn, but he ordered Maheu to scoop up the Sands, the Castaways, the Frontier, the Landmark, and the Silver Slipper. (Hughes could see the image of the glittery, flashing silver slipper atop the eponymous casino from his bedroom and wanted it dimmed or removed. Unable to get his way, he bought the Silver Slipper.) Next, he set his sights on the Stardust and was prevented from buying it only because the SEC thought such a purchase would give Hughes monopolistic control of the gaming industry in Vegas. (Had he been permitted to buy it, the mob would not have gotten control of it and perhaps the movie and book *Casino* never would have come to be.) Frustrated by the SEC, Hughes decided to buy Harold's Club in Reno; but when Frank Sinatra sent out feelers about selling the Cal-Neva Lodge in Lake Tahoe to Hughes, he was rebuffed. Hughes had a long-standing hatred of Sinatra since Ava Gardner had chosen the singer over the billionaire years earlier.

Hughes wound up owning 20 percent of Vegas and providing a livelihood for thousands of people. He was celebrated by employees, casino operators, and politicians. He regarded himself as the biggest fish in the pond. As such, he was honored not only for being a major economic force, but also for allegedly driving the mob out of Vegas, a claim that was erroneous, for the mob continued to profit not only from casinos not owned by Hughes, but also from ones he owned. The mob managed to finagle their way into continuing the skim; and since the Mormons did not gamble and had never run casinos, they were often blind to the mob's chicanery. The formerly mob-owned casinos, which had poured forth rivers of profits, suddenly began losing money. Under the noses of Hughes' Mormon Mafia, the mob fleeced his casinos as if shearing sedated sheep.

Yet, Hughes believed that his Vegas deals made him respected as a financial genius. Such a belief was confirmed by national and international magazine and newspaper articles that acclaimed him as the man who bought and changed the culture and image of Vegas. He was pictured as a white knight, driving out the mob at the point of his lance. Yet, none of the major publications that celebrated Hughes as a heroic businessman and as a brilliant investor noted that he was debilitated by a variety of illnesses. According to Sergio Lalli in an essay about Hughes in Vegas, Hughes

> had a tumor on his head. He had rotten gums in the back of his mouth, which ached all the time. He was emaciated weighing from 115 to 120 pounds. Insomnia prevented him from getting enough sleep. Since Hughes refused to rest on his side or on his stomach, his back and his rump were pocked with painful bed sores. He was anemic and allergic to sunlight. He had a peptic ulcer. The constant injection of dope over nearly twenty years had overworked his kidneys, which could barely purify his blood. Hughes suffered from a prostrate [sic] blockage, which made it difficult to pass urine. He had a severe case of piles [i.e., hemorrhoids].[5]

As if all of that were not sufficient to make Hughes a candidate for an assisted living facility, his peculiar diet of Campbell's chicken soup and banana nut ice cream left him constipated, so he would have to sit on a toilet for hours, attempting painfully to squeeze out a tiny fecal specimen. He was so exhausted by the effort that he often fell asleep on the bowl as his head flopped forward and down like a believer praying.

This once handsome aviator and movie producer, considered one of America's most desirable bachelors, had shrunk from 6'4" to 6'1"; his fingernails, long and ridged and yellow, curled like the claws of a mythical monster. His hair was unwashed and uncombed; his face was unshaved. His cheeks were sunken. His eyes were red rimmed and bleary from lack of sleep. He refused to bathe, but only purified himself with alcohol rubs every few weeks. He was so fearful of germs that he refused to let any of the Desert Inn's cleaning staff into his fetid bedroom.

Yet, from the privacy of his filthy room, sitting in his ratty and stained bathrobe, he dictated his demanding memos or barked orders into a phone. He was like a king who expected utter obedience from those who served him and hop-to-it celerity in carrying out his orders. Those who didn't follow his orders or who argued with him were sent packing. He ran his company of complaisant minions without ever having face-to-face conversations with them, and that included Maheu.

With phone in hand or scribbling demands on a yellow legal pad, Hughes issued orders to buy casinos, ranches, mines, and other properties as casually as a man ordering his stockbroker to purchase shares of a company. Such a voracious appetite to buy whatever excited his imagination also impressed Vegas boosters who claimed that Hughes was improving the image of the city from one that was populated by mobsters, con artists, prostitutes, thieves, and hustlers to one that could be home to average American families wanting a healthful environment in which to raise families. Politicians would also list the attractions and amenities of Vegas and the state of Nevada. They made a point of waxing non-poetically like conventional chambers of commerce members about the favorable business climate that awaited all companies that wanted to operate in Nevada: the state has no personal or corporate income tax, no inheritance tax, and real estate taxes are low. They were careful, however, not to mention the state's high sales tax. They went on to commend Hughes for also opening the door for publicly traded companies and farsighted investors to come to Vegas. And numerous legitimate entrepreneurs did indeed follow the Hughes' example: there was Steve Wynn, Kirk Kerkorian, and Sheldon Adelson, to name three of the most prominent.

But few mentioned, either sotto voce or aloud, that mobsters, such as Frank Costello and Meyer Lansky, secretly maintained their points in numerous casinos that had been financed by the Teamsters Central States Pension Fund. They knew that mobsters would secretly continue to control the skim, while the man in the ratty bathrobe would be celebrated as a brilliant tycoon and savior of a city.

Things changed on the surface, but not where vast sums of money could be stolen. Casinos had historically attracted underworld characters because of the opportunity to skim tax-free dollars. But even the legitimate amounts of money that were collected were enormous. The money came from customers who bought nothing but the allure of big winnings. Each casino was a store without any inventory that sold no merchandise. Customers flocked to their premises in the belief that there were no odds they couldn't beat. True believers, they relied on their good luck to turn pie-in-the-sky promises into earthly realities.

What mobster would want to give up ownership of such profitable enterprises? It was a question never posed to Hughes. In his naivete, Hughes had created a perfect setup for the mob: there were no Mormon casino managers, no Mormon pit bosses, no Mormon dealers. Those positions were filled by men with gambling experience. They were the men who had managed to keep their records clean, but who had nevertheless spent decades working for the mob. As long as the mob could continue the flow of the skim, the eccentric billionaire landlord in his germ-free penthouse bedroom could continue to take credit for cleaning up Vegas. It is no wonder that Hughes was dismissively thought of by mobsters as akin to an overgrown boy with his collection of toys. As long as he continued playing his part, ignorant of what the mob was doing, the mob would leave him alone. They knew that Hughes would not derail their gravy train. One mobster even joked that a toy company should come out with a Howard Hughes Vegas Monopoly game in which no one went to jail.

Yet, Hughes continued to think of himself as the Lord of Vegas. When he flung open the drapes of his bedroom windows (which was rarely done), he could behold all that he owned. He was a lord admiring his vast domain. It was breathtaking. In a reverie of self-satisfaction, he may have recalled some lines from his childhood reading of Shelley's "Ozymandias": "Look on my works, ye Mighty, and despair! . . . The lone and level sands stretch far away."

But it wasn't enough. He was on a roll. He had a winning streak that he wanted to continue. The more he bought, the more the politicians and business owners praised and admired him. Yet, they still couldn't get in to see him. The secretive germaphobe, secluded in his penthouse, drew up lists of properties he wanted to buy, including a mansion for his estranged wife, Jean Peters. According to columnist Jack Anderson, Peters was the only woman Hughes really loved.[6] And nothing was too good for her.

Hughes and Peters had married in 1957, shortly after Peters had divorced Texas oil man Stuart Cramer. Peters and Cramer had known each other for only a few weeks before they married. The couple soon realized that marriage was a mistake, and so they separated a few months after their nuptials. During her marriage to Hughes, which lasted until 1971, Peters retired from acting and withdrew from the Hollywood scene: no parties, no premieres, no screenings. Instead, she devoted herself to taking courses in psychology and anthropology at UCLA and doing charitable work. Though Hughes deeply loved her, he could not bring himself to live with her. In Beverly Hills, for example, they lived in separate bungalows at the Beverly Hills Hotel. When Hughes bought a mansion for Peters in Nevada, she refused to reside in it unless Hughes joined her. He said no, but as he had begun long before they married, he phoned her every day. He would tell her how much he loved her and ask about her health and well-being. Though she would have remained married to Hughes if he had agreed to live with her, she said that since they were living apart and Hughes refused to alter their arrangement, she would divorce him. The divorce took place in 1971, and Hughes agreed to pay her $70,000 a year in alimony for the remainder of her life. She regretted that people still referred to her as Mrs. Howard Hughes and would probably do so for many years. "I'm a realist," she said. "I know what the score is, and I know who the superstar is."[7]

For no one, neither former wives nor lovers, would Hughes leave his lair. He adamantly refused to grant visits to local politicians, who panted after his largesse. Though refusing to grant them visits, he generously gave to their campaigns with the understanding that he could rely on them to do his bidding. As a result, he was never compelled to appear in person before the Nevada Gaming Commission and Nevada Gaming Control Board in order to become a licensed casino owner. All others who wanted to own casinos had to appear in person and reveal their holdings. Hughes was always the exception. He believed he had paid to live beyond the grasp of laws, rules, and regulations that often stymied the ambitions of other men. And for his generosity to political campaigns, he accepted the public encomiums from those he had secretly supported. It was the least they could do for him.

He was like a man in a bubble. But for Nevadans, Hughes had become a Vegas brand, the symbol of all that was positive about the city. If the city had been a box of pancake batter, Hughes' picture and name would have been on the box. Imagine then how stunned were politicians and business owners to learn that the symbol of the new Las Vegas, a onetime Hollywood Lothario, who had seduced many stars and starlets, was now intent on turning Vegas from a hedonistic playground into a nearly dour, chaste, rigid resort for the most eminent examples of wealthy Protestant America.

In his attempt to remake Vegas, Hughes decided he wanted it to be a city as fashionable and elegant as Monte Carlo. It would attract beautiful and rich people. There would be beautiful women in elegant and expensive gowns who arrived in long sleek limos and were escorted into the casinos by handsome millionaires in tuxedos. Those men would drop hundreds of thousands of dollars at the gaming tables and think nothing of it. For the entertainment of such customers, Hughes wanted only classy, clean-cut singers, dancers, and comedians. If Jews were to entertain, then he didn't want any loud Borscht Belt performers. And certainly no blacks and no Hispanics. And the call girls who often kept high rollers betting hundreds of thousands of dollars at the gaming tables were banned. It didn't matter that they had often played an important role for the casinos for which they might receive benefits. The Hughes casinos were to be run like exclusive, expensive department stores of gambling where only the best people handed over their money. And dealers, who may have operated in cahoots with call girls, were now treated as if they were potential embezzlers. They, like retail salesclerks, had to reach certain levels of profitability; if they repeatedly fell below those levels, they were dismissed. To increase efficiency, the dealers were told not to waste time kibitzing with bettors. They had to know their places in society. Within a short period of time, Hughes had managed to mute, and in some cases completely block out, the sounds of fun that had existed in his casinos. The high rollers could no longer joke with dealers and pit bosses, could no longer be tempted by sexy hookers. The casinos were pure business, not social gatherings. Under the austere edicts issued by Hughes, the old colorful, fun-loving Vegas had turned dull and gray for high rollers. So the high rollers and the hookers emigrated from the Hughes casinos to the mob-run ones, where the parties never ended.

One dramatic incident showed the effects of Hughes' attitude toward high rollers. It would have unforeseen consequences but would not alter the way Hughes did business. Following his purchase of the Sands, a confrontation occurred that would grow to mythological proportions. It was the result of the pit bosses not being permitted to extend credit to longtime customers and high rollers without senior management approval. The primary victim of the new Hughes edict was the most popular and celebrated entertainer the Sands had ever employed: Frank Sinatra. Because he was denied a line of credit, there would be a violent, curse-infused blowup between Frank Sinatra and Carl Cohen, manager of the Sands. It not only changed the course of Sinatra's engagements in Vegas, but it also focused unwanted attention on the mob. (This will be fully dealt with in chapter 7.)

Sinatra was not the kind of entertainer Hughes wanted in his casinos. He suggested hiring clean-cut performers such as Bob Newhart, Debbie Reynolds, and Dinah Shore; but not Sammy Davis Jr., who Hughes referred to as a nigger, whose race had set back civilization a millennium. Such bigotry was not revealed to the public. In a memo to Maheu, he wrote: "I can summarize my attitude about employing more negroes very simply—I think it is a wonderful idea for somebody else, somewhere else." Hughes continued: "I feel the negroes have already made enough progress to last the next 100 years, and there is such a thing as overdoing it."[8]

In another memo to Maheu, Hughes wrote that his ambition was "to make Las Vegas as trustworthy and respectable as the New York Stock Exchange—so that Nevada gambling will have the kind of reputation that Lloyds of London has, so that Nevada on a note will be like Sterling on silver."[9] And that meant keeping the hookers, the blacks, and the Hispanics out of the city.

In addition to keeping his casinos free of minorities and prostitutes, Hughes was determined to change the programming of a local TV station. He wanted one that that would show his favorite movies about a mythical Old West, where heroic white settlers and courageous cowboys defeated ravaging, raging savages and rescued and protected sexy, beautiful white women sporting elaborate hairdos and dressed in shimmering, low-cut, elegant gowns. As an insomniac, Hughes was frustrated that the local TV station went off the air at midnight. And even before it went off the air, it did not show the Western movies that Hughes wanted to see. He therefore decided to buy station KLAS, the local CBS station. Having done so, he then asked the president of CBS, William Paley, to send reels of his favorite movies to the Vegas station. Paley obliged, and the movies arrived with the reliability of the cavalry riding to the rescue. And why shouldn't Paley have obliged? Hughes had just spent $3.6 million to buy KLAS.

Next, Hughes was in a rage that the ABC show *The Dating Game* had featured what he thought was an interracial couple. In fact, both people were African American, but one of them was very light skinned. Hughes went to war against ABC. He was intent on ridding the airways of programs that could promote miscegenation. He proceeded to make the life of the network president, Leonard Goldenson, miserable with his demands and threats. But Goldenson soon discovered the Achilles heel of his opponent and aspiring corporate predator. In order for Hughes to get a go-ahead from the FCC, he would have to appear in person and reveal his holdings. Hughes figured that he had enough politicians in his pocket to get the FCC to exempt him from making an appearance and revealing his holdings. Try though he did, Hughes was flabbergasted, then furious that the politicians he had so generously supported were unable to run interference for him. Hughes would have to appear and make public revelations. Just in case the FCC might be inclined to waver in its demands, Goldenson sent a barrage of attorneys to demand that Hughes abide by all rules and regulations. Goldenson was relentless. He made his own demands known not only to the FCC, but to congressional representatives with influence over the FCC. He demanded that Hughes appear. For Hughes, the very idea of appearing before the FCC would be like an accused witch appearing at the Salem Witch Trials. He would self-immolate in humiliating flames. However, should he overcome his fears and resistance and agree to reveal the full nature of his wealth, he would no doubt be permitted to buy ABC. But for a man as secretive and as paranoid as Hughes, such a revelation would be impossible. In addition, he was terrified of leaving his penthouse and venturing into a world of bacteria and viruses. So Hughes, as Goldenson expected, refused to accept the demands of the FCC, and the deal died.

Hughes, however, was not finished with his purchases. Though he now owned 20 percent of Vegas, he decided as one of the century's most celebrated aviators (having set numerous air speed records, survived several plane crashes, and created brilliant design innovations for commercial and military airplanes), he should also own the city's airports, plus Alamo Airways. The $65 million he had spent in Vegas was a small portion of the money he had received for the sale of TWA. He had plenty left over for many more purchases. Though Moe Dalitz would be declared "Mr. Las Vegas," Hughes thought of himself not only as the most important personage of Vegas, but of the entire state of Nevada.

Yet, he was unrecognizable from the celebrated Hollywood tycoon who made so many hit movies, such as *The Outlaw*, starring Jane Russell, for whom he designed a special cantilevered bra to show off her breasts; *Scarface*, starring Paul Muni; *Hell's Angels*, starring Jean Harlow; *Flying Leathernecks*, starring John Wayne and Robert Ryan; *Macao*, starring Jane Russell and Robert Mitchum; and one that presaged his own adventure in the casino business, *The Las Vegas Story*, starring Jane Russell and Victor Mature. He was also unrecognizable from the dashing, daring aviator who designed, built, and flew the biggest wooden plane in the world, the *Spruce Goose*. Its wingspan, featuring eight Pratt & Whitney engines with propellers, was longer than a football field. During its one and only flight, it was airborne for a mere twenty-six seconds and traveled for about one mile at an altitude of seventy feet. Though its venture into the air was brief, its flight added considerable luster to Hughes' reputation. As a proud inventor, who believed he had achieved the unachievable, Hughes kept his prized *Goose* meticulously clean and in perfect running condition in a climate-controlled hangar with a full crew at standby. It was so maintained at a cost of hundreds of thousands of dollars annually, until Hughes' death in 1976.

Hughes made sure that his beloved behemoth of a plane was better cared for than himself. In fact, it is amazing that Hughes lasted as long as he did. By the time he died of kidney failure, Hughes had the body and organs of what one would expect to ascertain in an examination of a drug-addicted homeless person who had been living on the streets for decades. Not only had his 6'4" frame shrunk to 6'1", but he was as emaciated as a concentration camp inmate. His skin-and-bones body weighed a mere ninety pounds. His long gray hair was filthy, had not been barbered, and was a matted and tangled mess. His fingernails were grotesquely long, misshapen, and curled. Dirt was caked where the nails met the skin of his fingers. His body was covered with bedsores, and X-rays revealed the presence of five needles from broken glass syringes embedded in his arms: the signs of his drug addiction. Police and medical examiners found it difficult to believe that the corpse of such a dissipated derelict could be that of Hughes. The FBI had to be called in to match his fingerprints with those on file, thus enabling the agency to conclusively identify the corpse. Hughes, the daring young man of aviation, the producer of Hollywood movies, and the biggest landowner in Vegas, is buried—as if he never left home—next to his parents in Glenwood Cemetery in Houston.

Because he died without having executed a will, his $2.5 billion estate was divided in 1983 among twenty-two cousins. The states of Texas and California brought suit against the estate for unpaid inheritance taxes; however, the estate battled against those claims and finally prevailed. One who did not walk away empty-handed was the actress Terry Moore, who had claimed that she and Hughes had secretly wed on a yacht off the coast of Mexico in 1949 and that they had never divorced. The court rejected her claim because she had previously indicated she was married to another man during that period of time. However, there was no doubt that the two had been lovers for a number of years and a palimony suit could have been initiated. Therefore, the estate's heirs agreed that Moore was entitled to a settlement, the exact amount of which remains unknown, though it has been reported to be anywhere from several million dollars to $350,000. Moore herself said that the settlement was "not more than eight figures,"[10] and a biography of Hughes implies that the settlement was $350,000.[11]

The Hughes estate took over the running of the Summa Corporation, which controlled all of Hughes' assets. Hughes did not like the name of the company, but he hadn't disliked it enough to change it. Hughes' home in the Desert Inn was for years a tourist attraction for those fascinated by the reclusive billionaire, whose penthouse was off-limits during Hughes' life. The Desert Inn remained for years a valuable holding of the Summa Corporation. Though Hughes had ordered that it be expanded, he died before it could be done. Following his death, however, it was expanded from 16 acres to 165 acres and a fourteen-story tower was built on the property, a symbol of Hughes' posthumous effect on the city he called home. But in 1986, Summa sold the renovated and expanded Desert Inn to entrepreneur Kirk Kerkorian and his Tracinda Corporation (named for his two daughters, Tracy and Linda). Kerkorian would go on to be the builder of the largest casinos in Vegas, and in 1993 he realized a huge profit when he sold the Desert Inn to ITT-Sheraton for $160 million. While the casinos that Summa sold continued to generate fabulous profits, the mines that Hughes had purchased in Nevada had been losing money year after year and so were sold shortly after his death. The Hughes Sports Network and KLAS-TV were sold in 1978, and the Summa Corporation refocused its operations on being a massive real estate development company. In honor of the man who made it all happen, the directors of Summa changed the name of the company to the Howard Hughes Corporation, a tribute to the man whose eccentric brilliance made them all wealthy. The newly named company was bought in 1996 by the Rouse Company and was then sold to General Growth Properties in 2004. In its current incarnation, the Hughes Corporation is a developer and operator of master-planned communities.

Howard Hughes transformed Las Vegas, not by ridding it of the mobsters who built the city, but by making it respectable for financial institutions to invest in it. Once that happened, Fortune 1000 companies began to see Vegas and its casinos as an important and integral part of the American capitalistic system. While millions of dollars were lost by individual bettors, those millions went into the coffers of companies that tore down many of the old casinos and built huge fantasy edifices that attracted visitors from all over the world. Vegas became the entertainment capital of the world, where the biggest stars performed for sums of money that would have amazed and perhaps shocked Hughes (e.g., Celine Dion was paid $30 million a year). Everything in Vegas grew more and more outsized since the brief era of Hughes: the money, the entertainers, the buildings, the boxing matches, the floor shows, the reputations of its gangsters, and even trade shows such as the Consumer Electronics Show. And the movies added to the myth of the city; *Viva Las Vegas*, *Oceans 11*, and *Casino* transfixed audiences.

While the city continued to grow and thrive after Hughes' death, the mob had one more go at the city. The Chicago Outfit was not about to turn over the skim to Corporate America, at least not without the Department of Justice putting the gang's major operatives in prison. The mob would breathe its last breath in Vegas and die an ignominious death, though its ties to the city would be memorialized and celebrated in the city's Mob Museum. In the mob's absence the city became a safe playground for moms, dads, their kids, and grandparents. It is a destination as American as Disneyland and Disney World.

Or as Tom Wolfe wrote: "Las Vegas has become as Bugsy Siegel [and Howard Hughes] dreamed, the American Monte Carlo—without any of the inevitable upper-class baggage of the Riviera casinos."[12]

NOTES

1. *Bangor Daily News*, January 10, 1972, https://news.google.com/newspapers ?id=giA0AAAAIBAJ&sjid=NOEIAAAAIBAJ&pg=2362%2C3036959 (accessed August 10, 2021).

2. *Bangor Daily News*, January 10, 1972, https://news.google.com/newspapers ?id=giA0AAAAIBAJ&sjid=NOEIAAAAIBAJ&pg=2362%2C3036959 (accessed August 10, 2021).

3. Comment made by Morris Kleinman to the author in 1977.

4. Sergio Lalli, "Howard Hughes in Las Vegas," in *The Players*, ed. Jack Shee-han (Reno: University of Nevada Press, 1997), 133.

5. Sergio Lalli, "Howard Hughes in Las Vegas," 134.

6. Jack Anderson with Les Whitten, "Hughes and Jean Peters," *The Gadsden Times*, April 13, 1976, p. 4.

7. "Jean Peters Asserts Hughes Secret Safe," *Register-Guard*, December 6, 1972, 5A, https://news.google.com/newspapers/p/register_guard?nid=4pF9x-cDGs oC&dat=19721206&printsec=frontpage&hl=en; Elaine Woo, "Jean Peters; Actress in Film, TV Married Howard Hughes," *Los Angeles Times*, October 21, 2000, https://www.latimes.com/archives/la-xpm-2000-oct-21-me-39956-story.html.

8. https://lasvegassun.com/news/2015/dec/28/a-peek-into-the-mind-of-howard -hughes/ (accessed August 10, 2021).

9. Lalli, "Howard Hughes in Las Vegas," 141.

10. https://www.upi.com/Archives/1983/05/24/Howard-Hughes-wife-claims -settlement/1055422596800 (accessed August 10, 2021).

11. Richard Hack, *Hughes: The Private Diaries, Memos and Letters* (Beverly Hills: Phoenix Books, 2007), 387.

12. Tom Wolfe, "Las Vegas (what?)," in *Smiling Through the Apocalypse*, ed. Harold Hayes (New York: McCall Publishing Company, 1969), 209.

7

THE ENTERTAINMENT CAPITAL OF THE WORLD

For years, the magnetic names of Frank Sinatra and Elvis Presley drew in hundreds of thousands of fans to Vegas and generated millions of dollars in receipts for the casinos where the two singers performed. Their appeal was decidedly different. Sinatra was cool, irreverent, a lover of booze, broads, and gambling. He always appeared in tuxedo, elegant, debonair, and a man other men wanted to be, while their wives might vicariously be his sex partners. Elvis, by contrast, was all glitz and explosive energy. His appeal was to younger audiences than Sinatra's. From the 1950s through the 1960s, their Vegas gigs overlapped. They had become representative of Vegas. In a four-week engagement at the International Hotel, Elvis drew in 101,000 fans. The only performer more glitzy than Elvis was Liberace, and it's not surprising that the two became Vegas pals.

Sinatra made his first appearance at the Desert Inn in September 1951, when his career was in the doldrums. He could barely get singing gigs at major nightclubs, which previously had open invitations for him to perform at enormous fees. In 1951, Sinatra accepted some singing engagements at third-rate clubs for fees that ranged from a few hundred dollars to a couple of thousand. So when one of his New Jersey gangster pals contacted Moe Dalitz and asked him to hire Sinatra for a few weeks at the Desert Inn, Dalitz obliged. Attendance, however, was sparse, and Sinatra was sinking into a depression. The descent from the king of the Bobby Soxers to has-been was a depressing but not an untypical celebrity story. For Sinatra,

1951 was a year of just staying relevant, but he would become the brightest star in Vegas, a man whose very name drew in the high rollers from around the country. By 1980, he easily commanded $400,000 a week. He was a man of extraordinary contradictions: he could be a generous friend or a violent and unforgiving enemy; he could tip a stagehand $500 and a bellhop $200. After performing in Israel, he donated his fee to an Israeli charity. His friend Kirk Douglas cast Sinatra in the movie *Cast a Giant Shadow*, and Sinatra donated his salary to another Israeli charity. When the actor Lee J. Cobb was hospitalized, Sinatra paid all of Cobb's hospital bills. When the Sands Hotel and Casino would not let Sammy Davis Jr. stay in one of the hotel's suites, Sinatra informed management that he would not perform unless Davis and other black entertainers were permitted to stay at the hotel. Management relented. When Sinatra was served a hamburger not cooked to his liking in a casino restaurant, he furiously flung it against a wall and had the waiter and cook fired. He would, when angry, call dealers and pit bosses pimps. Waitresses were labeled two-dollar whores. His crude and demanding treatment of waiters, waitresses, pit bosses, and dealers was legendary. It was no wonder that many casino employees disliked Sinatra and tried to avoid being near him, especially if he was losing at blackjack.

Though Sinatra was one of the highest paid entertainers in Vegas, five years after his death in 1998, salaries for entertainers in Vegas had skyrocketed beyond anything that the stars of earlier years had received. In 2003, Celine Dion, for example, was hired to perform for forty weeks a year and paid $30 million. Her performances from 2003 to 2007 generated $240 million a year in casino revenue, and her Vegas concerts were the highest grossing concerts in the history of Vegas. Tickets for front-row seats at her concerts sell for more than $1,600. And the resale price is even higher.

The heady days of sold-out performances began in the 1960s when Sinatra appeared as leader of the Rat Pack, comprising Peter Lawford, Dean Martin, Sammy Davis Jr., and Joey Bishop. They were the hottest ticket in town: people bribed waiters, bellhops, hotel and casino managers to get them tickets. Vegas had never seen anything like it. Though the shows were seen as spontaneous, ad-libbed performances, many of the jokes and routines were devised by the dour-faced Joey Bishop.

For six years, audiences filled every seat in the Copa Room of the Sands for Rat Pack performances. Not only did the Pack attract fans from all over the country, but they also attracted dozens of celebrities who wanted to partake of the excitement. The biggest stars in Hollywood sat near the stage, laughing and applauding with the rest of the audience. There, one could be in proximity of Cary Grant, Marlene Dietrich, Lauren Bacall, Tony Bennett, Milton Berle, Kirk Douglas, Shirley MacLaine, Angie Dickinson, Jill St. John, and the list went on.

Sinatra's name on the Sands marquee, with or without his sidekicks, opened so many wallets of gamblers that management gave him two points in the casino. It grew to nine points, though it has been reported that Sinatra was fronting those seven extra points for mobsters who couldn't be licensed to own casinos. If Sinatra was gambling, a crowd would form around him; gamblers who wanted to impress him would casually drop $50,000 while drawing losing hands at blackjack. But it didn't matter to the gamblers: they were in the presence of the coolest, hippest man in town, the man who had the world on a string, who could snap his fingers and women would drape themselves on him. His great appeal to middle-aged and older men was that they could vicariously imagine being part of Sinatra's circle, a drinking buddy, the man who could have any woman, Mr. Machismo, the most charismatic man in town, who did it his way.

Up on stage, with a glass of Jack Daniels in one hand, a cigarette dangling from between his lips, and his tie undone, his presence proclaimed he didn't give a damn what the squares did or said. He was Frank Sinatra. And when he didn't get what he wanted, he would shout "I'm Frank Sinatra." One half expected the heavens to open up. At the Sands, he was a king. He drank excessively, seduced and paid for women who lit the flame of his desire, stayed up all night, threw punches at those who upset him (though his bodyguards were always around to protect him from retaliation), and slept most of the day. He was the most emulated swinger going, a man whose life other men in their nine-to-five routines could only dream about becoming, while laughing, applauding, and drinking in the Copa Room.

In 1963, Sinatra's Vegas adventure almost came tumbling down. The Gaming Control Board revoked his license for associating with gangsters and breaking other rules of the gaming industry.

Sinatra's plight dates from the 1950s when Joe Kennedy, through fronts, bought the Cal-Neva Lodge. By the time Jack Kennedy was being groomed to run for the presidency, the mob wanted to solidify its relationship with the future president, and Sinatra would be the perfect vessel for that role. Jack and Sinatra admired each other, enjoyed sharing stories about their various sexual conquests, and Kennedy relished hearing gossip about the sexual carryings-on of celebrities. Sinatra offered to buy 49.5 percent of the Lodge and apparently Joe Kennedy had no objection. The FBI believed that Sinatra was fronting for Chicago Outfit boss Sam Giancana, who became the actual owner of the Lodge. The Chicago Outfit would be

instrumental in providing the votes necessary for Jack's election. Outside of
the mob, no one seemed to know that the father of the president and Giancana were partners. Another kind of partnership emerged when Giancana
and Jack Kennedy shared a mistress, Judith Campbell Exner.

By 1963, the Cal-Neva Lodge was seen as Sinatra's joint. Unbeknownst
to Nevada gaming officials, however, it welcomed numerous mobsters who
wanted a few relaxing days away from the stresses of their illegal operations.
For their pleasure, a prostitution ring was run from the front desk, and
prostitutes were regularly flown in from San Francisco to service the guests.
While prostitutes were being flown in, money from the Lodge's skim was
bagged and flown out. For sex and gambling and the skim, the Lodge was
a bank and playland for the mob.

Sinatra was always discreet about the presence of guests at the Lodge,
so he had tunnels built connecting several of the Lodge's cabins. Guests
could move underground without anyone knowing their movements. Each
favored quest had a reserved cabin connected to other cabins by the tunnels. Sinatra's cabin was number 5, which was often used by Jack and Robert Kennedy. Marilyn Monroe, when present, was in number 3. Though
Sinatra was discreet, some of his employees may have been less so. Word
got back to J. Edgar Hoover at the FBI about the tunnels and the frequent
presence of mobsters, particularly the presence of Sam Giancana. Hoover
reported this to Robert Kennedy, who was intent on protecting his brother
from negative publicity. And so began the unraveling of the Kennedy-
Sinatra relationship. As bad as that was for Sinatra, he worried even more
about the consequences of his relationship with Giancana, for the gangster
would hold Sinatra responsible if he jeopardized the smooth running of the
Lodge.

In his book, *When the Mob Ran Vegas*, Steve Fischer writes,

> On June 30, 1962, an intoxicated Chuckie English, a Giancana hood, stag-
> gered out of the Armory Lounge and bumped into one of the FBI agents tag-
> ging Giancana. English told the agents that if "Bobby Kennedy wants to know
> anything about Momo [one of Giancana's nicknames], all he had to do was ask
> Sinatra." The agent reported the conversation back to Hoover, who brought
> the comment to Robert Kennedy's attention, who told Hoover to increase the
> FBI's surveillance on Sinatra and the Cal-Neva (The previous information and
> quotes are from the Frank Sinatra FBI files).[1]

Robert Kennedy was worried that his brother's ties to Sinatra and hence
the mob could ruin Jack's chances for reelection in 1964. Robert certainly
didn't want the world to know that his brother was a whoremonger and

had an affair with Marilyn Monroe. Though Jack's affair with Monroe is now well known, it was kept secret during his presidency by a censorious media that admired and protected the image of the handsome, dashing young president. Had they been on daddy Joe's payroll they couldn't have done a better job protecting Jack's image. What the media did not know at the time and which would have added to Sinatra's woes with the FBI and gaming officials were a series of photos taken in the Lodge of Monroe with Giancana. Whether drunk and/or drugged, Monroe was photographed on her knees with her head hanging over a toilet bowl. Astride her was Giancana. When the photographer gave Sinatra the photos, Sinatra asked what he thought of them. The photographer advised Sinatra to burn the photos, which Sinatra promptly did. According to Anthony Summers and Robbyn Swan in their biography of Sinatra, "The Mafioso told several people he and actress had sex at the Cal-Neva. Monroe said so, too, according to Jeanne Carmen, who was her friend. Giancana mocked her poor performance and she spoke of the episode with disgust."[2]

A worse event haunted Sinatra's reputation and career. One of his former girlfriends, Toni Anderson, a cocktail waitress at the Lodge, had married a Lake Tahoe deputy sheriff named Richard Anderson. Toni continued to work at the Lodge, and her husband would often pick her up after work. One night, Anderson arrived to pick up his wife and heard Sinatra making suggestive comments to her. Anderson warned Sinatra to refrain from making such remarks and to keep his distance from his wife. Sinatra apologized and walked away. However, on a subsequent night, after Anderson arrived at the Lodge to pick up Toni, Sinatra snarled at him: "What the fuck are you doing here?" Sinatra then attempted to throw Anderson out of the Lodge, but Anderson—who was bigger and stronger than the singer—punched Sinatra, knocking him to the ground. Sinatra's injuries were sufficient to keep him from performing at the Lodge for several days. Sinatra was not a man who let a grudge fade away. A grudge was like a fire onto which Sinatra would pour the alcohol of his brooding anger.

At 10:26 on the night of July 17, 1962, Dick Anderson and his wife were driving on Highway 28 not far from the Cal-Neva. They were on their way to the Crystal Bay Club for dinner after a day spent working on the house they were building. Coming toward them at high speed was a late-model maroon convertible with California license plates. The Andersons' car went off the road and smashed into a tree. Dick Anderson was killed instantly. His wife was thrown from the car and suffered multiple fractures. The occupants of the maroon convertible never stopped, and the deputy sheriff investigating the crash could not determine the cause of the accident.

"We have not found any reason why Anderson should have lost control of his car or driven off the road as he did," he said, adding that Anderson might have been blinded by the bright lights of the oncoming car or deliberately forced off the road.

"It's still a mystery," said Dick Anderson's mother, Louise, twenty-four years later. "An FBI man and some people in the community thought that Frank Sinatra had something to do with the accident. That's something they didn't prove or didn't try to prove."[3]

Another violent incident almost led to Sinatra being jailed. On June 7, 1966, Sinatra, Dean Martin, and their guests arrived at the Beverly Hills Hotel to celebrate Martin's birthday. The boisterous group, drinking and telling jokes, sat in a booth in the Polo Lounge. Frederick Weisman asked the exuberant partygoers if they could cease their loud obscenities. A moment later, having been hit on the head with a large, heavy object, Weisman lay bleeding on the floor. The police were called, but before they arrived, Sinatra, Martin, and their friends had quickly departed. Weisman had a fractured skull, was rushed to a nearby hospital, and remained in a coma. Following brain surgery he revived but suffered from amnesia about what had happened to him. Sinatra was in hiding in Palm Springs nervously receiving reports on Weisman's condition. If he died, Sinatra could be criminally responsible. While Sinatra stayed secluded in Palm Springs, Martin hid out in Lake Tahoe. They both breathed sighs of relief when the district attorney announced there was no evidence of a crime. However, Weisman's "family was so outraged by what had happened to him that they wanted to press criminal charges against Sinatra. But, as they later confided to friends, they had received anonymous phone calls threatening to harm their children, so they were afraid to act.

"Frank's long history of violence so intimidated the Weismans that they decided to forget the whole affair."[4]

Though Sinatra's impulsive acts of violence would get him into trouble, his biggest problem continued to be his friendship with Sam Giancana, who had been spending time at Cal-Neva with his mistress, the singer Phyllis Maguire of the Maguire Sisters. The sisters were performing at the Lodge, and so it was not unusual for their manager, Victor LaCroix Collins, to be present. During a party in her suite, Phyllis playfully would punch Collins' arm whenever she passed his chair. He got annoyed and told her to stop. She continued, and Collins quickly rose from his seat, grabbed her shoulders and pushed her down, attempting to put her on a chair. She missed and fell to the floor. She yelled at Collins, and Giancana ran across the room like an angry charging bull. He punched Collins, ramming a large diamond ring into one of the manager's eyes. Blood streamed down one side of Collins' face. The two men wrestled onto the floor, Giancana under Collins, who had a tight grip on Giancana's balls with one hand and with his other a grip on Giancana's neck. At that point, an unknown assailant hit the back of Collins' head with a small, hard object, opening a deep gash that would require seven stitches. Suddenly Sinatra and his valet, George Jacobs, rushed into the room and pulled Collins off of Giancana, who ran out of the room.

That should have been the end of it, but during his visit, Giancana had been under FBI surveillance that included photos and taped telephone conversations. The agency compiled a report and gave it to the Nevada Gambling Control Board's chairman, Ed Olsen. The agency leaked the story to local papers, and Olsen phoned Sinatra, asking him to come in for an interview. Sinatra refused, and Olsen said that, if necessary, he would issue a subpoena. That ignited Sinatra's fury, who cursed at Olsen, also calling him a cripple, and then slammed down the phone. The next day several agents from the board visited the Lodge to observe the count from gambling in the casino, but the count had already begun. "Frank had them ejected."[5] The next day, agents from the board showed up again, and Paul "Skinny" D'Amato (a gambler and casino manager who owned 13 percent of the Lodge) offered each of them $100 to leave. The board now had all the evidence it needed.

The board decided to revoke Sinatra's license, noting that he permitted a known gangster, Sam Giancana, to be a guest of the Lodge, he had attempted to intimidate Olsen, he had his employs attempt to bribe state gaming officials, and he resisted subpoenas. Sinatra couldn't have been angrier: he was forced give up his interest in the Lodge and sell his nine points in the Sands.

Sinatra's anger was exceeded by Giancana's fury. The loss of the Cal-Neva Lodge infuriated Giancana and ended his friendship with Sinatra. He wanted to kill Sinatra and spoke of putting a contract on his life.

Sam Giancana never did forgive Frank for his role in the failed relationship with the Kennedys or for the loss of the Cal-Neva. According to a member of the mobster's family, only the intercession of East Coast [mob] associates persuaded Giancana not to have Frank killed in 1963. "That motherfucker," he said when Frank arrived unexpectedly at the Armory Lounge, "is lucky to be alive." . . . Giancana continued to speak from time to time of having Frank killed.[6]

He said,

> "That bastard and his big mouth. All he had to do was keep quiet, let the
> attorneys handle it, apologize, and get a thirty- to sixty-day suspension . . .
> but, no, Frank has to get on the phone with that damn big mouth of his and
> now we've lost the whole damn place." He read him off for using all that filthy
> language with Ed Olsen and said he was a stupid fool. He never forgave him.
> He washed Frank right out of his books.[7]

Though Giancana had previously put a contract out on the life of Sinatra,
he subsequently rescinded it. Following the Cal-Neva debacle, however,
Giancana decided to do it again.

> The hot-blooded boss did not take the loss of his getaway lying down. Accord-
> ing to the source, who wishes to remain anonymous, the idea of killing Sinatra
> was again revived by Mooney [Giancana] himself. "From what I was told," the
> source says, "Mooney was furious that Sinatra refused to give back the invest-
> ment, so he put out a contract. Frank begged New York boys to intercede for
> him again and Mooney called it off."[8]

The New York boys were Frank Costello and Meyer Lansky.

A few months after Sinatra had his license to operate a casino revoked,
Sammy Davis Jr. crossed paths with Olsen in the Sands Casino. Olsen
expected to be a target of Davis's wrath. For years, Davis was known as a
loyal member of the Rat Pack and a devoted friend to Sinatra, often teased
about being Sinatra's shadow. Instead of Davis berating Olsen, he said,
"That little son of a bitch, he's needed this for years. I've been working with
him for sixteen years, and nobody's ever had the guts to stand up to him."[9]

Though the loss of his gaming license was a professional loss for Sinatra,
he suffered another kind of loss. Other than his failed relationship with
Ava Gardner, the biggest blow to his machismo reputation as a tough guy
occurred when a bigger man would not fade away in the face of Sinatra's
attempted bullying. This incident was revealed to me by Tony Napoli (TN),
son of James (Jimmy Nap) Napoli, who was major bookmaker and a capo in
the Genovese crime family. Jimmy Nap had gotten his son Tony a job as a
manager in the Sands Casino.

Napoli told me that after Howard Hughes purchased the Sands, he
issued orders through Bob Maheu that no one would be issued lines of
credit without a financial check of them. Sinatra had always been issued
lines of credit; however, under Hughes (who disliked Sinatra since losing
Ava Gardner to him), Sinatra would be denied any credit until he paid off

his markers to the Sands. Some of those markers amounted to $200,000. In addition to not paying off his markers, Sinatra always pocketed his winnings. For Sinatra, it was a win-win arrangement. For the Sands, it was a loss-loss one. It was September 11, 1967, and Sinatra had been steadily losing. He was frustrated and getting increasingly irritable. The pit boss was not permitted to give Sinatra, who was standing with a group of Apollo astronauts, any credit. Sinatra felt embarrassed and humiliated in the presence of the astronauts. He blamed Carl Cohen for having his credit cut off. The more he brooded, the hotter he became, Napoli said.

Sinatra was furious. He yelled: "Where the hell is Jack [Entratter]? That Jew bastard Carl [Cohen] is trying to fuck with me again."[10] Cohen was the Sand's vice president, manager, and owner of several points.

Sinatra slammed his fist down on the front desk, demanding to know Carl Cohen's room number. When the clerk refused to reveal it, Sinatra threatened him. Sinatra then grabbed a security guard and demanded to be taken to the room of the switchboard operators. The guard refused and Sinatra threatened to take away the guard's pistol and shove it up his ass. Sinatra finally found the switchboard room on his own and pounded on the door. He screamed for the operators to open the door. When the operators refused to open it, he threatened to tear it down and beat up the operators.

Cohen, who had a do-not-disturb notation on his phone, was finally reached by the frightened telephone operators. He was told that Sinatra was yelling and threatening people who worked in the casino. Cohen said he would meet Sinatra in the Garden Room of the Sands. Sinatra was accompanied by pal and bodyguard Jilly Rizzo. They all sat at a table and Sinatra demanded to know why his credit had been cut off. He called Cohen an SOB.

"What did you call me?" Cohen asked.

"You heard me. You son of a bitch," Sinatra said. "What are you so nervous about?"

"You just got me out of bed," Cohen said.[11]

Cohen got up to leave. Sinatra started calling Cohen a rat fink, a cocksucker, a motherfucker. Sinatra then overturned Cohen's breakfast and said he would kill him.

"You kike," he screamed.

Carl Cohen, slow to anger, instantly drove his big right fist into Sinatra's mouth, smashing the caps off his two front teeth, knocking him straight to the floor.

Bleeding and furious, [Sinatra screamed,] "You broke my teeth. I'll kill you, you motherfucker, son of a bitch."

Frank got up and threw a chair at Cohen. It missed and hit a security guard in the head, then barked a command at Rizzo: "Get him Jilly, get him!" He did nothing.[12]

Ed Walters, a pit boss at the Sands, said: "You didn't fight Carl Cohen. There were a couple of guys that got on the wrong side of him who were never seen again. He had no fear of Frank Sinatra, whom he knew to be a hothead and nothing like a fighter."[13]

Tony Napoli told me that Sinatra called Jimmy Nap (Tony's father) to complain about Carl Cohen. He wanted something done. Jimmy Nap told Sinatra that "Carl Cohen is untouchable. He's one of us. You're an entertainer. Look who signs your checks. [Carl Cohen] It doesn't matter how much we pay you. You're just an entertainer, a nice amenity for the guests. Nothing more."[14]

Robert Maheu, describing Sinatra's behavior, sent the following memo to Howard Hughes:

> For two successive nights into the wee hours of the morning, Sinatra has made a damn fool of himself in the casino of the Sands. He moved around insulting people with vile language. Last night, he drove a golf cart through a plate glass window and was disgustingly drunk. In an effort to protect him from himself, Carl Cohen stopped his credit after he obtained 30k plus in cash and lost approximately 50k. Sinatra blew his top and late this afternoon called me to tell me that he was walking away from the Sands and would not finish his engagement.[15]

Sinatra soon signed a $3-million contract with Caesars Palace that guaranteed him $100,000 a week.

Carl Cohen, meanwhile, was treated like a conquering hero. As he left the Garden Room, employees gave him round after round of applause. Posters went up around town and in the hotel that featured a photo of Sinatra with his front teeth blacked out. Below his image, in big letters, was the message: "Carl Cohen for Mayor."

The following letter appeared in the *Las Vegas Sun*:

> Now, after a few drinks, this sheer genius of a man staggers into the office and as he blurringly gazes about decides the phone on his desk doesn't match the new orange sweater he's wearing. He calls you and demands an orange phone immediately. But you don't respond quickly enough. He calls you some choice words and the filth pleases him so much, he directs them to the

female help as well. His reasoning is, no orange phone, no phone at all, and he proceeds to tear all the phones out before he sets fire to the office and breaks the windows.[16]

Later back in Los Angeles, when asked by Kirk Douglas about the incident with Cohen, Sinatra allegedly said that he should never have gotten into a fight with a tough casino Jew. Though as impulsively belligerent as Sinatra often could be, his popularity as an entertainer never would have approached the heights it did if he weren't one of the finest popular singers of the American songbook throughout a period of more than six decades. Furthermore, he garnered rave reviews for his performances in such movies as *From Here to Eternity*, *The Man with the Golden Arm*, *The Joker Is Wild*, *Suddenly*, and *The Manchurian Candidate*, among many others. Of course, it was *Oceans 11* that brought the Rat Pack to wide public attention and served as an advertisement for the Pack's appearances at the Sands. It also cemented Sinatra's reputation as a cool, confident, tough guy. Talented and charismatic.

Talent he certainly had in abundance, but it wasn't only his talent that offset his reputation for violence: it was his often extraordinary generosity. He would send large sums of money to those in need, whether friends, acquaintances, or victims of natural disasters. He often paid for the medical costs of old girlfriends, actors, and musicians down on their luck. He paid hospital bills for friends and musicians who didn't have medical insurance or the wherewithal to pay their bills. He raised millions of dollars for Israeli charities and defense. He was a diligent fighter against prejudice directed at minorities and backed up such fights with generous donations. His ten-minute, 1945 movie, *The House I Live In*, became a vehicle for teaching schoolchildren the importance of racial and religious tolerance, respect, and acceptance. Eleanor Roosevelt expressed her admiration for the movie and for Sinatra. But that was years before Sinatra made Las Vegas his kind of town.

Sinatra was an asset to the Sands, regardless of what Jimmy Nap said, because of his ability to fill a casino with high rollers. And the enthusiasm for attending Sinatra concerts was further enhanced when he appeared on stage with his Rat Pack cohorts. Tourists would pay top dollar for a seat in the Copa Room to see the Pack. Thousands regularly attempted to bribe anyone who could get them tickets to a Rat Pack show.

The original Rat Pack began in Hollywood and New York with Humphrey Bogart as its most prominent member, and it included scriptwriters, directors and producers, and nightclub and restaurant owners. But it was at the Sands that it became famous, comprising its commanding leader, Frank Sinatra, and his fun-loving pals: Dean Martin, Sammy Davis Jr., Joey Bishop, and Peter Lawford. From its initial appearance at the Sands in 1960, the Pack was a masculine dream come true, where you could drink, carouse, joke, have beautiful women at your beck and call, and have all the fun in the world.

Sinatra couldn't have picked a better assemblage of talented performers. Initially, Sinatra preferred Jerry Lewis to Dean Martin. He did not think much of Martin's singing. "The dago's lousy, but the little Jew is great," Sinatra said in 1948.[17] But after Martin's breakup with Lewis in 1956 and his performance at the Sands in 1957, Sinatra came to appreciate Martin's talent. Martin self-effacingly appraised his style of singing, saying he was not really a singer: he was a crooner. (Crooning is a style of relaxed and seemingly effortless singing.)

Sinatra's relationship with Sammy Davis Jr. dated from 1947 when Sinatra hired the Will Mastin Trio, featuring the young Davis, to be the opening act for his concert at the Capital Theater in New York City. Though owing a debt of gratitude to Sinatra, Davis was not above making public statements that offended Sinatra and got him frozen out of Sinatra's circle. One such comment particularly angered Sinatra: Davis had commented that "talent is not an excuse for bad manners. It does not give you the right to step on people and treat them rotten. This is what he does occasionally."[18] It required major acts of obeisance, penance, flattery, and abject apologies from Davis for Sinatra to even begin talking with him again.

Peter Lawford got off to an inauspicious start with Sinatra. The young debonair actor with British manners had run afoul of Sinatra after a photo appeared in several newspapers of Lawford having a drink with Ava Gardner. Sinatra and Gardner were separated at the time, but Sinatra still loved her and the breakup of their marriage sent his mood and career into a downward spiral. Five years later, however, when Lawford's brother-in-law, John Kennedy, was running for president, Sinatra re-initiated a friendship with Lawford, one that Sinatra would furiously end a few years later. That occurred after President Kennedy cancelled a visit to Sinatra's Palm Springs home and instead stayed at the home of Bing Crosby. Sinatra blamed Lawford for not persuading Kennedy to stay at Sinatra's home. Before that falling out, Lawford appeared on stage with the Rat Pack and in the movie *Oceans 11*, the rights to which Lawford owned. As a member of the Rat Pack on stage, Lawford contributed very little to their performances, joining in the fun and shooting out a line usually supplied by Joey Bishop.

Joey Bishop, known as the Frown Prince of Comedy, had been the opening act for Sinatra at the Copacabana in New York City. And since Jack Entratter had moved from being the manager of the Copa nightclub to being head of talent at the Sands, it was a natural for Bishop to make the move with him. Bishop wrote all of the sketches for the Rat Pack and rehearsed the acts before the group went on stage. In his dour manner, he was able to interject solemn but funny lines during Sinatra's routines, such as "Frank, why don't you tell us about all the good the Mafia does." The audience would crack up at such remarks, and Sinatra laughed along with them.

The album *The Rat Pack Live at the Sands* captures all of the exuberance, irreverence, and talent of the group and remains popular to this day. (However, it is not as popular or as highly regarded as Sinatra's solo album *Sinatra at the Sands*, which is considered one of the finest concert albums of the last seventy-five years not only by Sinatra fans but also by fans of the Great American Songbook.) Though myths about the Rat Pack drinking on stage and being drunk are still held almost as sacred truths, Joey Bishop, at age eighty, shattered that myth during an interview with *Time* magazine: "Are we remembered as being drunks and chasing broads? I never saw Frank, Dean, Sammy or Peter drunk during performances. That was only a gag! And do you believe these guys had to chase broads? They had to chase 'em away!"[19]

The Rat Pack, though seemingly carefree, could find itself in harness to the mob. Sinatra's relationship with Giancana had many ups and downs. And when Robert Kennedy began prosecuting the mob with the zeal of a Thomas Dewey, Giancana blamed Sinatra for not getting Attorney General Robert Kennedy to back off his prosecution of Mafia members. After all, it was Sinatra who had bragged to Giancana that his connections with the Kennedys would result in happy days for the mob. When that didn't happen, Giancana—who was being surveilled around the clock by the FBI—said to Johnny Rosselli that Sinatra had to be hit.

Gus Russo, in his book *The Outfit*, writes:

In the fall of 1962, Mooney [Giancana] was ready to exact his pound of flesh from Frank Sinatra, the man who had sold him a bill of goods regarding the Kennedy "deal." Throughout 1962, Mooney had overseen a massive remodeling of his Villa Venice Restaurant, and according to some of his cronies, the entire undertaking was aimed at making a onetime killing with Sinatra's Rat Pack as bait.

Starting on November 26, and for the better part of a month, Dean Martin, Frank Sinatra, Eddie Fisher, Sammy Davis, Jr. and Jimmy Durante appeared for free at the Villa Venice. During the sold-out run, there were lavish parties and receptions in Mooney's suite while the suckers were being ferried to the Quonset Hut [nearby to the Villa] to be relieved of their money at the craps, blackjack, and roulette tables.[20]

Following the event, which netted Giancana more than $3 million, the FBI attempted to question Sammy Davis Jr. about it. He said: "I can't talk about it. Baby, I got one eye, and that eye sees a lot of things that my brain says I shouldn't talk about. Because my brain says that if I do, my one eye might not be seeing anything for a while."[21] Months later the Villa burned to the ground, and one can only assume that Giancana had fire insurance.

Whether performing for the mob or at the Sands, the Rat Pack was as popular as ever. But Frank, furious at the way his credit was cut off at the Sands and embarrassed about his encounter with Carl Cohen, left the Sands for greener pastures. (His Rat Pack dispersed.) Sinatra found a temporary venue for his performances at Caesars Palace, where he was guaranteed $400,000 a week during engagements that would last for eight weeks. In addition, he was given $10,000 in chips to play blackjack, his favorite game. If his losses exceeded that amount, he would sign a marker, but he would never pay it off. He believed that his presence brought so many people into the casino, who dropped hundreds of thousands of dollars at the gaming tables, that he was entitled to have his losses forgiven.

On November 27, 1968, more than a year after leaving the Sands, Sinatra made his debut to raucous applause at Caesars Palace. However, his enthusiastic welcome was marred by the FBI, which had been investigating the relationship that casinos had with the Mafia. And, unfortunately, Sinatra became one focus of the agency's investigation. As at the Sands, Sinatra had large amounts of markers he had signed over to Caesars. The money was not being deducted from his salary, and he was not, as expected, paying the money back from his winnings. An undercover FBI agent called the casino manager, Sanford Waterman, at five in the morning and told him Sinatra wanted to sign another marker. Waterman confronted Sinatra, telling him that if he wanted chips, he would have to pay cash for them. The two got into a nasty argument, Sinatra calling Waterman a kike, and Waterman calling Sinatra a son of a bitch guinea. They traded punches then grappled on the floor. Sinatra placed his hands around Waterman's neck and Waterman pulled out a pistol and pointed the barrel between Sinatra's eyes, who then called Waterman a crazy Hebe. The two men were separated by security guards. Sinatra said that the mob would take care of Waterman and that he would not work at Caesars again. He walked away from his contract. Waterman was held in jail overnight for pulling a gun on Sinatra. Sheriff Lamb later decided that Sinatra had been the aggressor and said that if he returned to Vegas he would be arrested. He added: "I'm tired of him intimidating waiters, waitresses, and starting fires and throwing pies. He gets away with too much. He's through picking on little people in this town."[22]

The district attorney stated: "My reports indicated that Waterman still had finger marks on his throat where Sinatra grabbed him. There seems to be reasonable grounds for making the assumption that Sinatra was the aggressor all the way."[23] No one mentioned the fact that Waterman had been a partner of Sinatra and part owner of the Cal-Neva Lodge, having bought Dean Martin's share of the Lodge in 1961. So much for the kind and generous gestures of former partners.

Back in Los Angeles, Sinatra said he had "suffered enough indignities. . . . If the public officials who seek newspaper exposure by harassing me and other entertainers don't get off my back, it is of little moment to me if I ever play Las Vegas again." That was a precursor to a show business "retirement" that lasted from 1971 until a ballyhooed return to Caesars Palace on January 25, 1974.[24]

He made his triumphant return to Vegas and Caesars Palace in 1974, after Waterman had been arrested for racketeering and the district attorney had been defeated in his re-election bid. Sinatra's mother had initially been against his return engagement at Caesars, but with the district attorney and Waterman out of the picture and with Sheriff Lamb saying Sinatra would be welcome in Vegas, she gave her approval for her son's return. And what a return visit it proved to be. If Caesars had rolled out a red carpet strewn with rose petals, it would have been an understatement of the intensity of their welcoming embrace. Sinatra, the Vegas king of entertainers, sang to an audience of 1,300 wildly appreciative fans on opening night. And each of those fans received a medallion with the following inscribed message: "Hail Sinatra, The Noblest Roman Has Returned." This time the casino provided Sinatra with free bodyguards and sufficient credit for him to gamble as long as the cards held his interest.

By 1981, there was no question but that Frank Sinatra was an institution in Vegas, admired, sought after, and honored. Rather than being run out of town or coming to blows with casino moguls, Sinatra was finally being re-evaluated for a gaming license, which would be his badge of approval, obviating his previous licensing revocation and connections with mobsters. So sure was Sinatra that he would be granted a license that he listed President Reagan as a character reference, who said, through his attorney, that Sinatra was "an honorable person—completely honest and loyal."[25] The commission also heard favorable testimony from Gregory Peck, Kirk Douglas, and other Hollywood luminaries. Sinatra was treated like a visiting potentate from the land of make believe. He denied any association with mobsters, and the commission did not follow up with any probing questions. It was as if the commissioners were gently tossing Wiffle balls at Sinatra, who just as gently batted them away. The Gaming Commission, as expected, approved Sinatra's license to be an entertainment consultant at Caesars Palace. The Sinatra slate had been wiped clean, and he was now an honored member of Las Vegas society. People packed into Caesars to hear the greatest pop song singer of the last fifty years. For Sinatra, the love of his audience was like a shot of potent drugs that vanished his insecurities and shot him into euphoria. The casino didn't even have to post his name on a marquee to announce his appearances; it could simply inscribe the message, He's Here!

As the toast of the town, Sinatra sang not only at Caesars but also at the revitalized Golden Nugget, Bally's, and the Riviera. And on his seventy-seventh birthday, he was the subject of a gala celebration at the Desert Inn, where he had first performed in 1951. However, it was a sad day for his fans, for Sinatra was already suffering from dementia and had a difficult time remembering the lyrics of songs he had been singing for decades. His voice was no longer as crisp and clear as it had been. There was a hoarseness present from years of smoking and drinking.

One of my friends, who was a friend of the Sinatra family, was invited to accompany Sinatra to the Meadowlands in New Jersey, where Sinatra was scheduled to sing. Before the concert, my friend was invited to join Sinatra for drinks in his suite at the Waldorf Astoria. After his knock on Sinatra's door, the door was opened and there was Sinatra in his tuxedo. He extended his hand and said, "Hi. I'm Frank Sinatra." The two then retired to the living room, where Sinatra had five glasses of Jack Daniels bourbon. At the Meadowlands, Sinatra required a teleprompter, for he could no longer remember all the lyrics of his most popular songs.

Though honored in Vegas and a frequent guest in Reagan's White House, Sinatra's Mafia associations would continue to haunt him, especially after he was photographed in his dressing room with Carlo Gambino and members of the Gambino crime family at the Westchester Premier Theater. Anthony Summers and Robbyn Swan write that an employee at the Palm Springs Hotel overheard Tommy Marson, one of the men pictured in the photograph, saying into the phone: "Frank I need you at the Westchester Premier Theater. Frank, I don't give a fuck what you gotta do. You be there." And Frank obeyed.[26]

One of the men not in the photograph was Louis "Louie Domes" Pacella, who owned a restaurant in New York. Summers and Swan write in their biography of Sinatra:

> Pacella's attorney put it more strongly. "You will find," he told the court, "that Frank Sinatra and Louis Pacella were very, very, very close and dear friends. In fact, the evidence will show you that they were brothers, not because they shared the same mother and father but because they shared love, admiration and friendship for many years."[27]
>
> Pacella was reportedly a capo in the Genovese crime family and, according to the Drug Enforcement Administration, a heroin dealer. He had inherited a special assignment. "After Sam Giancana was murdered," said Philip Leonetti, a high-ranking mafioso who later turned FBI informant, Pacella "took over control of Frank Sinatra."[28]

Regardless of his connections, music aficionados continued to praise Sinatra as a sui generis artist. My former neighbor and acclaimed jazz critic Arnold Shaw told me at the time he was writing a biography of Sinatra that the singer was one of the finest vocalists of the classic American songbook; he was like no other. No one could match him. Shaw's book, *Sinatra: Twentieth Century Romantic*, of course, pleased the singer, who sent a gracious thank-you note to Shaw.

Another neighbor and friend, Guy Wood, wrote the song "My One and Only Love," which Sinatra recorded on his albums *Nice 'n' Easy* and *This Is Sinatra*. Wood said he was honored that Sinatra recorded his song and that Sinatra had one of the finest pop music voices.

Though others have written books about Sinatra's life, the singer—though offered millions of dollars to write his autobiography—refused. He told a literary agent that he wouldn't write his autobiography because he wasn't proud of many things he had done. Then, after a pause, he said that the only thing that really mattered about him was his singing and that he had made popular music into an art form. Of all the entertainers of Vegas, Sinatra was the apotheosis of the charismatic entertainer, the man who was the beau ideal of the cool, hip, swaggering swinger.

Elvis Presley was a different story. Though his siren call drew thousands to his concerts, he was not the cool, swinging sophisticate who would draw in the fans of the Rat Pack. He was smart enough to have realized that his early image as "Elvis the Pelvis" would not be a hit in Vegas. Screaming teenage girls were not the typical casino customers. So Elvis transformed himself from good ole Southern boy with a leather jacket, greasy hair, a snarl, and guitar to one of the glitziest performers on a Vegas stage. His audience had grown with him; they had not been Sinatra fans. They grew up listening to rock 'n' roll; their most popular singers were Fats Domino, Little Richard, Jerry Lee Lewis, and various doo-wop groups. For them, Sinatra was old hat, a representative of their parents' generation. Sinatra and members of the Rat Pack never would have appeared in the glitzy bejeweled jumpsuits that Elvis wore. Sinatra's usual Vegas attire consisted of a bespoke tuxedo that fit as perfectly as if worn by a mannequin in a Rodeo Street boutique window. His bow to casualness consisted of untying his black bow tie and letting it hang below his shirt collar. He was Mr. Cool; the man never even owned a pair of jeans. He was a product of the elegant New York and Chicago nightclubs of the 1950s and 1960s. Seeing a scruffy young man in jeans and chukka boots, Sinatra would let his displeasure be known.

For him, the counterculture was without culture.

It's no wonder that Sinatra hated rock 'n' roll and only appeared on a television special with Elvis to increase his ratings. Sinatra's attitude about rock music was reflected in the kind of entertainers who appeared in Vegas. In addition to the Rat Pack, there was Tony Bennett, Eddie Fisher, Tony Martin, Andy Williams, Perry Como, and comedians Buddy Hackett and Shecky Greene. Their appeal was to middle-aged and older customers, the ones who had big bucks to leave at the gaming tables.

It's no wonder that Elvis initially rejected the idea of appearing on a Vegas stage. He knew the customers were not his audience. They would rather hear "I Left My Heart in San Francisco," "Volare," "Don't Let the Stars Get in Your Eyes," "Put on a Happy Face," "My Way," "Come Fly with Me," "The Lady Is a Tramp," and "I've Got the World on a String" than "Hound Dog," "Don't Be Cruel," and "Jailhouse Rock." Nevertheless, Elvis's manager, Colonel Tom Parker, talked his client into appearing at the New Frontier in 1956. "Elvis cut such an incongruous figure . . . that *Newsweek* likened his appearance to a 'jug of corn liquor at a champagne party.' The Las Vegas audience was described as sitting through Elvis's act as 'if he were a clinical experiment.'"[29]

It all changed, however, in 1968 when Kirk Kerkorian announced that he would build the world's largest and most luxurious hotel/casino, the International. The hoopla generated by the announcement was enough to get the Colonel to book Elvis, as "The World's Greatest Entertainer," into the hotel. Elvis was not happy about it; he was worried and apprehensive about being rejected again. But the Colonel managed to convince Elvis that this time would be different. The Colonel, known for his greed and sharp practices, would not have booked Elvis into the hotel if he thought it would be a money-losing performance. Though the Colonel still conceived of his client in a leather jacket, backed by a five-piece band, singing "Heartbreak Hotel," Elvis said he would have no part of that old routine. He had moved on and was no longer interested in his early image, looking like a greasy-haired juvenile delinquent. Much to the Colonel's dismay, Elvis would make a dramatic change. He would become the Liberace of Rock, but first he needed another kind of role model.

Albert Goldman, in his biography of Elvis, writes:

> One night he walked into the lounge at the Flamingo and found the solution to his problems. The performer was a young and virtually unknown Welsh singer named Tom Jones. . . . His stance was commanding. As he would hit the long high notes, he would bend back from the waist, giving the women at ringside a good long look at his crotch. . . . In the strong stage lights, you could clearly see the outline of his dick and balls.[30]

Elvis had found his Vegas inspiration, though he thought that Jones went too far, that his performance was lewd. He copied the Jones style without thrusting his genitals out as if a gift to the women in the audience. Instead of a lewd conclusion to his songs, Elvis would highlight his performances with dramatic karate moves. He was a black belt and so he delivered the karate moves like exclamation marks. As Goldman writes: "He didn't jiggle and jerk anymore. He took his stand and held it, firm as a statue. He didn't walk in the old butchy style. He padded back and forth like a cat-footed karate killer."[31]

Colonel Parker, now on board with the new Elvis act, extensively advertised his client's upcoming performances in newspapers, on television, on radio, and on huge billboards. It was the biggest advertising campaign in the history of Vegas. Elvis fan clubs from around the world learned of the concert, and thousands of their members flocked to hear him. They did not come to Vegas to gamble, but to see their hero. Everyone in the entertainment world knew that Elvis would soon be performing. And his performances, backed by a large orchestra, earned a huge profit for the International, greater than anything that Sinatra had ever generated. But while Sinatra was paid $400,000 a week at Caesars, Elvis was paid only $125,000, of which 50 percent went to the Colonel, plus an agent's commission. Elvis's wily old manager was not sufficiently wily, however, to negotiate a more generous contract with the International. Instead, the Colonel was given unlimited credit in the hotel's casino and a rent-free suite. The hotel also paid for many of the Colonel's living expenses. Elvis would appear twice a year at the International for the same weekly salary, which was never renegotiated. Year after year, he would appear in his bejeweled tight-fitting jump suit adorned with ropes of pearls, more exhausted year after year from the grueling schedule of his performances.

The hotel could not have been more pleased. In his first four weeks at the International, Elvis drew in an audience of 101,000 fans. And during a period of seven years, he drew in more than two million fans. They went crazy for him, shouting and cheering as if watching Muhammad Ali winning a heavyweight boxing championship. Richard Zoglin writes,

> The set reached a climax with Elvis's feverish, seven-minute no-holds-barred performance of a song almost no one in the audience had heard before . . . "Suspicious Minds," which nearly brought the house down.
> The show lasted an hour and fifteen minutes, and Elvis worked himself to a frazzle; pacing the stage like a panther, crouching, lunging, leaping, doing karate kicks and punches.[32]

During his performance, he would drop down on one knee or bend forward from the waist and kiss women near the stage. Some of them squealed with excitement. A few women threw their panties onto the stage. Elvis was in heaven. The love of the audience was a tsunami that rolled over and engulfed him.

Sammy Davis Jr., Cary Grant, Carol Channing, Fats Domino, and Pat Boone, who were in the audience, were effusive in their praise. They had never seen such an enthralling performance by a singer. So impressive was his performance that RCA released *From Memphis to Vegas/From Vegas to Memphis*, a double album of his live performance.

Elvis was the most powerful magnet the city had ever seen. He was a financial bonanza for the International. Management couldn't believe they got him at such a modest price, by Vegas standards. He was the biggest draw in Vegas for seven straight years.

He became such a Vegas institution that there were Elvis wedding chapels, Elvis slot machines, and a life-size statue of Elvis in the lobby of the International's successor hotel, the Hilton. And should tourists walk around the city, they would often encounter Elvis impersonators. One could walk over to a street named for Elvis and expect to see a few impersonators in jumpsuits, each with dyed black hair combed into a large pompadour.

The real Elvis was more complex and less extroverted than what people saw on the stage. He was sincerely religious, even spiritual, which was reflected in the books he chose to read. As Richard Zoglin writes in *Elvis in Vegas*: "Elvis's room was always piled high with books of spiritual and religious seeking."[33] Elvis had been befriended by his hairstylist, Larry Geller, who gave his friend books about self-realization and spirituality. Elvis loved speaking with Geller about spiritual matters and the role of religion in one's life. However, Elvis's friends and hangers-on found Geller's presence a hindrance to their good times, and so they forced him out of Elvis's life. For them, nothing should get in the way of letting their good times roll. Religion was a downer.

Too enthralled by religion, his performances might become dull, even sedate. Better to keep on rocking. The success of the Presley phenomenon rested upon wild and seductive performances. His friends flattered and encouraged him. They were a chorus of sycophants. And Elvis responded to their adulation as if it were his due. His ongoing success was so spectacular that it opened the door for other rockers, the first being Blood, Sweat & Tears. More rock groups followed, changing the entire performance culture of the town. Other than Blood Sweat & Tears, which had performed at Woodstock, there were plenty of counterculture performers who had been at Woodstock, but who would not set foot in Vegas. For them, Vegas was vulgar, inauthentic, and tawdry. Only philistines would find the entertainment enjoyable.

Elvis, who would not have set foot in Woodstock, performed for four straight weeks, two shows a night, as if mainlining adrenaline. Yet, the pace exhausted him. He began taking drugs to keep himself energized, and then drugs to put himself to sleep. The more he took, the more he needed.

By October 9, 1973, Elvis's health was in obvious decline. His breathing was labored, he had become fat, and his eyes were bloodshot. Twice that year, he took an overdose of barbiturates and spent three days in a coma. He had developed an addiction to pethidine, a synthetic opioid, that put him into another coma in 1973. His primary care doctor, George C. Nichopoulos, said Presley "felt that by getting drugs from a doctor, he wasn't the common everyday junkie getting something off the street."[34]

Guitarist John Wilkinson said, "He was all gut. He was slurring. He was so fucked up. . . . It was obvious he was drugged. It was obvious there was something terribly wrong with his body. It was so bad the words to the songs were barely intelligible. . . . I remember crying. He could barely get through the introductions."[35]

Tony Scherman wrote that by early 1977, "Presley had become a grotesque caricature of his sleek, energetic former self. Grossly overweight, his mind dulled by the pharmacopia he daily ingested, he was barely able to pull himself through his abbreviated concerts."[36]

The increasingly large doses of drugs made him paranoid, so that he started carrying pistols wherever he went. When angry, he might shoot at the sky, or for fun just fire off a few shots.

When high, he would do the same thing. His mood swings went from high to low, from kind to snarling mean. High on drugs, he spent his money almost as quickly as it came in. Month by month, he continued gaining weight. His performances became grim pastiches of his usual hits; as an attempt to shock his audiences, he would occasionally insert pornographic comments into the lyrics of his love ballads. As his health continued to decline, he cancelled more and more shows. At times, he couldn't even walk onto a stage. Or if there, he would have to sit in a chair. Gone were the rave reviews from his early performances at the International. Everyone who was close to Elvis believed that he was soon to stagger into death's embrace. He would not die like his contemporary 1950s teen idol, James Dean, in a car crash, or be shot by a jealous husband. His death would lack drama, be without dignity. Elvis died like many other addicts. On August 16, 1977, apparently having fallen off a toilet bowl, he landed in fetal position on the floor. It was the sad, undignified end to a man who changed popular music beginning with his big hit, "Heartbreak Hotel," in 1956.

He had created a new era in Vegas: gone were the old nightclub sophisticates listening to the classic American songbook and Broadway show tunes. Elvis served to revitalize Vegas, helping to make it a bigger, more booming entertainment center than it had previously been. Thanks to him, Vegas immodestly calls itself the Entertainment Capital of the World.

Since his death, the singers come and go in Vegas; yet, another kind of entertainment has remained steadfast: the siren call of beautiful showgirls. Men have not only been drawn to Vegas by the dreams of winning big at gambling, they have also looked forward to satisfying their fantasies in the company of showgirls. Many have heard about the availability of showgirls after their performances have ended. They could often be seen in the company of high rollers.

The come-on of sexual fun began in the early days of Vegas with burlesque shows, followed by famous strippers, such as Candy Barr, Tempest Storm, and Lili St. Cyr. However, as men grew tired of those kinds of shows, the casinos tempted them with glamorous Las Vegas showgirls: tall statuesque beauties (at least 5'8" and as tall as 6'1") with voluptuous figures. The showgirls appeared either topless in big reviews or as nude dancers. Some showgirls who wore topless gowns of feathers and rhinestones also wore enormous bejeweled headdresses that could weigh as much as thirty pounds as they balanced on four- or five-inch heels. Slowly gliding across a stage to a musical accompaniment, bathed in a light show that highlighted their beauty, they were careful not to stumble. They were meant to be billboards of desire, inviting men to fantasize about the intense sensual pleasures of a sexual romp with such gorgeous creatures. Mario Puzo said that Vegas had the most beautiful women of any city in the world. It is a city that has objectified women, turning them into assets that encourage men to gamble and be reckless with their money. They are manifestations of dreams of conquest and winning. And it's not only the allure of beautiful showgirls who are often encouraged to befriend high rollers and get them to gamble away large sums, to puff up their dreams of wining big; there are also prostitutes, who are chip hustlers practiced in partaking of the winnings of high rollers by being their gambling muses. Since the 1940s, if not earlier, prostitutes have been so much a part of Vegas that they are as integral to the culture of gambling as slot machines. During the 1970s, the number of prostitutes working the Strip allegedly exceeded ten thousand.[37] In addition to the women who daily work as hustlers in the casinos, there are others who fly in for weekends. Mario Puzo wrote that there is a phenomenon known as weekend call girls, who are secretaries, receptionists, manicurists, teachers, single mothers, divorcees, failed actresses, and models past their prime; all come to town to cash in. They make connections with dealers and pit bosses, who will put them in touch with gamblers looking for some sexual fun. The weekenders give a percentage of what they make to the dealers or pit bosses who set them up. Back home, the weekenders resume their normal lives; their friends, relatives, and neighbors ignorant of their weekend adventures. The once popular advertising slogan, "What happens in Vegas—Stays in Vegas," was the perfect come-on not only for men seeking adventures of the flesh, away from wives or girlfriends, but also for enterprising women in need of money and a desire for a little danger to spice up their lives.

As seen in the movie *Casino*, Ginger (played by Sharon Stone) hustled high rollers out of large sums of money with the implicit promise of sex. Showgirls, of course, could also be successful chip hustlers, who—when finished with their performances—would make themselves available to high rollers, especially if the gamblers were big winners. A showgirl would arrive at a gaming table and say that management wanted to provide the gambler with free drinks. In such cases, the showgirl would keep her target drinking and gambling, making larger and larger bets, reckless in his efforts to win big. But, of course, the odds are always against the gamblers, and eventually the casino would not only recoup its losses, but also make a killing. The showgirl would be tipped with chips until the gambler ran out of money. His wallet drained, his credit cut off, the losing gambler was left to return home like a wounded animal.

The high rollers were either the aristocrats of gamblers or the highest level of suckers among gamblers. They came in junkets, flying first class, then driven in style from the airport to the hotels and given free rooms, drinks, meals, and tickets to all the events at the hotels. They would not be invited back, however, unless they had lost large sums of money. The Las Vegas Junket was a brilliant maneuver that was invented by Big Julie Weintraub, who got his name because he stood 6'5" and weighed 260 pounds. His nose had been broken several times, giving him the look of a retired boxer. Though he had the look of a tough guy, he was sweet and good humored. The *Las Vegas Sun* referred to him as the Las Vegas Junket King. In the 1970s, Weintraub told me that he loved playing craps but had lost a lot of money at the tables. He decided that there was more money to be made in running junkets of high rollers to Vegas casinos than in losing money at the craps tables. Though he was a New York jeweler by profession, he loved Vegas and loved catering to planeloads of high rollers. He brought thousands of them to Vegas, and because they lost such large sums of money, the casinos loved Big Julie.

Though the casinos loved the high rollers, they also wanted to attract families. To do so, they would have to change the image and reputation of Vegas from a city of prostitutes and gangsters and degenerate gamblers to one that was wholesome Americana. They thought they could convert Sin City into a Disneyland for families. So casinos offered carnivals, roller coasters, fighting pirates, cowboy duels, and the like. Casinos had become theme parks. But there were few families that attended the new theme park extravaganzas. Instead, they could go to the real Disneyland or Disney World, to the numerous amusement parks throughout the country, to circuses, and to other family-oriented events. Families did not have to drag their kids to casinos; there were less costly venues in proximity to their homes where kids could ride merry-go-rounds, carousels, whips, and roller coasters and eat cotton candy and jellied apples.

Quick to realize its mistakes, the casinos reverted back to traditional attractions: showgirls, strip shows, and entertainment extravaganzas. Larry Gragg writes in *Bright Light City*,

> By the early years of the twenty-first century, there was a rapid proliferation (forty by one count in 2004) of so-called gentlemen's clubs not far from the strip hotels. . . . Many customers also opted for up close and personal lap dances at the clubs. . . . Some of the clubs were enormous, Sapphire, for example, could hold 2,000 customers and 250 dancers. . . . Because the Strip's hotels could not offer "exotic dancing," they quickly opened explicitly themed shows like Skin Tight, Midnight Fantasy, Crazy Girls, Zumanity, and La Femme, all of which were quite successful.[38]

And so Las Vegas continues as the Entertainment Capital of the World, where Celine Dion can earn $30 million and gamblers can go on the prowl for any kind of carnal pleasure that will fulfill their fantasies. What happens in Vegas, still stays in Vegas.

NOTES

1. Steve Fischer, *When the Mob Ran Vegas* (Las Vegas: Berkline Press, 2005), 149–50.

2. Anthony Summers and Robbyn Swan, *Sinatra: The Life* (New York: Alfred A. Knopf, 2005), 190.

3. Kitty Kelley, *His Way: The Unauthorized Biography of Frank Sinatra* (New York: Bantam Books, 1986), 315.

4. Kelley, *His Way*, 355.

5. Summers and Swan, *Sinatra*, 291.

6. Summers and Swan, *Sinatra*, 295.

7. Kelley, *His Way*, 327.

8. Gus Russo, *The Outfit* (New York: Bloomsbury, 2001), 449.

9. Kelley, *His Way*, 327.

10. Fischer, *When the Mob Ran Vegas*, 170.

11. James Kaplan, *Sinatra: The Chairman* (New York: Doubleday, 2015), 730.

12. Kaplan, *Sinatra: The Chairman*, 730.

13. Kaplan, *Sinatra: The Chairman*, 729.

14. Tony Napoli, interview with author, March 2019.

15. Kaplan, *Sinatra: The Chairman*, 729.

16. Kelley, *His Way*, 374.

17. Richard Zoglin, *Elvis in Vegas* (New York: Simon & Schuster, 2019), 63.

18. Zoglin, *Elvis in Vegas*, 65.

19. Joey Bishop interview with *Time* magazine, http://www.time.com/time/magazine/article/0,9171,139509,00.html (accessed August 25, 2021).

20. Russo, *The Outfit*, 433–34.

21. Russo, *The Outfit*, 434.

22. Kelley, *His Way*, 399.

23. Kelley, *His Way*, 399.

24. https://www.reviewjournal.com/news/frank-sinatra/ (accessed August 26, 2021).

25. Summers and Swan, *Sinatra*, 368.

26. Summers and Swan, *Sinatra*, 364.

27. Summers and Swan, *Sinatra*, 367.

28. Summers and Swan, *Sinatra*, 367.

29. Albert Goldman, *Elvis* (New York: McGraw-Hill Book Company, 1981), 434.

30. Goldman, *Elvis*, 437.

31. Goldman, *Elvis*, 439.

32. Zoglin, *Elvis in Vegas*, 198–99.

33. Zoglin, *Elvis in Vegas*, 175.

34. Alan Higginbotham (August 11, 2002), "Doctor Feelgood," *The Observer*, https://www.theguardian.com/theobserver/2002/aug/11/features.magazine27 (accessed September 10, 2021).

35. Jerry Hopkins, *Elvis: The Final Years* (New York: Berkley, 1986), 136.

36. Tony Scherman (August 16, 2006), "Elvis Dies," *American Heritage* 57, no. 4, https://www.elvisinfonet.com/spotlight_elvisdies.html (accessed September 16, 2021).

37. *U.S. News and World Reports*, March 9, 1981, p. 66.

38. Larry Gragg, *Bright Light City: Las Vegas in Popular Culture* (Lawrence: University Press of Kansas, 2013), 174.

8

THE ANT, LEFTY, AND GENIUS

Tony Spilotro's 1971 arrival in Vegas was the beginning of the end for the Chicago Outfit and for the Vegas careers of Lefty Rosenthal and front man Allen Glick. Spilotro was known as Tony the Ant after FBI agent William Roemer referred to the diminutive gangster as a Little Pissant, which the media shortened to Ant. And so Spilotro, much to his annoyance, was forever identified with an insect. Just as Bugsy Siegel hated being referred to as a bug, so Spilotro hated being referred to as an ant.

He had been sent to Vegas to keep watch on the Outfit's interests in the Stardust, the Hacienda, the Marina, and the Fremont. He had been preceded by a revolving door of two other Outfit gangsters, Johnny Rosselli and Marshall Caifano, both of whom seemed to trade places in an ongoing game of musical gangster chairs, each replacing the other in accordance with the whims of the Outfit. While Rosselli was a smooth-talking charmer, Caifano was a violent psychopath, who enjoyed killing people with a blowtorch. Having been tossed out of the El Rancho Vegas casino for his drunken behavior, he went back three weeks later and burned the place down. Spilotro, who also enjoyed killing people, would not resort to such destructive activity. He was considered smart enough to avoid bringing heat down on the mob. But, that was a major misreading of his attributes.

To create the appearance of legitimacy, Spilotro purchased the rights to open a gift shop at the Circus Circus casino from owner Jay Sarno (who had also built Caesars Palace). As a favor to the Outfit and the Teamsters, Sarno let Spilotro buy the gift shop for the bargain basement price of $70,000. However, Spilotro didn't have the $70,000 and the Teamsters, which had financed numerous of Sarno's operations, said it couldn't make a loan as small as $70,000. It typically made loans in the tens of millions of dollars. Such a small loan would raise eyebrows. However, where there is a will to make a deal, there will always be a way to make a deal happen. A company named the American Pail Corporation was incorporated in New Mexico. The owners received a $1.4 million loan from the Teamsters Central States Pension Fund. The owners of American Pail and Allen Dorfman of the Teamsters divided up the $1.4 million and then sent a check for $70,000 from the loan to Spilotro, who incorporated the gift shop as Anthony Stuart Ltd. Stuart was the maiden name of Spilotro's wife, Nancy.

The gift shop, in addition to selling vastly overpriced items, was the center of Spilotro's bookmaking and loan-sharking operations. An illegal loan-sharking operation was a necessity for those gamblers who could not get credit at the casinos. At the gift shop, desperate gamblers could borrow money from Spilotro and then bet with him. For the bettors, it was usually a lose-lose situation; but for Spilotro, it was win-win: he would not only collect on the lost bets but also on the interest (vigorish) for the money he had loaned. And if a gambler was slow to pay or attempted to flee without paying, Spilotro's gang of thugs would quickly collect. The most fearsome of Spilotro's collectors was Fat Herbie Blitzstein, who weighed 320 pounds and stood 6'6". All he had to do was pound his right fist onto the palm of his left hand and snarl at a recalcitrant borrower. Suddenly the deadbeat would fork over his money and apologize for any misunderstanding. Blitzstein, now sneering at the former deadbeat, would snatch up a few additional bills as payment for his trouble.

Blitzstein was not the only gangster who Spilotro imported from Chicago. Other members of the gang included well-known Chicago burglars Wayne Matecki and Sal Romano, psychopathic killer Larry Neumann, hit man Paulie Schiro, childhood friend and hit man Frank Cullotta (who ran the Hole in the Wall Gang for Spilotro), and Spilotro's brother Michael. For added protection, Spilotro recruited former Metro detective Joe Blasko. These men became the notorious Hole in the Wall Gang, which robbed high-end homes and jewelry stores. They made legendary Old West gangs such as the James-Younger Gang look like laid-back amateurs. The Hole in the Wall Gang was a volatile hurricane of thieves who tore through every obstacle in their lust for big scores. Safes, burglar alarms, steel-reinforced-concrete walls, attack dogs, private security guards never stood in the way of the gang making a big score. Nothing stood in their way. Using informants, such as bellboys, waiters, desk clerks, dealers, pit bosses, receptionists, and secretaries, they gained inside knowledge of when and where to drill the biggest break-in holes in the history of Vegas burglaries.

Heisting hundreds of thousands of dollars of jewelry, the Hole in the Wall Gang needed an outlet to sell their swag, and so Tony had his brother Michael open the Gold Rush, a jewelry store that did a hand-over-fist business selling hot merchandise to customers and fences. While the downstairs had well-stocked display cases of glittering and bejeweled bangles, rings, and necklaces, the upstairs was a defensive fortress of listening devices, scans, police radios, binoculars, night vision scopes, and an armory of guns—everything from pistols to machine guns to hand grenades. From his fortress, Spilotro was able to surveil the police who were surveilling him.

It was no surprise that Spilotro was cautious to the point of paranoia about cops and FBI agents. Before leaving Chicago, he had developed a reputation not only as a thief and loan shark but also as a cold-blooded killer. Cops had a file of circumstantial evidence plus gossip from snitches that Spilotro had shotgunned his own boss and mentor, the notoriously sadistic Mad Sam DeStefano. DeStefano so loved torturing his victims that they would beg to be killed rather than endure being skinned alive with a razor, having electric wires attached to their testicles, or being dropped into a vat of acid.

So when the man who ended the career of Mad Sam arrived in Vegas, he was not perceived as an entrepreneur looking to make a killing in a legitimate business. Instead, cops figured he might be willing to make killings part of his Vegas modus operandi. He certainly had a reputation for killing deadbeat gamblers and witnesses to his homicides. They also knew that Spilotro had been kicked out of a couple of European cities after he and an accomplice attempted to rob a pair of jewelry stores. As far as the Gaming Control Board (GCB) was concerned, Spilotro was as welcome in Vegas as a contagious deadly virus. He should be quarantined (i.e., not permitted in any casino) and then sent back to the place whence he came.

The Gaming Control Board wanted to put Spilotro's name into its Black Book (aka List of Excluded Persons), which would be like dumping his Vegas career into a grave. In 1978, former Gaming Commissioner Chairman Peter Echeverria said: "Tony Spilotro is a very dangerous individual and the reports I hear . . . is that Tony Spilotro is supposed to be in Las Vegas watching after the mob's interests."[1] The commissioners finally succeeded in placing the name Anthony Spilotro onto the pages of the Black Book, though it was fought by Spilotro's lawyer, Oscar Goodman. They lost the case, and so Spilotro could not see how the various skims were being carried out.

It came as no surprise to Spilotro that his career as gift shop owner at Circus Circus was about to come to an end. He sold his gift shop for $700,000. And when the new owners complained that Spilotro had falsely inflated the value of the store, he asked them if they knew who he was and of all the bodies supposedly buried in the desert. The new owners of the gift shop swallowed their misgivings and walked away. Spilotro pocketed his profit without having to repay his $70,000 loan. Spilotro then moved on to the Dunes Casino, where he operated from a poker room. There, the GCB made sure his stay was short lived.

Though barred from entering casinos, Spilotro attempted to make sure that the skims were running smoothly. He did so by checking in with Lefty Rosenthal. However, the government was beginning to take a close look at casino operations. This made the Outfit nervous. Wanting to keep a low profile, the bosses decided that the installation of a squeaky-clean front man as the owner of their four casinos (the Stardust, the Fremont, the Hacienda, and the Marina) would throw the Department of Justice blood-hounds off their trail.

Enter thirty-four-year-old Allen Glick (aka "Genius" in coded mob talk), a San Diego real estate developer. "Glick's look and style—he was short, balding, and owlish—belied his tenacity. Few around him knew that the youthful, studiously mild-mannered Glick—who spoke so softly that he was sometimes barely audible—had spent two years hanging out of a Huey helicopter in Vietnam, where he won a bronze star."[2] Mild-mannered though he was, he was determined to be a big player in Vegas. He let it be known that he wanted to buy the Stardust, but—unfortunately—he did not have the necessary funds. Word got to Del Coleman, a large shareholder in Recrion, the company that owned the Stardust. Coleman met with Glick, who next met with Al Baron of the Teamsters Union. Next in line was Frank Balistrieri, the mob boss of Milwaukee. Glick would get as much as $62 million from the Teamsters Central States Pension Fund, but Balistrieri said Glick would have to hire certain people if he wanted the money. Glick was also pushed to retain Balistrieri's two sons as his lawyers. He also signed an option agreement that gave the sons the right to buy the new company for $30,000 if—at some point—Glick decided to sell.

For day-to-day operations, Glick was told in no uncertain terms that he had to hire Frank "Lefty" Rosenthal. Though not identified as such, Rosenthal would serve as general manager of the Stardust casino, and Tony Spilotro would be his outside muscle. Rosenthal could not be a key employee because he had a record as a felon for fixing a college basketball game. Glick, a perfect front man, was the mob's valuable investment. With Rosenthal overseeing the skim and Spilotro keeping troublemakers away, the mob felt secure. They would do whatever was necessary to protect their investment, while keeping Glick in a cocoon of ignorance. The time would come when the veils of his chrysalis would be torn off and a cold reality would surround him with murderous implications.

Meanwhile, he was to be protected at all costs, for he was the mob's camouflage. No one could be permitted to endanger the mob. One day, Marty Buccieri, a Caesars Palace casino manager, went to see Glick. Buccieri had introduced Glick to important people in Vegas when Glick first said he wanted to buy the Stardust. After Glick got his money from the Central States Pension Fund, Buccieri insisted that he deserved a finder's fee for putting Glick on the road to riches. Buccieri was hot to partake of Glick's bonanza. So hot, in fact, he didn't just ask for a fee, he demanded it—or else: he grabbed Glick by the throat and squeezed until Glick's face turned red. A pair of security guards ran to Glick's defense and pulled Buccieri away from him. Buccieri, pointing an angry fist at Glick, yelled, "We're not done here!" Glick gulped for air, then straightened his collar. Something would have to be done about Buccieri. Glick believed that Buccieri had no legitimate basis for demanding a fee. He wasn't entitled to anything. Glick called on Rosenthal and reported the alleged basis of Buccieri's demand and the threat that went with it. Buccieri never realized that his demand went beyond Glick and was, in fact, implicitly directed to the highest echelons of the mob. One week after his visit to Glick, Buccieri was found slumped over the steering wheel of his car, which was parked in the Caesars World parking lot. Someone had fired two .22 caliber bullets into his brain. No one was going to mess with Glick and certainly not with the Outfit's casino investments; the skim was a waterfall of cash and no one was going to interfere with its flow. The Stardust, the Fremont, the Marina, and the Hacienda, which were fronted by Glick as assets of the Argent Corporation (an acronym of Allan R. Glick Enterprises, and French for money), were as valuable to the mob as oil wells to Saudi Arabia.

Buccieri wasn't the only threat to Glick. The other was Tamara Rand. She had claimed to be Glick's real estate partner and wanted her share of the Stardust. She began a lawsuit to recover what she believed she was owed. Such a lawsuit, if permitted to go forward, would shine a light into the dark doings of the Teamsters and the mob. Rand's lawyers would demand that the court order Glick to turn over the financial records of the Stardust and give a deposition about how he obtained money to buy the casino. The lawsuit had to be killed. Spilotro was handed the mission; this was an example of why he had been sent to Vegas: his role was to protect the skim and the actors who ran it.

Rand, sipping coffee and reading legal documents, sat at a kitchen table in her home in the Mission Hills section of San Diego. She did not hear the shoeless intruder come in behind her. His left hand tightly covered her mouth, muffling her startled scream. His right hand, holding a silence-enhanced .22 caliber pistol, squeezed the trigger and fired five bullets into Rand's brain. Nicholas Pileggi quotes Metro homicide detective Beecher Avants saying,

> The morning after the murder, I began getting calls from the press. It turned out that Tamara Rand had just been to Las Vegas and had an argument with Allen Glick.
>
> Shades of Marty Buccieri! You can't have an argument with this man and not wind up somehow getting yourself killed. It turned out Rand had claimed to be kind of partner of Glick's and had gone to court to ask for a piece of the Stardust.[3]

The FBI later concluded that the murder was ordered by Frank Balistrieri after he learned that Rand had won a court decision to subpoena Teamster documents about its loan for Glick to buy the Stardust. Once that happened, all those connected to the loan would be subpoenaed to give depositions. The skim from the Stardust would be revealed and the law would come down on them like a sledgehammer. With Rand dead, the lawsuit would be dead too. Her murder was never officially solved, though the police believe Spilotro either pulled the trigger or ordered it done.

Lefty Rosenthal presented a different kind of problem to the bosses and to himself. Perhaps because he was considered the best handicapper in Vegas and treated like a celebrity guru, who was also feared by employees, he carried himself with the arrogance of a potentate. In addition to thriving on his reputation, he—unlike mob bosses—was a publicity hound. His capacity for anger was always apparent to those whom he bossed. When he was denied a gaming license as a key employer, his anger was apparent to everyone, especially to the commissioner of the GCB.

This could prove to be a major headache for the mob. Attempting to avoid an avalanche of negative publicity that could result in FBI scrutiny, the mob had Glick assert that Rosenthal had nothing to do with the gaming operations of the Stardust. Instead, he had been hired as the casino's public relations director. When that ruse failed (not least because of Rosenthal's vociferous accusations of being a victim of the board's hypocrisy), Glick appointed Rosenthal as the casino's food and beverage director. "With Lefty, the job title didn't matter. As the mob's man, he would be involved in every aspect of Stardust management."[4]

Gary Jenkins, a former Kansas City intelligence detective and author of *Leaving Vegas*, writes: "Chicago Outfit bosses had sent Lefty to Las Vegas to oversee their interest in the Stardust casino. Of course, part of that was to ensure a steady stream of money was skimmed from the gambling proceeds and sent back to Chicago. Lefty Rosenthal was exactly the kind of person the GCB was mandated to keep out of gaming employment."[5] What neither the GCB nor the mob knew was that Rosenthal was a top-echelon informant for the FBI. In other words, he tried to cover potential losses by protecting his downside and ensuring an upside.

As Steve Fischer writes in *When the Mob Ran Vegas*,

> Lefty Rosenthal was running the Stardust Hotel. Tony Spilotro was taking care of the casino and any other problems that might arise, and Allen Glick was off playing golf down at La Costa on the California coast. Everyone seemed to be in place. Rosenthal had understood from day one what was expected of him. Chicago was deadly serious about making the Stardust and their other Las Vegas properties more profitable.[6]

Rosenthal kept changing titles at the Stardust. He was like a Kabuki actor switching masks for each role he played, but the GCB easily discerned the face beneath the masks, and each one was the face of the infamous felonious gambler. The GCB issued an order barring Rosenthal from holding any position at the Stardust. This was too much for Rosenthal's ego; he was a fighter and he would vociferously fight back, causing outrage and unease among the mob bosses. Rather than getting permission from the Outfit, he started his own TV show, *The Lefty Rosenthal Show*, based at the Stardust. One of his frequent guests was Frank Sinatra, often accompanied by Don Rickles. On his show, Rosenthal announced that he was going to hold a press conference during which he would enumerate his charges about the hypocrisy and mendacity of the GCB commissioners. As if that were not sufficient to generate agita among the bosses, he was conniving to blackmail the governor-elect of Nevada as a way to get a gaming license. If that became public, Rosenthal would be of no use to the mob. The more Rosenthal openly fought against the GCB, the hotter grew the flames of the mob's fury. Nick Civella, the boss of the Kansas City mob, which was—in effect—a subsidiary of the Outfit, was furious. Yet, he knew what a valuable commodity Rosenthal was to the Outfit, and he believed that he could endanger his own position with the Outfit if he confronted Rosenthal.

In a bugged conversation with underboss Carl "Tuffy" DeLuna, Civella says,

> I just wonder how much it would disturb, uh, Two (Joey Aiuppa [boss of the Outfit]) if I call Lefty myself. I remember the first time, you know, when I brought up something about him snitching on that commissioner. They, they first said, well, had, had to do something, he didn't have to snitch. You know the, the reputation he's gonna have with the public officials; nobody's going to trust the motherfucker. (Unintelligible) I guess he shouldn't have done it. I guess he wasn't smart (stutters) I feel, I feel, I've got a right to call left and, ah, express my, you know, I wanna ask him what the hell he's doing first, hear his, try to hear his side of it.[7]

Civella finally says that he believes Rosenthal may be a snitch, revealing information to the local police and/or the FBI. But DeLuna dissuades him of the possibility. Then Civella raises the issue of Rosenthal having a press conference. DeLuna says, "It's hard for me to conceive that Frank this Lefty, would go have a press conference and, and utter remarks that you are, that are damaging to the la familias (the families) in total. It's just hard for me to conceive that."[8] Civella then wonders if he should call Rosenthal without getting permission from Aiuppa. He thinks he could just make a courtesy call.

> DeLuna responds: "If you wanted to call him, Nick, I don't see a fucking thing wrong with it and they did tell you that, they told you that before."
> Civella: "I know, I remember."
> DeLuna: "But I wouldn't holler at him if I were you."
> Civella then wonders if he could get Rosenthal's lawyer to call him and ask Rosenthal to get back to him. He then responds to DeLuna's advice not to holler at Rosenthal.
> Civella: "I'm not going to holler at him, I'm just gonna ask him what he's doing, you know, does he know what he's doing."
> DeLuna: "From that, if he tells you he's gonna have a press conference well then good. If he doesn't tell it to you, you can ask him. 'Well what is your position gonna be?'"[9]

It's remarkable that the powerful and feared head of the Kansas City Mafia family was so hesitant to confront Rosenthal. Though Rosenthal was overseeing the skim of millions of dollars, he wasn't a made man of any family. Though the Outfit was multiethnic, unlike Mafia families in the East and Southwest, Civella believed that in a showdown between himself and Rosenthal, the Outfit would side with an Italian over a Jew. But Rosenthal's ethnicity mattered little or not at all to the Outfit: he was as protected as if he were a Mafia prince. And Rosenthal betted on that, which is why he could ignore any entreaties from Civella and treat Glick as if the front man were nothing but a servant.

When it came to Glick, there was no hesitancy on the part of Civella. This was revealed when Glick later testified in court. The mob had grown disillusioned with Glick after the Securities and Exchange Commission (SEC) discovered that Glick had used Argent funds for noncorporate ventures. In other words, he was using money that should have gone into the skim to pay for personal expenses. It was not long before the SEC brought suit against Argent. All of the charges, plus the name of Nick Civella, were printed in the *Wall Street Journal*. This was too much for Civella. The mob's control of the skim at the Argent casinos could be revealed. Glick had to go. Civella then ordered DeLuna to threaten to kill Glick unless he sold the mob the casinos owned by Argent. Following is an excerpt of trial testimony about the mob and Glick:

Prosecutor: "Mr. Glick can you tell the jury about the Defendant Carl DeLuna?"

Glick: "Yes it was in . . . April 1978."

Prosecutor: "Where was the meeting?"

Glick: "I was asked to come to Oscar Goodman's office in downtown Las Vegas."

Prosecutor: "Who is Oscar Goodman?"

Glick: "Mr. Goodman is an attorney who represented Argent Corporation at one time."

Prosecutor: "When you entered the office, who did you observe?"

Glick: "I saw Mr. DeLuna sitting behind Mr. Goodman's desk with his feet on the desk."

Prosecutor: "Tell the jury, as best you can recall, what you remember about your conversation with Mr. DeLuna."

Glick: "Mr. DeLuna's demeanor was very vulgar, coarse, and he used many profanities."

Prosecutor: "What was the topic of this conversation?"

Glick: "He said that he and his partners were sick of having to deal with me and having me around. He wanted me to know this would be the last time I would hear from him, or anybody else, unless I abided by what he said. He informed me that it was their desire to have me sell the Argent Corporation immediately and to announce the sale as soon as possible. He said that, in the event I did not take his threats seriously, and that I may find my life expendable, he went on to inform me that I would not [*sic*] my children's lives expendable. He looked down on a piece of paper and gave me the names and ages of my sons. And he said that if he did not hear from me, within a short period of time, that I announced the sale, that one by one he would have each of my sons murdered."[10]

Not long after that meeting, Glick told the GCB that he intended to sell the Argent Corporation. And it was Rosenthal who wanted to be president of whatever the new controlling corporation would be.

Glick's unsettling encounter with DeLuna was not the first time he had been threatened by the Kansas City mob; at an earlier time, he was flown at three o'clock in the morning to Kansas City for a meeting in a hotel suite with Nick Civella. There, a belligerent Civella demanded a $1.5 million finder's fee as what was owed to him for getting Glick his Teamsters loan. When Glick said he couldn't pay, he was warned that he would be killed. Finally, it was settled that Rosenthal would arrange for the money to be paid to Civella from the skim at the Stardust. Glick was also informed that Rosenthal was running the Stardust and all the other casinos in the mob's portfolio. Civella ended the meeting by telling Glick that if he hadn't agreed to the deal, he would have been killed on the spot. The harsh reality of Glick's position as a puppet front man was made depressingly vivid. Glick would do what he was told to do for as long as Argent owned the mob's casinos.

While Rosenthal had supplanted Glick in the actual running of the mob's casinos, he was having a personal problem that would destroy his relationship with Spilotro. Rosenthal, who had arrived in Vegas in 1968, and Spilotro, who arrived in 1971, were supposed to work together to ensure that the skim ran smoothly for the benefit of the Outfit and its smaller outposts in Milwaukee, Cleveland, Detroit, and Kansas City. But Rosenthal's wife, Geri, a former topless showgirl and chip hustler, was having an affair with Spilotro. And Spilotro, rather than operating sub rosa, flaunted the affair; it was as if he was broadcasting to all the mobsters in Vegas, "You think Lefty is running things. I'm more important. I'm the biggest, toughest guy in the city and I'm fucking the man's wife." Throughout the affair, Geri fought night and day with Lefty, accusing him of trying to control her every move, calling him a tight-ass, and questioning his masculinity. The more they fought, the more pills she took, the greater the amount of alcohol she consumed. And Lefty, with ready and easy access to all the showgirls he employed, had one fling after another. As if that weren't bad enough, on the morning of September 8, 1980, Rosenthal had locked Geri out of their house the previous night. When Geri arrived, high on drugs, she went berserk, screaming and ramming her Mercedes Benz into Rosenthal's Cadillac.

She was also waving around a pearl-handled, snub-nosed .38, which was a gift from Spilotro. Neighbors called the police. Geri shouted she was going to the FBI and would tell them everything about her husband's illegal activities. Gossip of the event spread, and Rosenthal knew he had to protect himself—perhaps Geri too. The next day, he flew to Chicago, where he met with Joey Aiuppa and his second-in-command, Jackie Cerone. They were increasingly worried that the skim was in jeopardy. Rosenthal assured the two men that he could cool down the situation and return things to normal. However, both Rosenthal and Spilotro had detoured dramatically from the roles set out for them by their bosses in Chicago. Rosenthal was unable to keep his volatile marriage quiet. The marriage, which was near death, was a tabloid sensation. Reporters loved news and gossip about the alleged casino boss and his former showgirl wife having blowout fights in public. Lefty realized he had to save himself and eliminate gossip about Geri's affair with Spilotro. He decided to divorce Geri. He and Spilotro—though no longer trusting each other—knew they had to continue working together, or both of them would be killed. The Outfit kept tabs on the two. One misstep and they would both die.

Back in Chicago, Joey Aiuppa worried that all the gossip and notoriety of the affair would cause the FBI to scrutinize the operations of the Stardust. He was not alone. Civella told DeLuna that the skim might be in jeopardy. Of course, the FBI had been keeping a record of the Lefty, Spilotro, and Geri triangle. But that wasn't all: they hoped that Rosenthal's vociferous dispute with the GCB would reveal information about the running of all the Argent casinos. The agents were like hungry wolves, licking their chops and circling their prey, all of whom had successfully managed to wound themselves.

Driven by boundless greed and arrogance, Spilotro made his situation worse by dealing dope, and the burglaries of the Hole in the Wall Gang were getting more sensational, not only generating stories on the nightly TV news shows, but also putting pressure on local officials to catch the thieves and put an end to the burglaries. Before going to Vegas, Spilotro had been warned by the Outfit to operate discreetly, not act like publicity-prone Al Capone. He paid no attention. He believed that his power, his reputation, and his willingness to resort to any tactic would ultimately save him. His history of avoiding convictions led him to feel invulnerable. If pride goes before a fall, Spilotro's pride was that of a psychopathic narcissist; but the inevitability of his fall was obvious to Rosenthal and even Cullotta. Had Spilotro known what the mob had in store for him, he wouldn't have believed it. He thought of himself as not only an exceedingly valuable commodity to the Outfit but also irreplaceable.

As Spilotro's inability to curb his excesses added to the volume of his notoriety, the Outfit watched in ever-increasing anger. He was often hauled in for questioning about this or that burglary, but just as often he smilingly skipped to freedom accompanied by his lawyers. Yet, an invisible noose was tightening around his neck in 1979 when the bosses learned that Spilotro was charged with the murder of mobster Sherwin Lisner. He was killed because Spilotro had learned that Lisner was a confidential informant for the Metro police department. Lisner's murder was committed by Frank Cullotta on orders from Spilotro. When Cullotta later discovered that Spilotro would sell him out to save himself, Cullotta decided to accept a deal from prosecutors and testify against his former boss. Furious bosses demanded to know why Spilotro hadn't killed Cullotta, for the mob often kills its killers so that they can't later testify. Cullotta made his deal and went into the Witness Protection Program. Spilotro couldn't believe that he was the victim of such betrayal. Then, almost as an insult, he was charged with operating an illegal sports betting and loan-sharking operation. The bosses were now holding a stopwatch and counting the time till they could finally rid themselves of Spilotro.

To top it off, the bosses in five cities (Chicago, Milwaukee, Kansas City, Detroit, and Cleveland) had learned from their sources that the government was compiling mounds of evidence about the skim and other crimes. The FBI had hours and hours of bugged conversations, which defense lawyers would scrutinize and later challenge. But their challenges would be perceived as pro forma, lacking in substance, and leaving jurors ready to convict. As convincing as were the tapes of the bugged conversations, the testimony of witnesses with firsthand information would be even more so. The bosses didn't need palm readers to tell them what the outcome of their trials would be. They were as jittery and scared as goats tied to a post waiting for a lion to tear them to pieces. Nevertheless, like many desperate mobsters before them, they attempted to halt the inevitable by killing off potential witnesses. Their strategy was to get rid of those who could possibly flip and those who might be confidential informants.

First on the list was Rosenthal. Civella had been convinced that Rosenthal would flip and snitch to save himself. He managed to convince Balistrieri too. Balistrieri was known to use car bombs as a successful disposal method. On October 4, 1982, Rosenthal left Tony Roma's restaurant about 8:30 p.m. with his usual take-out order of ribs. He got into his Cadillac and turned the ignition key and flames shot out of the car's air-conditioning and defroster vents. He grabbed the door handle, pushed the door open, and rolled out of the car. The car was blazing, fire filled the entire interior.

Then, as Rosenthal rolled away on the ground, the car exploded, rising several feet off the pavement. If it hadn't been for a steel plate installed by the manufacturer beneath the driver's seat, Rosenthal would have been torn to small particles of bone and flesh by the explosion. With the mob's failure to silence Rosenthal, they knew that they had to be more scrupulous in the murder of other potential witnesses. At least, they felt they had delivered a warning to Rosenthal. Indeed, they had. When the government offered Rosenthal an opportunity to enter the Witness Protection Program, he turned down the invitation. No further attempts were made on his life, not only because the bosses were about to go on trial but also because a second attempt might be traced back to them.

Though Geri Rosenthal had threatened to inform the FBI about Lefty's handling of the skim, the mob needn't have worried. Four days after the bombing of Lefty's car, Geri McGee was seen stumbling along a sidewalk in the early morning hours in front of the Sunset Motel in Los Angeles. She was stoned, wildly screaming, her words completely incoherent. She stumbled a few more steps, then landed on the lobby floor of the motel. She passed out, and a clerk from the motel phoned the police. It was November 16, and Geri never recovered from her coma. She was dead at age forty-six. The Los Angeles coroner ascertained that Geri had died of a lethal overdose of cocaine, Valium, and whiskey. Her body was badly bruised. Police believed she had been beaten by a pimp or someone who had stolen her money. Her apartment had been ransacked; all of her jewelry and cash were gone. Her safe-deposit box contained $15,000 in silver dollars and various rare coins. That was it. The millions Lefty had given her for spending sprees had long vanished. She ended her days as a bruised, drugged derelict.

And then there was poor Allen Dorfman, an associate of Jimmy Hoffa, the Outfit, and owner of an insurance agency connected to those two entities. He had always remained in the good graces of Hoffa and the Outfit, so no one even considered that he might wind up murdered. But he was. On January 20, 1983, Dorfman was shot several times in the head; he had just left a restaurant with Irwin Weiner, an insurance agent and former bail bondsman. Having disposed of Dorfman, the shooters strode away, leaving Weiner unharmed. Dorfman had been facing a fifty-five-year prison sentence and was sixty years old. The mob had believed that to save himself from dying in prison, Dorfman might flip and testify against them. Former FBI agent William Roemer quotes top Outfit member Joey Lombardo in a bugged conversation saying: "Allen Dorfman is not that type of guy, but the people that got a piece of him are that type of guy. Allen is meek and

Allen is harmless. But the people behind him are not meek and they are not harmless. Do you understand what I mean?"

Roemer goes on to write:

> That put to bed any illusions about the status of Allen Dorfman as far as control of him by the mob was concerned. Not that anybody I ever knew had any such illusions. It also was a good indication of why the mob would thereafter kill Dorfman. He was "meek" and "harmless." They did not want some sweet-talking FBI agent taking a run at Allen to make an informant out of him.[11]

A dead Dorfman had no effect on the outcome of the trial.

Unlike Dorfman, Spilotro could not be sweet-talked by an FBI agent. He would never flip. But he had been the cause of all the mob's troubles in Vegas. He was the lightning rod that drew down a bolt of wrath from the FBI and Justice Department. He would have to be made an example of what happens if you do not obey the mob and if your disobedience draws down the wrath of the government. Spilotro had, indeed, screwed up badly. As a result of his affair with Geri Rosenthal, he and Lefty were no longer talking to each other. That split meant the mob could not depend on them to work in tandem to protect the skims. Frank Cullotta relates in his autobiography:

> One night Tony and Frank were in the Jubilation having a few drinks. Lefty walked in with six showgirls and a couple of his male stooges. Tony said, "Look at that Jew cocksucker. You'd think he'd at least wave at me, or wink, or something. He don't do shit. Look at him, who the fuck does he think he is, this guy? Believe me, Frankie, he's got me so fucking mad that if he didn't have the juice he's got, I'd have corked him a long time ago."[12]

The anger that existed between the two old pals, however, was nothing compared to the rage of the bosses. Since all the bosses were in their late sixties or seventies, they knew that, if convicted, they would surely die in prison. Spilotro was the maniac who lit the fuse that would blow up their world. The Vegas media poured fuel on the mob's fiery rage when it speculated that once the bosses were behind bars for life, Spilotro would take over the Outfit and become the biggest mob boss not just in Vegas but probably in the entire country. It's not surprising that of all the Vegas-related executions, that of Tony "The Ant" Spilotro would be the most gruesome. The death of his brother Michael was collateral material.

According to FBI agent Roemer, who had been assigned to investigate Spilotro for several years, Tony and his brother Michael were being driven

by a pair of Outfit thugs to their deaths. The Spilotros thought they were
on their way to an important meeting with the top echelon of the Outfit.

> When the car was about twelve miles east of St. Anne, heading away from
> Aiuppa's hunting lodge, the driver turned onto Newton County Country
> Road. He then pulled off the rural road and onto a cornfield alongside the
> Willow Slough Preserve, 12,000 acres of state-owned land located ten miles
> into Indiana. Two other thugs were waiting for them. The driver exited the
> car as these two opened the doors for Tony and Michael, covering both with
> .38s and .45s. A hole about six feet long and five feet deep had been dug into
> the cornfield. Tony reacted immediately. He turned to throw a punch. But
> the thugs were ready for that. For his trouble Tony got the butt of .45 across
> his face. One of the other thugs stepped forward and brought his gun down
> swiftly on the top of Tony's head.[13]

Much of this information was related by Albert Caesar Tocco to his wife,
Betty. On the day after the murders, Tocco phoned his wife, asking her to
drive to Indiana and pick him up. He was anxious and nearly hysterical. He
told his wife that he had dug the graves for the Spilotro brothers. When
Tocco learned that his wife was speaking to the FBI, Betty went into the
Witness Protection Program. It is not clear if Tocco participated in the
murders or just dug the graves. Pathology reports of the murders surmised
that the Spilotros had been "beaten with fists and feet about 11 PM on June
14, 1986 and that each was buried unconscious but still alive."[14]

In his book *Casino*, Nicholas Pileggi quotes Roemer saying: "The killers
must have carried a tremendous grudge. Usually it's one hole, two holes,
three holes point-blank in the back of the head, probably [with] a twenty-
two. It's quick and the guy doesn't suffer. These guys were beaten to death.
Tortured."[15]

The Ant's death left him unindicted for the murders of Danny Seifert,
Emil Vaci, Marty Buccieri, Tamara Rand, Sam DeStefano, Frank Bompen-
siero, Billy McCarthy, Jimmy Miraglia, Sherwin Lisner, Allen Dorfman,
and at least a half dozen more. While the death of the Spilotro brothers
voided their court dates, mob bosses could look forward to a slow withering
of their lives in prison.

Unfortunately for the bosses, DeLuna was a superb bookkeeper and
legal secretary. He kept notes about every transaction made by the Kansas
City boss, Nick Civella, and the distribution of money to the Outfit. When
the FBI began its warranted search of DeLuna's home, he guided the
agents from room to room as if he were a real estate agent showing a prospective buyer the best features of the house. Agents found guns, silencers,

and stacks of cash. After showing the agents all the rooms, DeLuna directed them to the basement. As Gary Jenkins writes:

> In the walkout basement of DeLuna's middle-class brick home, they found an office containing handwritten notes and numbered notations. . . . They found that DeLuna had kept accurate notations about the distribution of the skim, dates and activities verifying his trips to Las Vegas and Chicago and other significant details about his personal activity in connection with exercising control over the Stardust and the Tropicana casinos.[16]

Following the discoveries, DeLuna confessed to a pair of cohorts that he expected to spend a couple of years in prison and needed to prepare his wife for his absence. In fact, DeLuna was shocked when he was sentenced to thirty years in prison, a sentence for which neither he nor his wife was prepared.

Civella would escape the outcome of DeLuna's lack of discretion, for the mob boss was dying of cancer. On March 13, 1983, he died of lung cancer. The trial commenced in September 1985 in Kansas City. Prior to the trial, the government was able to get numerous of those involved to testify. They included Allen Glick; Roy L. Williams, the Kansas City boss of the Teamsters; Cleveland underboss Angelo Lonardo; and Frank Cullotta, who agreed to testify after Spilotro had issued a contract on his old pal's life.

Those on trial included Outfit boss Joey Aiuppa, age seventy-seven; his underboss Jack Cerone, age seventy-one (each sentenced to twenty-eight years in prison); Milton Maishe Rockman, age seventy-three, acting boss of the Cleveland mob, sentenced to twenty-four years in prison; and Frank Balistrieri, age sixty-seven, head of the Milwaukee mob, who received ten years after agreeing to help the government. His two lawyer sons, John and Joseph, were both acquitted.

Rosenthal retired first to California, then to Boca Raton, Florida. Of their days in running Vegas, Frank Cullotta told Nicholas Pileggi: "It should have been so sweet. Everything was in place We were given paradise on earth, but we fucked it up."[17]

NOTES

1. https://lasvegassun.com/news/1978/jun/26/nevada-probes-spilotro-gaming-blackbook/ (accessed October 14, 2021).

2. Nicholas Pileggi, *Casino: Love and Honor in Las Vegas* (New York: Simon & Schuster, 1995), 120.

3. Pileggi, *Casino*, 183.

4. Gary Jenkins, *Leaving Vegas: The True Story of How the FBI Wiretaps Ended Mob Domination of Las Vegas Casinos* (Scotts Valley, CA: CreateSpace Independent Publishing, 2016), 78.

5. Jenkins, *Leaving Vegas*, 104.

6. Steve Fischer, *When the Mob Ran Vegas: Stories of Money, Mayhem, and Murder* (Las Vegas: Berkline Press, 2005), 207.

7. Jenkins, *Leaving Vegas*, 125–26.

8. Jenkins, *Leaving Vegas*, 126.

9. Jenkins, *Leaving Vegas*, 127–28.

10. Jenkins, *Leaving Vegas*, 35–36.

11. William F. Roemer Jr., *The Enforcer* (New York: Donald I. Fine, Inc., 1994), 280.

12. Dennis N. Griffin and Frank Cullotta, *Cullotta: The Life of a Chicago Criminal, Las Vegas Mobster, and Government Witness* (Las Vegas: Huntington Press, 2007), 151.

13. Roemer, *The Enforcer*, 320.

14. Roemer, *The Enforcer*, 325.

15. Pileggi, *Casino*, 346.

16. Jenkins, *Leaving Vegas*, 221.

17. Pileggi, *Casino*, 348.

9

THE OUTFIT CRAPPED OUT

The ouster of the mob in Vegas took decades and began in 1963 when Attorney General Robert Kennedy attempted to investigate casino skimming. He believed that gambling was the mob's major source of income. In order to end it, he decided to crack down on casinos that the mob controlled. He attempted to deputize state gaming agents to participate on raids of casinos. However, Governor Grant Sawyer, nervous about adverse publicity that could scare off tourists, attempted to persuade Kennedy not to go forward with his crackdown on casinos. With or without gaming agents, Kennedy said he was determined to proceed, and that meant wiretapping the offices of casino bosses. He then attempted to convince casino employees to flip and testify against their bosses, but the employees were more frightened of angering their bosses than of angering the FBI. After all, the bosses had it in their power to kill you. Kennedy, as attorney general, could threaten to send them to prison, but he was unlikely to win any convictions. And the employees knew it.

Evan Thomas, in his biography of Kennedy, writes:

In the spring of 1963, Kennedy finally insisted that [J. Edgar] Hoover send him a report on casino skimming that could be passed along to other agencies. The skimming report arrived at the criminal division of the Justice Department on Wednesday, April 24, 1963—and, incredibly, leaked right back to the mob by Monday. FBI agents, monitoring the bureau's bugs in the casinos, listened in horror as mobbed-up casino owners read aloud from the FBI's highly confidential report. The leak, never adequately explained, was a tremendous setback to the war on organized crime. It effectively blew any chance of making criminal cases in Las Vegas—indeed, the casino owners sued the FBI for violating their civil liberties.[1]

The casinos must have been smirking as the FBI and Kennedy continued to point fingers of blame at each other for the leak. The Justice Department went so far as to claim that Hoover had intentionally leaked the information so that he could claim it had been leaked by the Justice Department before Kennedy could claim it was leaked by the FBI. One piece of evidence in defense of Kennedy not leaking vital information is that his crusade against the mob was unremitting. He won hundreds of indictments and convictions and was the most zealous prosecutor of the mob in the history of the Justice Department. Hoover, however, was said to be a pal of Frank Costello, known as the Prime Minister of the Underworld, who allegedly gave Hoover tips on fixed horse races. Hoover loved the track and loved walking away with his winnings. Costello was happy to oblige as long as Hoover continued to hunt for communist spies and ignore the mob.

Kennedy, however, was like a guided missile. He could not be deterred from his targets. He not only vigorously pursued Jimmy Hoffa, whose Central States Pension Fund made millions of dollars of loans to casino owners, but he also went after Sam Giancana, the head of the Chicago Outfit and the behind-the-scenes owner of the Cal-Neva Lodge and Casino. As noted in an earlier chapter, Giancana's front man was his on-again, off-again friend Frank Sinatra. Thomas continues:

> [Kennedy] encouraged them [the FBI] to lean hard on the Mafia boss, and they did, tailing Giancana right onto the golf course. Frustrated, one of Giancana's henchmen confronted his FBI shadows in the Giancana hangout, the Armory Lounge in June 1963. "If Bobby Kennedy wants to talk to me," said Chuckie English to the G-men, "I'll be glad to talk to them and he knows who to go through" (The gangster was referring to Frank Sinatra).[2]

Kennedy would not give up; he was still determined to go after the casinos, which he called "the bank of America's organized crime."[3] And this time Governor Grant Sawyer threw up another objection: he opposed the federal government getting involved in a "states' rights" issue. Sergio Lalli writes that

> Sawyer was particularly incensed by the FBI's secret wiretaps of Nevada citizens—wiretaps that were operating without court approval and therefore

illegal. . . . [The Justice Department] had refused to turn over information to the state. And it continued to conduct investigations without indictments. . . . Sawyer said [it's] "a shocking story of espionage and harassment against the state . . . determined to damage or destroy the major business of the state—without regard to morality or law."[4]

Nevertheless, recordings from the wiretaps made evident that front men had been installed so that the feds could not claim that the casinos were run by mobsters. The wiretaps also revealed the enormity of the mob's skimming operations. The count rooms were like the mob's private treasury departments, pouring forth continuous waves of money. When presented with that evidence, the state mandated that an electronic viewing system be installed in all count rooms.

After Kennedy left his position as attorney general, things cooled down a bit for the mob. They felt that skimming could continue as it had with no one looking over their shoulders.

They installed Tony Spilotro and Lefty Rosenthal to make sure there would be no obstacles to the skim. But, as reported in the previous chapter, Spilotro was a hurricane of disaster for the mob. He generated enough self-destructive evidence that the FBI was able to bring down a sledgehammer that would smash the mob's presence in Vegas. Before Spilotro drew heat from law enforcement in Vegas, the Outfit had been a master of flexibility; it had always endeavored to bend with the winds of new laws and regulations. It was the ideal method for not attracting attention. The mob was also exceedingly generous in its financial support of politicians. It's a common belief among mobsters that every politician comes with a price tag. In fact, political campaigns are so expensive that the money donated by mob-front organizations proved essential to successful campaigns. Spilotro, however, was another matter. He never graduated from his early years as a tough bruiser. His attitude was not to give a shit about politicians. Rather than pay off politicians, he paid his very clever lawyers to keep him out of prison. His lawyers, however, could not keep him out of the spotlight of media coverage. And that media coverage made the Outfit nervous, then angry. The guy was out of control. Instead of protecting the skim, he and his Hole in the Wall Gang were knocking over jewelry stores and bringing heat on the Outfit. Spilotro was not only angering the Outfit, he was infuriating many legitimate business leaders in Vegas, who made their anger known to their Outfit contacts in Chicago and Kansas City. Spilotro was fast creating an image of Las Vegas as a putrid swamp out of which crawled rapacious jewel thieves, fences, and loan sharks, all of whom were fed information by a few renegade cops, private security guards, hotel check-in clerks, and chip hustlers who seductively massaged their victims into spilling costly revelations. Anyone who read news accounts of the Hole in the Wall Gang knew that Vegas was a dangerous place. Many wives of wealthy gamblers were warned before going to Vegas to leave their jewelry at home. Safes were no longer safe. Gangs of jewel thieves with acetylene torches, high-powered drills, varieties of explosives, police scanners, night vision goggles, and machine guns were on the prowl.

The Hole in the Wall Gang had become a more dangerous threat to the Outfit's smooth-running skim than Bobby Kennedy had been. The mob knew how important it was for Vegas to be free of murders, muggings, break-ins, and other forms of theft, for those kinds of crime would bring police scrutiny and that scrutiny would spill over to mobsters and their operations. Indeed, beginning in the late 1940s, mobsters hired public relations professionals to project an image of Vegas as a crime-free city. If Vegas mobsters were killed, such as Bugsy Siegel and Gus Greenbaum, the murders took place in states other than Nevada. Susan Dalitz told the author that when she was growing up, Vegas was a safe city: no muggings, no murders, no mayhem. You could walk the streets at night and no one would mug you. Residents were like those who lived in small towns and never locked their doors at night.

Spilotro was destroying that image. He and his wrecking crew of thieves were operating like anarchists high on dope. They didn't care about anything but satisfying their greed. The more brazen Spilotro and his gang became, the more the Outfit realized that Spilotro had to be eliminated. It was the only way they could protect themselves. Spilotro never realized that he was sending out invitations to his own execution. The RSVPs would be brutally hand-delivered in another state (as expected).

To hasten Spilotro's end, his second-in-command, Frank Cullotta, decided to accept an invitation from the FBI to testify against his onetime boss as well as top guys in the Outfit. Having flipped Cullotta, thus turning him into a government witness, the FBI secured him a place in the Witness Protection Program. Like all gangsters who flip, Cullotta was motivated by fear and an intense desire to survive. The FBI had given him a recording of a wiretapped conversation in which he listened to Spilotro complaining about the dirty laundry in his gang and that it was time to clean house. Cullotta figured that he and his fellow thieves were the dirty laundry. Cullotta, who had been a boyhood pal of Spilotro's, stated to investigators that such betrayals are part of mob life. There was nothing sacred in Spilotro's friendship with Cullotta. After all, they had each killed friends and mentors.

In addition to testifying against Spilotro and the Hole in the Wall Gang members, Cullotta gave evidence against one of the Outfit's top Vegas enforcers, alleged boss and consigliere Joey "the Clown" Lombardo. Cullotta claimed that Lombardo had protected Spilotro from being killed by the Outfit, but once Lombardo was sent to prison, Spilotro was a dead man walking, oblivious to the fate that awaited him.

Of course, defense lawyers who had worked for the Outfit attempted to discredit Cullotta's credibility by bringing up his past; but Cullotta, as a part of his plea agreement, matter-of-factly admitted to his vast resume of crimes that included fifty armed robberies, two hundred burglaries, twenty-five arsons, and participation in two murders.

Such an admission was typical of Cullotta's blasé attitude about all sorts of crimes. He was a man who had spent his life coldly evaluating criminal opportunities and weighing the odds for success. That ability to unemotionally glance at crimes did not result in anger toward Spilotro. He understood that Spilotro did what he thought was necessary, but the Outfit had gone beyond its traditional methods of execution in the way it had Spilotro murdered. Cullotta said that "the way Tony and Michael were killed was terrible. They were beaten to death! Not shot, no cut throats. They were beaten to death, beaten to death. That's a hell of a way to die. Nobody should go like that. That was the Outfit's way of showing Tony wasn't that tough a guy.

"The Outfit didn't intend for the bodies to be discovered so soon; they weren't looking for any more heat. The bodies were buried okay; no mistakes were made there. It was just that the farmer knew his land too well and spotted the fresh dig."[5]

Though the mob finally got rid of Spilotro, Cullotta was an agent of destruction they couldn't silence. He was an eager witness who exchanged his testimony for a two-year sentence in a federal prison. He was paroled into the Witness Protection Program in 1984 and given two years of probation, which ended when he was forty-eight years old. He died, at age eighty-one, in Las Vegas of complications from COVID-19 on August 20, 2020. Earlier that year, he had started his own YouTube program titled *Coffee with Cullotta*. Like Lefty Rosenthal, he loved the limelight, taking bows as a former mobster. He also took tourists on bus rides to the mob sites of Vegas. He had become a minor celebrity, who signed copies of his memoir and was photographed by his fans. Best of all, the Outfit was not gunning for him. The bosses were all in prison.

While Cullotta was earning a modest living and bathing in the limelight of his brief celebrity in Vegas, the remnants of the Outfit were in full retreat. They bitterly complained that their paradise on earth had been destroyed. It was nearly biblical; they had been expelled from their garden of Eden and then sent on a one-way trip back to whence they came.

Just to survive, the Outfit was forced to downsize. At one time, it had thousands of soldiers in major cities, such as Chicago, Detroit, Milwaukee, Cleveland, Miami, Las Vegas, and Los Angeles. After its expulsion from Vegas, it was reduced in size to no more than a few hundred soldiers and even fewer associates. It had once been a large American conglomerate with subsidiaries and franchises in Vegas, but it had expanded without sufficient due diligence, relying on the wrong emissaries to carry out its goals, and was now superseded by more powerful entities who were far-seeing, innovative, legitimate entrepreneurs and investors: junk bond kings, investment bankers, and high-priced attorneys at white-shoe law firms. They may have had the hearts of buccaneers, but they had ivy-league brains.

Wall Street and the Justice Department had brought forth a new era in Vegas, and so the old men of the Outfit returned to their roots in Chicago. The Outfit's core businesses would still make them wealthy. The Outfit continued to deal in construction, labor unions, real estate, offshore gambling, stock fraud, loan-sharking, extortion, and drugs. Drugs, in particular, though ostensibly disavowed, had been the basis for large fortunes. The underwriting, importation, and distribution of drugs were too profitable to abandon. So, if the Outfit could avoid the common pitfalls of the drug trade, its top echelon members could continue to add to their fortunes. Those members made every attempt to remain invisible, keeping plenty of distance between their financing operations and the basic mechanics of drug dealing.

While drugs were a major source of income, other traditional mob ventures also remained as significant sources of cash. One such source was labor relations. Gus Russo, in his book *The Outfit*, writes of the new downsized Outfit as "Mob Lite," yet he notes its traditional grip on labor relations remained as tight as ever. "One such labor union believed to be controlled by Chicago's Mob Lite is the nineteen-thousand-member Laborers' International Union of North America, which sits on a $1.5 billion treasury. Controlling the unions allows the Mob Lite to have implicit, and usually legal influence on work contracts."[6]

(There were branches of Laborers' International Union of North America [LIUNA] that had been infiltrated by organized crime in the 1990s. For example, Local 210 of LIUNA was controlled by the Mafia family of Buffalo, New York; however, a long-running and exhaustive investigation finally drove organized crime out of the union in 2006.)

Once out of Vegas, downsizing and keeping low profiles were not the only routes taken by the Outfit's top men to diminish chances of government indictments. The convictions of mob bosses in five cities had given impetus to the idea that not only should those who finance drug operations remain invisible but also those who would become bosses. The Outfit's hierarchy decided that each new boss should strive to be invisible, anonymous, elusive, or—if possible—take on the camouflaged colorations of local businessmen. Denial of being a mobster was the song they sang when confronted by reporters, cops, FBI agents, and prosecutors.

The next step in their obvious public relations campaign was to convince law enforcement that the Outfit no longer even existed. Oh yes, they would say, there were still some old members around, but they were really too old for the sort of thing that went on years ago. The old guys would smile like benevolent grandfathers and say they were just old retired men or ROMEOs (retired old men eating out). Some said they did a little bit of legitimate gambling, would gather now and then to play cards and gossip about politics and business and reminisce. It was all said so sweetly and with such cheerful looks of innocence that FBI agents responded with derisive smiles.

Though the old men's declarations, attestations, claims, protestations, and assertions were met with disbelief, their lawyers said you couldn't prove a negative. Old gamblers were not compelled to prove that they were not criminals. Yet, the Outfit had obviously not only learned a lesson from the recent convictions and long prison sentence of its bosses, but also from the historic examples of the flamboyance of Al Capone and John Gotti. Name recognition brought forth heightened risks. One's name in lights tended to turn risks into surveillances that resulted in indictments. Anonymity was the way to go. Who in his right mind would want to be identified as a boss and run the risk of being indicted in a Racketeer Influenced and Corrupt Organizations Act (RICO) case, convicted, and sent to prison for life? Yet, as hard as the Outfit tried to avoid having the government identify a series of bosses, the names of bosses seemed to pop up like mushrooms after a steady rainfall. They were identified by informants and wiretapped associates. Information would be leaked to reporters, and embarrassing stories would appear in newspapers and on local television news programs.

Here is the line of post-Vegas boss succession of the Outfit that could have been prepared by a Dun and Bradstreet of the underworld but was compiled by the FBI.

Following Joey Aiuppa, the outfit was ruled by Joseph Ferriola, followed by Samuel Carlisi, followed by John DiFronzo, and it is now allegedly ruled by Salvatore DeLaurentis (though there is no firm evidence that DeLaurentis is a boss or even a member of the Outfit).

Ferriola ruled the Outfit after Aiuppa and Jackie Cerone went to prison for skimming the Stardust casino. But Ferriola's reign was short lived due to health problems and the heartrending stresses caused by baited legal traps laid out by the FBI and IRS; both organizations were hot to throw a net over their target and drag him into court. However, having received a second heart transplant at the Methodist Hospital in Houston, the sixty-one-year-old Ferriola succumbed to heart disease. Had he survived he would have been indicted for racketeering. His physician was an eminent transplant surgeon, Michael E. DeBakey. Ferriola is believed to have been the first gangster ever to have received a heart transplant. Being a boss had its perks.

After Ferriola died, Sam "Wings" Carlisi became the new boss of the Outfit. He was tagged with the sobriquet "Wings" for his extensive flights to do business with mob bosses in upstate New York and Pennsylvania. It was said that he had more frequent-flier miles than any mob boss in the country. However, in March 1996, his jets were turned off, and Carlisi was grounded. He was convicted of loan-sharking, arson, and racketeering, all related to illegal gambling operations he was running in Chicago and in a number of its suburbs. He was sentenced to thirteen years in prison and died there of a heart attack on January 2, 1997, at age eighty-two.

Carlisi's vacant executive suite was then occupied by John "No Nose" DiFronzo, so nicknamed because—as a young man—he dove through a plate glass window to avoid being arrested after burglarizing a clothing store. As he dove, a razor-sharp shard of glass sliced off a sliver of his nose; however, the bloody sliver was quickly recovered and returned to DiFronzo by an honest policeman. Soon thereafter, a skilled surgeon did a remarkably aesthetic job of re-attaching the sliver, and only a hairline scar was evidence of the daring attempted escape. DiFronzo, after that encounter, proved less impulsive and managed to steer clear of clothing stores and plate glass windows. His disposal of evidence and general elusiveness made it difficult for prosecutors to indict him for an array of serious crimes, such as murder, and so he served only a few short prison terms. He was so successful in avoiding indictments that he could have been known as Chicago's "Teflon Don." To maintain his low profile (nose and all), he instructed his cohorts not to use his name. Instead, as Vincent "The Chin" Gigante insisted that his capos and soldiers point to their chins when referring to him, so DiFronzo insisted on gang members pointing to their noses when referring to him. His caution and evasions paid off, for he was neither the victim of a hit nor the victim of a long prison sentence. He died at age eighty-nine from complications of Alzheimer's disease on May 27, 2018. He died having forgotten all the crimes he had committed.

His successor as Outfit boss is believed by the FBI to be Salvatore "Solly" DeLaurentis. (However, belief is not evidence for an indictment, and DeLaurentis, as far as one can tell, is an innocent man.) Yet, agents not only regard him as the boss but also as consigliere to the Outfit. He had served a long prison sentence for extortion, tax fraud, and racketeering before being released in 2006. Rather than being known for a physical feature, he is known for a metaphor that appears in many stories about him. When referring to the gurgling sound made by bloody homicide victims who have been stuffed into the trunks of cars, he uses the phrase "trunk music." His love of music has not deterred him from denying his past, but he claims that his present and future are crime-free. (And no prosecutor has proved otherwise. He may, indeed, be living a life untouched by crime.) In a TV interview, he claimed that he had gone clean.

"I'm in the carpet cleaning business," DeLaurentis told the I-Team, ABC7 News in 2018.[7] He laughed off those who said he was the boss or involved in mob rackets at all and said the FBI should know that because the bureau monitors his activities.

"DeLaurentis has long been a mob-denier. 'The Outfit is like a group that comes in here to paint the walls' he told investigative reporter Chuck Goudie during a 1993 interview. 'It's the painting outfit.'"[8] (One wonders if he ever heard the expression: "We paint houses.")

During that television interview in Chicago, DeLaurentis said he was "a bricklayer by trade" and a part-time gambler. "We gamble" he said "but as far as Mafia, I don't know what that is."

Goudie: "So you contend that if there is a Chicago Outfit it's an outfit of gamblers?"

DeLaurentis: "Yea. Right. An outfit of guys who gamble. If they were any other kind of businessmen they'd be in the chamber of commerce."[9]

The new head of the FBI in Chicago disagrees with the statement that there is no mob—or that it is washed up.

"Are they out there leaving people dead in the streets?" asks FBI special agent in charge Jeffrey Sallet. "No. But just because people aren't killing somebody doesn't mean that they don't represent a threat," Sallet said. "Mob guys or Outfit guys—whatever you want to call them—are resilient. Where there is an opportunity to make money, they will engage. The reason they don't kill people the same way they did twenty-five years ago is because it's bad for business."

"Regardless of what some see as an evolving lineup atop the Chicago mob, defense attorney Joe Lopez, who has represented numerous top hoodlums, says the Outfit is a thing of the past. 'I don't think anybody is ruling the roost. I think the roost was closed,'" Lopez told the I-Team.[10]

He disputes that DeLaurentis has succeeded John DiFronzo. "'He's old too,' said Lopez, who proudly carries his own nickname, 'The Shark.' Lopez said that Chicago mob leaders 'became obsolete' and were put out of business by the 'digital revolution [that] has changed the entire world.' Other mob experts differ.

"'The outfit is a criminal enterprise, it's still functioning' said John Binder, author of *The Chicago Outfit*. Binder maintains that the mob has a working relationship with Chicago street gangs. He says the Outfit is 'involved in the wholesaling and to some extent importation' of cocaine and heroin that gangs sell on city streets. 'Just because it's not the Outfit guys standing on the West Side or South Side selling it doesn't mean they aren't actively involved in making a lot of money off of narcotics themselves.'"[11]

Among those listed as mob bosses, there remains considerable dispute about whether Joey "The Clown" Lombardo may or may not have been a mob boss. While the aforenamed bosses attempted to keep low profiles or have no recognizable profiles, Lombardo was a media event onto himself. His picture was often in the tabloids, for he often grimaced, frowned, mugged, pouted, and grinned like a beaver. He would tear a hole in a newspaper and poke his face through it, then laugh uproariously.

After his pal Tony Spilotro was killed, FBI agents believed that Lombardo, whether a mob boss or not, took over Spilotro's rackets in Vegas. If so, his value to the Outfit was short lived, for he was convicted in 1986 of skimming more than $2 million from various Vegas casinos, such as the Stardust. For that crime, he was sentenced to ten years in prison and released on November 13, 1992. Upon his release, he attempted to convince the FBI and other law enforcement agencies that he was no longer a criminal. He, too, claimed to have gone clean, though not into the carpet-cleaning business. To emphasize the point that he was no longer a criminal, he took the unique step of taking out an ad in the *Chicago Tribune*. As his own copywriter, he composed and issued the following message:

I am Joe Lombardo, I have been released on parole from federal prison. I never took a secret oath with guns and daggers, pricked my finger, drew blood, or burned paper to join a criminal organization. If anyone hears my name used in connection with any criminal activity, please notify the FBI, and my parole officer, Ron Kunke.[12]

Mr. Kunke reportedly received a number of playful but anonymous phone calls.

Though Lombardo's ad generated considerable media attention, the FBI responded with smiles and skepticism. In fact, the ad had no effect on the FBI looking into a series of old, unsolved mob hits. The agents were determined to bring an indictment against Lombardo; they not only swabbed him for a DNA sample but also attempted to flip him, going so far as to warn him that there was a contract out on his life. Finally, on April 25, 2005, Lombardo, along with thirteen other defendants, was indicted in what the government called Operation Family Secrets, which revealed that the Outfit had been responsible for eighteen murders over a period of thirty-five years. (The investigation and trial were named "Family Secrets" because Frank Calabrese Jr. and his uncle, Nick Calabrese, testified against Frank Calabrese Sr., a notorious hit man for the Outfit. Their testimony was so thorough and exhaustive that the entire Outfit was indicted as a racketeering criminal enterprise. During the trial, jurors heard from 125 witnesses and were presented with more than 200 pieces of evidence. The top leaders who were convicted included not only Lombardo but also Frank Calabrese Sr., James Marcello, Paul "The Indian" Schiro, and Anthony "Twan" Doyle.)

Lombardo, who had earned his sobriquet because of his clownish behavior, now looked decidedly miserable as he was convicted of racketeering, extortion, loan-sharking, and murder. He took off like a horse galloping out of a burning barn. He was on the lam and intended to remain out of prison for the rest of his life. The FBI, however, had no intention of letting him flee justice. It posted a reward of $20,000 for information leading to his arrest. Finally on January 13, 2006, he was spotted and quickly arrested by FBI agents. Lombardo looked like a derelict; he was unshaven and dressed in crumpled old clothes. He had been nabbed outside the home of Dominic Calarco, his longtime friend. Prior to his capture, Lombardo had visited the dental offices of Patrick Spilotro to have an abscessed tooth extracted; the dentist was none other than the brother of the deceased mobsters Tony and Michael Spilotro. Agents found $3,000 in Lombardo's wallet and no other information. In court, when asked about his evasion of the law, he responded: "I was—what do they call it. I was unavailable."[13]

On February 2, 2009, Judge Zagel sentenced Lombardo, who slumped in a wheelchair, to life in prison. Lombardo, no longer clowning, neither grinning nor laughing, professed his innocence, telling the court, "Now I suppose the court is going to send me to a life in prison for something I did not do." That's exactly what the judge did, adding: "The worst things you have done are terrible and I see no regret in you."[14]

Having suffered from arteriosclerosis, Lombardo had several heart attacks while a prisoner in Chicago's Metropolitan Correctional Center. He was taken to Northwestern Memorial Hospital, put on a stretcher, and wheeled into an operating room. It would be the fourth time a stent was inserted into one of his arteries. On October 19, 2019, he died of heart disease and throat cancer in the ADX Florence Supermax Prison. He was ninety years old. Much as he hated being called a clown, his obituaries did not fail to use the hated sobriquet.

Lombardo was not the last Outfit man in Vegas. Though in decline and surveilled by government agents, the Outfit made one last attempt to control the skim in Vegas. The Outfit chose Donald Angelini, an enforcer with the charm of a professional diplomat. He was not the kind of mobster who would attract the attention of the media or run a gang of jewel thieves. He was well-spoken, diplomatic, and offered those he dealt with a friendly smile and warm handshake. He even looked as if he had been sent by central casting; he dressed elegantly in bespoke suits, had a trim physique, and carried himself with a sense of dignity. For his knowledge of gambling, he was known as the "Wizard of Odds." Among the Outfit and casino owners and managers, he was respected for his financial acumen, his memory of facts and figures, and his generosity to friends and relatives. To the FBI, however, he was just another member of the Outfit, though one of its smartest capos, whom many law enforcement officials considered to be several cuts above the average mobsters. In fact, some said that if Angelini had used his intelligence in the world of legitimate business, he could easily have been one of corporate America's respected chief financial officers.

As smart as Angelini was, he made a fateful error of judgment when in the late 1980s he and several senior members of the Outfit attempted to gain control of the gambling operations of the Rincon Indian Reservation near San Diego, California. Their objective was to skim their own profits from the casino profits. In other words, they attempted to reduce their taxable profits to unreported, untaxable ones. They were caught, indicted, convicted, and sent to prison. In 1989, Angelini was sentenced to thirty-seven months on gambling and RICO charges. On October 14, 1994, Angelini was released from prison.

Upon his death at age seventy-four from cancer on December 6, 2000, the following article appeared in the *Chicago Tribune*:

Dubbed the "Wizard of Odds" in the Chicago Outfit, the name organized crime members for decades have given to the city's Mafia faction, Mr. Angelini was viewed by authorities as one of the top moneymakers in Chicago crime syndicate history.

To those who knew him, the father of three and grandfather of five was simply a generous gentleman.

"He was one of the finest, most wonderful men I have ever met," said William A. Von Hoene Jr., an attorney at the Chicago firm of Jenner & Block who represented Mr. Angelini during the past decade.

"He was generous, kind, loving, devoted to his family and an extraordinary friend to many, many people," Von Hoene said.

Mr. Angelini pleaded guilty to federal gambling charges in 1989 and was sentenced to 21 months in prison.

Prosecutors alleged that Mr. Angelini, along with the late Dominic Cortina, reigned as gambling czar over a $20 million per-year sports betting empire.

Mr. Angelini and his attorney scoffed at the government's figures, but government agents insisted their numbers may even have been conservative.

It wasn't Mr. Angelini's first run-in with the law, nor was it his last.

As early as the 1960s, when he was arrested with the late syndicate boss John "Jackie the Lackey" Cerone, federal agents considered Mr. Angelini to be the brains behind the mob's vast sports gambling operation. They said he set nearly unbeatable "spreads" on sporting events and controlled the odds for football, baseball and hockey games.

"He's one of the, I hate to say, great minds . . . within organized crime," Wayne Johnson, the chief investigator for the Chicago Crime Commission, said in a recent interview.

Assistant U.S. Attorney John Burley, the federal organized crime prosecutor who secured Mr. Angelini's 1989 indictment, said he even grew to appreciate the man's mastery.

"He was a fast study, a very smart man," Burley said. "I came to appreciate his wizardry."

Mr. Angelini recently made headlines again when he became the third organized crime figure to be banned from riverboat casinos here by the Illinois Gaming Board under the "black book" provision of the state's casino law. According to law enforcement sources who tracked his activities, he was a regular at the Grand Victoria Casino in Elgin, where he wagered huge sums of cash.

Mr. Angelini and Cortina, both considered to be gentlemen by the government agents who tracked them, were never associated with the bloodshed that racked Chicago's underworld in the 1960s, 1970s and even into the 1980s.

Although he was known as a gentleman, Mr. Angelini once led authorities on a short chase along the Kennedy Expressway. They wanted to arrest him.

He wanted to board a plane at O'Hare International Airport—not to flee justice, but to take a previously arranged vacation in Florida.[15]

Angelini's exit was the end of the Outfit's adventures in Vegas. It had, indeed, crapped out. The Outfit would become a subject for mob buffs, television documentaries, nostalgic museum exhibitions, memoirs, and romanticized movies.

In place of old bootleg money and the Teamsters Central States Pension Fund, a new wave of financing casinos took off: junk bonds, junk bonds, and more junk bonds. Wall Street investment bankers proved as ravenous as their infamous predecessors, though the bankers' deals were legal and so were the recommendations of stockbrokers who sold bushels of stocks to those who believed that a new Las Vegas was about to become America's premier tourist city.

And it was not just gambling that would attract a flood of middle-class Americans. There would be all-inclusive packages of entertainment that the Outfit had never considered, such as those offered by Circus Circus and Treasure Island. Casinos would sell millions of dollars of overpriced luxury goods: furs, jewelry, bejeweled handbags; there would be musical shows as extravagant as (and, in many cases, even more extravagant than) anything on Broadway; there would be grand openings of some of the world's most expensive restaurants, serving exotic dishes that won the praises of professional gourmands. And, of course, there would be the old standbys that had been in Vegas even earlier than the Outfit: leggy statuesque showgirls, beautiful high-priced prostitutes, the magnetic presence of celebrities betting at nearby blackjack or baccarat tables, and freebies for high rollers. It was round-the-clock fun. One Outfit capo grumbled to a commissioner that no matter what the new Vegas offered its customers, they would still be drawn to the city as a gambling mecca. Gambling, with or without the mob's presence, would always be the foundation on which Vegas was built.

Indeed, it was gambling that was the siren call for tourists. Even when Sinatra and Elvis were dominant attractions in Vegas, people came to gamble. They came with dreams of beating the house, and they couldn't or wouldn't be convinced that gambling by its very nature always favors the house. Vast numbers of Americans would come with their credit cards, their checkbooks, their rolls of money and believe that they would return home wealthier than when they had arrived. Their dreams of big wins would die hard.

In his book *The Outfit*, Gus Russo quotes former Outfit soldier B. J. Jahoda:

All organized gambling, legal and illegal, is a zero-sum game intentionally designed so that, over time, the player ends up with the zero and the house ends up with the sum. It has always been so and so it will always remain.

Organized gambling creates and manufactures nothing except smoke, false promises, and hard dollars at the expense of the unwary. And while all forms of organized gambling are parasitic by their very nature, none, not even the Outfit's, can match or exceed the predatory and rat-hearted level at which many of the major casinos operate.[16]

Tourists continue to leave millions of dollars every week in Vegas. None of that money now goes into the pockets of the Outfit. Law enforcement agreed that the Outfit is no longer in business in Vegas. The casinos are free to operate as legitimate businesses (many publicly owned), enriching their new owners and shareholders. Nevertheless, federal law enforcement agencies as well as local police keep watch on casinos. The mob might attempt to sneak back in again, for no matter where casinos operate, gambling attracts mobsters. If they can't regain control of casinos, then perhaps they could gain control of labor unions whose members service the casinos, or they could own ancillary industries that the casinos rely on. The Outfit, like other organized crime groups, is opportunistic. If it can no longer tap into Vegas casinos, it might succeed in some of the states that have legalized gambling. To use a cliché: Where there is a will, there's a way, and where there's a way, the mob will find a way in.

The story of the Outfit's end in Vegas cannot be concluded without noting one final murder. It was directed at Fat Herbie Blitzstein, a member of the Hole in the Wall Gang and an enforcer for Spilotro. Though he was no longer robbing jewelry stores in Vegas, he established other illegal enterprises, including an auto insurance scam racket. In addition, he was raking in large sums of money from bookmaking and loan-sharking operations. He was not as brazen as Spilotro and not as cautious as the mob-lite Outfit in Chicago. And it did not take much time for Mafioso in Buffalo and Los Angeles to learn of Blitzstein's lucrative operations. They decided on an unfriendly takeover. The mobsters from the East and the West converged and took up their positions. In 1997, they murdered Blitzstein. It took a while, but two years later the FBI was able to arrest the killers. Of the seven men arrested and indicted in the plot to murder Blitzstein, four pleaded guilty to lesser charges and received reduced sentences. One man died in prison before he could be tried. Two were tried but acquitted. Newspapers in banner headlines reported Blitzstein's murder as the last Mafia hit in Vegas. They also editorialized that since the Outfit and all of its emissaries were gone from Vegas, tourists could feel safe; women could store their jewelry in hotel safes without having to worry about thefts; and Wall Street could rest assured that its investments in legitimately run companies would be as profitable as in any other major American corporation—maybe even more so.

With the Blitzstein case concluded and the Outfit gone, there was limited business for criminal defense lawyers in Vegas. As a result, the most colorful and prominent of those lawyers, Oscar Goodman, changed careers. Politics was his game: he ran for and was elected mayor three times. He served for twelve years; and because a Vegas mayor cannot serve more than three terms, Goodman was succeeded in office by his wife. While mayor, Goodman came up with the idea of the Mob Museum, which has a plethora of exhibition materials about the Outfit and other mob families who ruled Vegas for decades. It's where the Outfit and an assortment of Vegas gangsters still live on.

In an article in the *Las Vegas Review-Journal*, reporter Jeff German quotes Michael Green, a history professor at the College of Southern Nevada, saying, "In terms Bugsy Siegel would appreciate: Traditional organized crime may be gone, but there will always be organized crime of some kind here, as long as we have gambling and there's money to be made from it."[17]

Several businesses that deal with the casinos are whispered to be run by mobsters or secretly owned by mobsters or associated with mobsters. Are such whispers facts or mere rumors? Neither federal law enforcement officials, nor local ones, comment one way or the other. Though the mob is certainly gone from the count rooms, its shadowy hands may still be benefitting from collateral businesses, some of which were set up decades ago by Vegas mobsters now long dead.

The deceased and banished mobsters were replaced by men with more profound views about the possibilities that Vegas offers. They include Jay Sarno, Kirk Kerkorian, Steve Wynn, and Sheldon Adelson. They turned Vegas into the biggest tourist destination in the world for middle-class gamblers who have made slot machines the most profitable games of chance in town.

Indeed, everything in Vegas is now aimed at hordes of middle-class tourists. They want everything big and splashy and loud. And that's what they get. As a result, the smaller hotel casinos have been demolished, replaced with gigantic hotel/casinos, each of which has thousands of rooms. Each hotel, when fully occupied, has a population of a small town. Indeed, so popular are these new monster hotel/casinos that the city has outpaced Orlando, Florida, as a tourist destination, with six thousand more hotel rooms than those in the home of Disney World. And not only does Vegas have thousands of more hotel rooms than Orlando, but it has a higher occupancy rate: Vegas occupancies are at 90 percent, while Orlando's are 70 percent.

NOTES

1. Evan Thomas, *Robert Kennedy* (New York: Simon & Schuster, 2000), 257.

2. Thomas, *Robert Kennedy*, 257.

3. Jeff Sallaz, *The Labor of Luck: Casino Capitalism in the United States and South Africa* (Oakland: University of California Press, 2009), 171.

4. Sergio Lalli, "A Peculiar Institution," in *The Players*, ed. Jack Sheehan (Reno: University of Nevada Press, 1997), 13.

5. Dennis N. Griffin and Frank Cullotta, *Cullotta* (Las Vegas: Huntington Press, 2007), 269.

6. Gus Russo, *The Outfit* (New York: Bloomsbury, 2001), 475.

7. "With Top Chicago Mob Boss Dead, Outfit Looks for New Blood," I-Team, ABC 7 News Broadcast, June 1, 2018, https://abc7chicago.com/john-no-nose -difronzo-chicago-mob-outfit-boss/3550181/.

8. https://abc7chicago.com/john-no-nose-difronzo-chicago-mob-outfit-boss/ 3550181/.

9. https://abc7chicago.com/john-no-nose-difronzo-chicago-mob-outfit-boss/ 3550181/.

10. https://abc7chicago.com/john-no-nose-difronzo-chicago-mob-outfit-boss/ 3550181/.

11. https://abc7chicago.com/john-no-nose-difronzo-chicago-mob-outfit-boss/ 3550181/ (accessed October 28, 2021).

12. https://www.chicagotribune.com/news/ct-xpm-1992-11-13-9204120895 -story.html (accessed October 28, 2021).

13. Rudolph Bush, "Lombardo Pleads Not Guilty to Charges—Appearance Has 'Clowning' Moments," *Chicago Tribune*, January 18, 2006, p. 7.

14. https://www.nbcchicago.com/news/local/joey-the-clown-lombardo -sentenced-to-life/2091438/ (accessed November 7, 2021).

15. https://www.chicagotribune.com/news/ct-xpm-2000-12-08-0012080284 -story.html (accessed November 8, 2021).

16. Russo, *The Outfit*, 500.

17. https://www.reviewjournal.com/local/local-las-vegas/the-mafias-history-in -las-vegas-from-bugsy-siegel-to-anthony-spilotro-413833/ (accessed November 8, 2021).

10

NEW FACES OF VEGAS

Sarno, Kerkorian, Wynn, and Adelson

The era of mob control of Vegas was fading into history. Replacing the mob were risk-taking entrepreneurs, men of vision, who not only changed the economics of Vegas (including how casinos were financed), but who also changed the face and skyline of Vegas. They built resorts that were bigger, gaudier, more luxurious, and more compelling than anything previously seen on the Strip. They tore down the old casino-hotels and replaced them with magnificent themed resorts. The four most innovative and creative entrepreneurs responsible for the new Vegas were Jay Sarno, Kirk Kerkorian, Steve Wynn, and Sheldon Adelson.

JAY SARNO

Sitting atop an elephant and welcoming tourists was the 5'8", 200-pound-plus, jovial Jay Sarno, who seemed more of a carnival barker than a brilliant visionary. The persona on display disguised the driven visionary who was no buffoon indulging in fanciful theatrics. He was not a conjuror of chimeras. Rather, he was the first casino boss to envision casinos as more than gambling joints. He was the C. B. DeMille of Vegas, who created spectacles of fantasy, where the average middle-class American male could escape from his predictable, scheduled existence. Whereas DeMille directed a movie titled *The Greatest Show on Earth*, Sarno created the greatest casino on Earth; the world had never seen anything like it back in 1966.

So who was Jay Sarno and where did he come from? He was born in 1922 in St. Joseph, Missouri, to immigrant Jewish parents from Poland. During the Depression, his father struggled to make a living as a cabinetmaker. His mother was a homemaker. Sarno attended the University of Missouri, where he earned a degree in business, and where he formed a lifelong friendship with Stanley Mallin. The two joined the army during World War II and served in the Pacific.

After they were honorably discharged from the army, the two men opened a tile contracting business in Miami, Florida. From there, they ventured into real estate development, building government-subsidized housing in Atlanta. In 1958, they met Allen Dorfman, who introduced the two men to Jimmy Hoffa. It was not long before the Central States Pension Fund was lending them money to build motels not only in Atlanta but also in Dallas and Palo Alto, California.

Over the years, Sarno had established a sterling record for building luxurious and profitable motels; he decided it was time to ask his friends at the Teamsters for a loan to build the most luxurious casino in Vegas. They agreed, and in 1966, more than $10 million was made available for Sarno's dream casino, Caesars Palace.

It was a magnificent edifice that enclosed a world of decadent fantasy. And Sarno, a master of publicity and marketing, was able to captivate not only celebrities in Hollywood and Vegas but also the national media. Aroused and enticed by an avalanche of publicity, a stampede of high rollers dashed to Caesars.

Sarno had created in Caesars a hedonistic reflection of ancient Rome as imagined by a twentieth-century Casanova. Beautiful gregarious hostesses welcomed male guests to the hotel by seductively saying, "Welcome to Caesar's Palace. I can be your slave." Security guards were dressed as gladiators and pit bosses dressed in togas. Even eating had to have a decadent Roman theme, which is why Sarno named his restaurant the Bacchanal. There, gentlemen gamblers were served wine in goblets by gorgeous goddesses, who seductively massaged their necks and backs. The men could also ogle hundreds of sexy babes in minitogas that accentuated their long legs and voluptuous breasts. High rollers seeking more sexually active encounters could be accompanied by cocottes to their suites, where a price list of services was presented with a salacious wink. Men returning from a weekend at Caesars did not complain about the money they lost; instead, they told their friends about the fabulous experiences they had in the gaudiest, most decadent resort they had ever visited. Stories about Caesars proliferated, and Sarno sold out every room.

Jay's daughter September told the author:

> Jay built a hotel-casino that is the opposite of home. He made it transforma-
> tional, a departure from the daily drudge of real life. Men would like to be like
> Caesar, if they could. Jay provided them with that fantasy. Though my father
> didn't originate the statement "what happens in Vegas stays in Vegas," the
> principle was his. He believed that he provided an opportunity to do in Vegas
> what you could not do at home.[1]

Even the exterior of Caesars excited visitors. September Sarno commented that "Caesars was the first hotel-casino not built directly on the
street. Jay created a fantasy for people to enjoy before even entering the
casino. With his lavish fountains, he brought water to the desert. Guests
transitioned from the fountains into the fantasy world of the casino."[2] As
limos drove up long, serpentine driveways, passengers looked in wonder
as water shot into the sky from sixteen enormous phallic fountains. Visitors
would later exhale their oohs and aahs as they admired the outdoor swimming pool, which had been meticulously modeled on an ancient pool in
Pompei. To build that pool, Sarno had imported eight thousand pieces of
marble from an Italian quarry.

For entertainment, Sarno had ordered the building of an eight-thousand-
seat auditorium, which he named Circus Maximus, and a small lounge
named Nero's Nook, where comedians performed.

Architectural writer Alan Hess writes: "Caesars Palace needed only a
sumptuous array of Classical statuary and a host of marble-white columns
to establish its theme. The visitor's imagination, in league with well-placed
publicity, filled in the opulence."[3]

No expense was too great for Sarno. Money was for spending (and for
gambling), and he spent what was needed to ensure that Caesars' grand
opening on August 5, 1966, would be more magnificent than a Hollywood
premiere. Sarno and one his partners, Nate Jacobsen, spent $1 million to
make sure the opening would be the event of the year. That money paid
for thousands of pounds of caviar, tons of filet mignon, hundreds of pounds
of crabmeat, and thousands of bottles of champagne. And while spending
freely, Sarno gambled at his dice tables with the abandon of a man unconcerned about debts. He lost hundreds of thousands of dollars at his favorite
game: craps.

Money was not Sarno's primary interest. He was a creator, a showman,
and a visionary. Having created the hottest casino in the world was an

achievement that satisfied his ego. Money had been the means for achieving his goal. Caesars quickly set a standard for luxury, fantasy, fun, and escapism. Other entrepreneurs looked in awe at what Sarno had accomplished, and they were inspired to build their own big, specially themed resorts. They would build mega resorts that would be even more luxurious and trend-setting than Caesars. But, it was Sarno, the Frank Lloyd Wright and the P. T. Barnum of Vegas, who inspired others to follow in his footsteps.

Sarno's son Jay told the author:

> Jay was a compulsive gambler, and as a customer of casinos he knew what other customers would value. He didn't need a marketing plan to decide what kind of hotel-casino to build. He built Caesars based on his own tastes, of what made him a happy casino customer. He didn't need a designer to tell him what to include in his casinos. Everything in Caesars was custom designed: the costumes for the waiters and waitresses, the letterhead, the ashtrays, the menus, etc. He built Caesars based on what he saw in Hollywood spectaculars of ancient Rome. He was also influenced by Disneyland, where one could leave the real world and become immersed in a fantasy world. When he sold Caesars, the lawyer for the buyers asked his clients why they paid so much for the hotel-casino. They replied that Jay would lose whatever the overage was while gambling.[4]

As a risk-taker and maverick, Sarno would inevitably make some mistakes. To begin, he never considered that his loan from the Central States Pension Fund would shine an investigative spotlight on him. The Department of Justice (DOJ) had opened an investigation in its ongoing pursuit of mobsters who controlled casinos. Lawyers at the DOJ wanted to know why Sarno hired some people with unsavory reputations. His Pension loan had come with certain conditions. He had to hire Teamster-designated people or he never would have gotten the loan. Historian Ovid Demaris declared that Caesars was mob controlled from the day it opened. Some of the hires were known associates of the Chicago Outfit, yet Sarno seemed unconcerned. He believed that his enormous success would overcome any negative results from the outcome of the investigation. At worst, perhaps some men would have to be fired. The Pension Fund and the Outfit would understand, and Sarno could continue raking in the millions of dollars that Caesars generated.

Optimistic and undeterred, Sarno next began building an entirely different kind of hotel-casino that would be even more newsworthy than Caesars. He named it Circus Circus. While Caesars represented Sarno's fantasy about decadent ancient Rome, Circus Circus would be a wild incarnation of childhood fantasies about circuses. He opened it, with great fanfare, in 1968. By utilizing all of his marketing and publicity skills, he was able to generate newspaper and magazine stories from coast to coast and beyond. He thought that the casino, built to look like a circus tent, would be a runaway success. Unfortunately, he had failed to build any hotel rooms.

Without hotel rooms, he could not comp high rollers. And, of the few that came, they were distracted from their gambling by all the tumult of cascading circus events. Not only were the high rollers distracted, but so were the employees. It was difficult to keep one's attention focused on dealing cards while a pink elephant flew overhead in a girdle of straps. And as if the elephant weren't enough, there were daring young men and women trapeze artists who performed acrobatically over the head of dealers, pit bosses, and gamblers. The only ones who seemed to benefit from the daredevil spectacles were those who came to cheat: as dealers ducked their heads and beheld men and scantily clad women defying gravity while flying overhead, they were sufficiently distracted to create opportunities for gamblers to cheat.

No one in Vegas had ever seen anything like it. It was a casino themed to attract families, and Sarno himself was its ringmaster. He created a theme park with enough circus acts and carnival games to keep the most energetic kids entranced for hours while their parents poured their money into the slot machines. Though budget-minded families came in droves, the high rollers stayed away. They preferred Caesars, where they dropped millions of dollars playing blackjack, baccarat, and craps, thus making the place one of the biggest successes on the Strip. Circus Circus was another story.

Sarno realized his mistake and was soon speeding ahead, building the necessary hotel rooms. On top of his original $15 million loan to build Circus Circus, he borrowed $23 million from the Teamsters Central States Pension Fund. (At that time, he believed there were no other lenders he could go to. Banks regarded casinos as too risky, especially since casinos were thought to be mob controlled.) Sarno, with the kind of single-mindedness that characterized Bugsy Siegel's building of the Flamingo, opened the hotel part of Circus Circus as contractors feverishly installed plumbing and light fixtures. Fortunately for Sarno, neither his lender nor mobsters were waiting with guns for him to turn a profit. Though Circus Circus had four hundred hotel rooms, it still failed to turn a profit. High rollers still preferred Caesars, where there were no circus distractions.

Not one to moan and groan about failure, Sarno decided that Circus Circus had become such an important destination for families that he could charge admission. Parents didn't object, for they could give their kids access to a midway full of games and sideshows. It was paradise for kids. They could even watch a baby elephant named Tanya pull the handle on a giant slot machine. Parents not mesmerized by the spinning reels in slot machines could sit at a bar that was part of a merry-go-round as their kids circled around on wooden horses. If the parents wanted to go into the casino and gamble, they could slide down a fireman's pole. It was all unrelieved fun. Unfortunately for Sarno's reputation, he had sold numerous midway concessions to less than honorable purveyors of fun. As A. D. Hopkins writes,

> One Las Vegan remembers stopping at a midway game, on the way in, and winning. His prize turned out to be a deck of cards—with every card cleverly marked so it could be read from the back. Flagrant disrespect for the honest game, flaunted only a few feet from the casino, did not inspire $1,000 bets. That gambler never bet another $2 at Circus Circus.[5]

Throngs of budget-minded families could not make Circus Circus profitable. Having run out of options, Sarno and his partners decided to lease the casino in 1974 to Del Webb, William Bennett, and William Pennington, all seasoned casino operators. They managed to turn it into a successful venture and soon bought it from Sarno. Five years earlier, in 1969, Sarno and his partners had been forced to sell Caesars following a Federal Organized Crime Task Force investigation that discovered that one of Sarno's partners had ties to organized crime figures. There were also a number of financial irregularities. Caesars had been bought by Lum's restaurant owners Stuart and Clifford S. Perlman for $60 million. From both sales, Sarno had more than enough money to pay for a new dream casino. While he was dreaming and planning, he dipped into his bulging bank account to gamble. He proceeded to lose millions of dollars at a rapid pace. From 1969 to 1971, he lost $2.7 million. It was all tremendous fun. The losses didn't distract him from planning to build a new mega resort. He said it would be bigger and more luxurious than any resort he had previously built. In fact, it would be bigger and more luxurious than any resort in the world. It would be called Grandissimo. While he had built four hundred hotel rooms at Circus Circus, he would build six thousand luxurious rooms and suites for the Grandissimo. It would be heaven on earth for gamblers and not just for men who gambled, but also for women.

Unfortunately, it was not to be. Sarno, who had a gluttonous appetite for food, women, and gambling, died of a heart attack, age sixty-two, on July 21, 1984, in his suite at Caesars Palace. He died having been unable to attract investors to his dream of building the Grandissimo. However, his dream did not go unnoticed by future developers of mega resort casinos. Five years after his death, the daring and brilliant Steve Wynn created the Mirage, Treasure Island, the Bellagio, the Wynn, and others.

There were rumors that Sarno had died in the arms of two beautiful young women. A. D. Hopkins writes

> One of the mysteries of Jay Sarno was how a balding man in his 50s, who stood five-feet-eight and weighed more than 200 pounds, could repeatedly attract beautiful young blondes whom other men only dreamed about. Part of his success was making a great first impression. "If most men meet you and like you, they buy you a drink," explained one woman. "If Jay Sarno met you and liked you, he bought you a mink. He really did that, more than once, on a first meeting."
>
> His skirt chasing was something the women who loved him simply came to accept. Joyce, who remarried after their 1974 divorce, said, "When we were married I couldn't have a boyfriend, but he wanted me to play golf with his girlfriends. I had to divorce him so we could double date."
>
> Even after the divorce, Joyce was an honored guest at dinner parties given for Jay's girlfriends. He continued to buy Joyce splendid presents—a full-length mink, even another Rolls-Royce, and he never married anybody else.[6]

The following article from the *Las Vegas Review-Journal* neatly summed up Sarno's career in Vegas.

> You can get an argument over who started the Las Vegas Strip, but there's no question it was Jay Sarno who changed it forever. The fast-living genius behind Caesars Palace and Circus Circus invented the fantasy resort and the modern family resort, twin ideas that have guided the past three decades of Las Vegas' growth.
>
> "He lived so large that it is difficult to exaggerate his appetites for gambling, women or food. Or, for that matter, his creativity and generosity."
>
> (Unlike most casino moguls, Sarno was himself a gambler.)
>
> But there were more subtle innovations. All the amenities—like showrooms, shops, restaurants, and pool entrance—radiated off the casino. "It meant that to go anywhere you had to go past the casino, and it gave a sense of being around the action all the time," said [Joy] Harris [Sarno's interior decorator].
>
> "We hit lightning in a bottle with Caesars," recalled [Sarno's partner] Mallin happily. "It took right off. It was the nicest thing in Las Vegas and maybe in the country."
>
> From the time Caesars opened in 1966, the most successful new gambling resorts would be those that, like Caesars, carried out some escapist theme.
>
> Caesars cost $24 million and sold in 1969 for $60 million.[7]

KIRK KERKORIAN

Another visionary of a different variety, Kirk Kerkorian played on a larger and more diverse field of dreams than Sarno. While Sarno did not husband his wealth, Kerkorian became one of the richest men in America. It was not only hard work and risk-taking that led to his success, it was his nearly preternatural ability to perceive and take advantage of opportunities before anyone else. In addition, he was a superbly savvy negotiator who always managed to walk away from every negotiation getting precisely what he wanted. At that same time, he made friends of those he negotiated against, leaving them feeling that they gained what they wanted from the negotiation.

So where did this wizard of dealmaking come from? He was born to a poor Armenian immigrant family and dropped out of school after the eighth grade. He was a tough kid who belonged to a gang and spent a brief time in reform school. Then under his brother Nish's tutelage, he became a successful amateur boxer who won twenty-nine of his thirty-three fights using a powerful right cross. It earned him the nickname Rifle Right Kerkorian. That right cross proved essential in his winning the Pacific Coast Amateur Welterweight championship. Upon being told he was too slight of build and insufficiently aggressive to achieve success as a professional boxer, he trained his sights on a less physically demanding profession.

As the drumbeats of war grew louder and beat more rapidly, Kerkorian decided that those in the sky would play a more essential role than those on the ground. Furthermore, being a pilot required considerably more skill and intelligence than having to fire an M-1 rifle. If he could learn to pilot a plane, he figured he would not be drafted into the infantry.

In 1940, Kerkorian paid a visit to the Happy Bottom Ranch in the Mojave Desert, which was adjacent to Muroc Field, later to be better known as Edwards Air Force Base. The amusingly named Happy Bottom Ranch was owned by Florence "Pancho" Barnes, a highly regarded female aviator. Her ranch was a combination of dairy and cattle farm and a flight school.

Upon meeting Barnes, Kerkorian explained his desire to learn to fly planes and then confessed he had no money to pay for the necessary training. Barnes took a liking to the eager young man and made a deal with him. She would teach him to fly in exchange for his sweat labor: he would have to milk the cows and groom the horses. He immediately agreed. For the young ambitious Kerkorian who had gone no further than the eighth grade and had no skills but those of a boxer, Barnes's offer was like an acceptance letter from Harvard.

On his first ascent into the sunny sky above the clouds, he knew he had made the right choice. He fell in love with flying and thought this would be his life's vocation. After six months, he qualified as a licensed pilot. Soon thereafter, he applied for a pilot's job and was accepted by the British Royal Air Force, which was hiring pilots to ferry Canadian-built de Havilland Mosquito planes over the North Atlantic to Scotland. It was dangerous work, for the planes could be blown off course and pilots occasionally had to ditch them. But his pay of $1,000 for each flight was too attractive to pass up. After two and a half years, he had made more than thirty flights and was able to save enough money to buy a single-engine Cessna. That was the start of a small commercial airline. Kerkorian was now making money, flying gamblers from Los Angeles to Vegas and back again. One of his regular passengers was Bugsy Siegel. In fact, it was Kerkorian who flew Siegel one hot June night in 1947 back to Los Angeles, where Siegel expected to meet with some of his Eastern gangster partners. Instead of meeting his gangster investors, Siegel was shot multiple times in the home of his mistress, Virginia Hill, as he read the *Los Angeles Times*.

There were many others whom Kerkorian transported for gambling outings. As his business grew, he needed to add planes to his fleet. He bought as many small planes as he needed. Kerkorian's profits were increasing week by week. While the additional money didn't burn a hole in his pocket, it inspired him to test his luck and skill at the dice tables of various casinos. He fell in love with craps. As he played, he remained cool and collected with a barely perceptible smile on his face, regardless if he was winning or losing tens of thousands of dollars.

Though a gambler, he had no unrealistic expectations. He knew that money would be the foundation on which he could build the reality of what had only been his dreams; he was not going to throw it away on too many rolls of the dice. With the profits from his charter flights, Kerkorian bought Trans International Airlines for $60,000. Following that acquisition, he purchased a number of World War II surplus bombers, financing the deal with a loan from Seagram's. Because airplane fuel was in short supply, he sold the fuel that was in the bombers' tanks to other airlines and used the money to retire his loan.

As his charter service grew and its profits soared, he decided to expand beyond propeller-driven airplanes. He became the first aviator entrepreneur to provide jet service to and from Vegas, which further increased his business and added significantly to his bottom line.

His charter service was the envy of other companies that wanted to enjoy the profits that Kerkorian was generating. Rather than expanding his fleet and taking on additional routes, Kerkorian sold his charter airline to Transamerica Corporation in 1968. In so doing, he turned his $60,000 investment into an enormous profit: Transamerica paid him $104 million. The deal was just one of many of Kerkorian's outsized successes.

The deal had not been enough for Kerkorian. He hungered for more and bigger opportunities. As a gambler who had enjoyed the dice tables of Vegas, he decided that his next venture should be in the gambling capital of America. There, for $960,000, he bought the land on which Caesars Palace was to be built. He leased the land back to Caesars' owners for $190,000 a year, plus 15 percent of the casino's gross. However, after three years of adding to Kerkorian's wealth, the owners purchased the land for $5 million. It was a sweet deal for Kerkorian. His company also purchased Bugsy Siegel's Flamingo. He paid $12.5 million for Siegel's dream casino and was acclaimed in the media as a wizard of dealmaking.

Though the proud owner of the Flamingo, Kerkorian was aiming for something bigger, grander, and more daring. In 1967, he obtained a $30 million bank loan to build the biggest hotel in Vegas: the International Hotel. He invested $16.6 million of his own money in the project and then arranged for his company, Leisure International Corporation, to issue stock at $5 a share. Before the hotel opened, the stock had climbed to $50 a share. Though he had to sell off some of his stock to settle large gambling debts, his personal investment in the hotel rose in value from $16.6 million to $180 million! He decided to give up gambling—at dice tables.

To much hoopla, Kerkorian held the grand opening of the International Hotel in 1969. He was roundly admired (and in some cases regarded as a foolish optimist) for creating a new kind of Vegas, one that would be a vacation destination for middle-class families. It would not be another Circus Circus nor another decadent Caesars Palace. It would provide innocent fun for families and would have a youth hostel providing a wealth of activities for kids. Families would be able to go on tours to nearby attractions, such as Lake Mead, and take brief helicopter rides.

Within two years, he sold the International and the Flamingo to the Hilton Hotel chain. He was dreaming of something even bigger than the International. It would be the MGM Grand, and it was built at a cost of $106 million. The hotel opened on December 5, 1973. Due to its enormous success, he built another MGM Grand in 1978; this time in Reno, Nevada. The second incarnation cost $131 million. As with the International and the Flamingo, Kerkorian took no pride of ownership. It was the dealmaking that excited him, so he sold his two MGM Grand Hotels to Bally Manufacturing Corporation for $594 million in 1986. He was on a trajectory to become one of the richest men in America.

Though he loved making deals in Vegas, he had his eyes on a wider world. He returned to his first love and purchased a controlling interest in Western Airlines. That done, he moved onto another area, where he had no previous experience. Not knowing anything about the movie business, he bought Metro Goldwyn Mayer and United Artists. That made him an even bigger star in the financial news than he had previously been. That deal was somewhat minimized when he turned around and sold MGM/UA to Pathe Communications Corporation in 1990 for $1.3 billion. That same year, he decided to build the second MGM Grand, which would have a 330-acre theme park and a casino of nearly 180,000 square feet. It would be the biggest casino in Vegas. In fact, it would be the biggest casino in the world at that time. It was bigger than the Empire State Building. The MGM Grand, which opened in 1993, has five thousand rooms, eight restaurants, a health club, a monorail, the fifteen-thousand-seat MGM Grand Garden, and a theme park as big as Disneyland when it opened in 1955.

The original MGM Grand was a fork in the road for Kerkorian. It burnt to the ground, resulting in the deaths of eighty-seven people, most of whom died from smoke inhalation. Kerkorian was shaken by it. He felt he had to redeem himself to himself before he could make any additional deals. Months later, he completed the rebuilding of the resort.

"It's something I rarely ever talk about, because how do you talk about it?" [Kerkorian] says quietly. "I was in New York in a meeting with people from Columbia Studios, and I had an emergency call telling me that the hotel was on television, on fire, and in less than two hours I was at the airport and on my way to Las Vegas.

"The two people I really felt for at the time were Fred Benninger and Al Benedict, because they were on the front lines through everything that happened." Benedict was hotel president.

Benedict later told *Review-Journal* reporter Dave Palermo that when Kerkorian arrived a few hours after the blaze, his first question was, "Where do we start?"

"I figured there was no way we could come out of this," said Benedict. "I think the idea of walking away and forgetting about rebuilding the property was in the back of everybody's mind. That's what most people would have done."

But not Kerkorian. Eight months later, the MGM Grand re-opened.

"How could I walk away while that whole team was out there, taking the brunt from everybody? I had to be a part of it, I couldn't walk away, I just couldn't."[8]

Kerkorian remained focused. He rebuilt the hotel with every fire safety device installed. The devices were tested and retested to make sure that there would be no calamitous fires in the future, and no lives would end in fires.

Throughout, Kerkorian remained the man he had always been. Though his wealth touched the stratosphere, he kept to his simple Armenian ways. Arriving or departing one of his hotels, he carried his own bags. He drove his own cars, a Ford Taurus or a Pontiac Firebird or a Jeep Grand Cherokee. One of his few indulgences was the purchase of custom-made Brioni suits, for which he paid full price. He always made sure to tip service workers, and once while in a taxi taking him from the Pierre Hotel in New York City to LaGuardia Airport, he had the driver take him back to his hotel because he had forgotten to tip the maids. He earned a well-deserved reputation for always paying his debts. Not only did he pay off all of his debts, he never accepted things that he could pay for. No one would ever call Kerkorian a freeloader. Though rich beyond the dreams of most mortals, Kerkorian was invariably modest about his accomplishments and shied away from the spotlight of self-aggrandizement. During the grand opening of one of his casinos, he sat in the darkened back of the dining room sipping from a glass of scotch while his friend, Cary Grant, standing on a stage in front of a large audience of celebrities, lauded Kerkorian with a bounty of encomiums. He then called upon Kerkorian to stand and take a bow. Kerkorian flushed with embarrassment, stood for a moment, smiled, and quickly sat down. Grant knew better than to invite Kerkorian to join him on the stage. Moments after being introduced, Kerkorian departed. Some assumed that after he had ducked out of the hotel, he drove to the airport, enclosed himself in the cockpit of one of his planes, and took off for Los Angeles.

This modest man, who shunned the spotlight and never bragged about his wealth and never put his name on one of his casino-hotels, never forgot his Armenian heritage. Following an earthquake in northern Armenia in 1988, he gave more than $1 billion to that nation's charities. He also helped finance a movie, *The Promise*, about the Armenian genocide. For his generosity, Kerkorian was declared an honorary citizen of Armenia and named a "National Hero of Armenia," the country's highest award. In 2017, *Time* magazine, in a listing of donors, named Kerkorian the tenth largest donor in the United States.

In addition to being loyal to his heritage, Kerkorian was a loyal friend, especially to those who had helped him in times of need. One of his good friends was Vegas sheriff Ralph Lamb. One day, Kerkorian and Lamb had set out on horseback. As they road through the desert, Kerkorian was suddenly convulsed with sharp, shooting pains in his abdomen. He was suffering from appendicitis. He was about to fall from his saddle when Lamb grabbed him and hoisted him onto his own horse. He secured Kerkorian with a strap around the horse's girth and brought his ailing passenger back to Vegas, where Kerkorian was quickly wheeled into an operating room. A surgeon immediately went to work. Both he and Lamb had saved Kerkorian's life. Lamb would always be one of Kerkorian's closest friends.

On another occasion, Kerkorian's wife, Jean, was waiting in the cocktail lounge of the Riviera hotel for her husband to arrive. Two men, drunk and obstreperous, sat at the bar directing obscene and suggestive comments and gestures at Jean. She stood nervously by the window of the hotel, looking out at the street. At that moment, Manny Agassi, an Armenian immigrant, former featherweight Olympic boxer, Vegas restaurant waiter, and Kirk's tennis instructor, walked by. Jean gestured at him to come inside. He entered the lounge and asked what was wrong. She told him about the two men at the bar who wouldn't leave her alone. Manny, being a mere 5'5" and a lightweight, angrily strode toward the two men. As he did so, he shot left jabs in their direction and surprised them with a right cross that only hit the air in front of their now agitated mouths. Manny told both men to beat it or they would wind up unconscious on the floor. Both men, each more than six feet tall and as husky as linebackers, rapidly departed the cocktail lounge. After that, Kirk made sure that Manny would always be handsomely employed. Manny, in return, named his son after Kirk: Andre Kirk Agassi, the great American tennis champion.

People who met Kerkorian for the first time were invariably surprised by his modesty and seeming shyness. They expected to meet a gregarious, loud titan of business. And he was certainly one of the most honored businessmen in the United States. By 2008, he was worth $16 billion according to *Forbes* magazine. He was the richest man in California and the 412th richest person in the world. In addition to his competitive dealmaking, he was an intensely competitive tennis player. He played in many tournaments, and after each win he would graciously shake hands with his opponents, but he never gave interviews. His graciousness and decency, plus his amazing rise to stratospheric wealth, were ongoing subjects for magazine and newspaper stories. And though reporters and feature writers clamored for interviews, often besieging top executives in Kerkorian's employ to get them interviews with their boss, Kerkorian would simply smile and most often just say no. To all who knew him, he was thought of as a regular guy.

By the time he died on June 15, 2015, on his ninety-eighth birthday, he was celebrated as one of the great innovators of Las Vegas, one of a handful of men who had changed the face of a city that started with sawdust-on-the-floors gambling saloons and a reputation for being run by gangsters.

William C. Rempel, in his biography of Kerkorian, aptly summarized the qualities that defined his subject:

> Fellow casino owner Donald Trump called Kirk "the king" and told friends: "I love that guy." Kirk was, however, Trump's polar opposite in style and temperament. Kirk was soft-spoken and understated with a paralyzing fear of public speaking. He wished, he said, that he "could talk like Trump." Kirk also wanted his name on nothing—not on buildings, not on street signs, not even on his personal parking spot at MGM Studios. And Kirk never defaulted on a loan and always regarded his handshake as binding contract.
>
> Kirk travelled without an entourage. He carried his own bags and drove his own car, typically a Ford Taurus or a Jeep Cherokee. He jogged the streets of Beverly Hills and walked to lunches without a bodyguard. He refused comps, personally paying for meals and rooms in his own hotels.[9]

STEVE WYNN

While Kerkorian preferred to stay in the background, more puppeteer than actor, Steve Wynn played all parts: he was showman, dealmaker, visionary, celebrity, art collector; he appeared in his own commercials, and the one he made with Frank Sinatra made Wynn as famous as his casino. Like Sarno and Kerkorian, he was brilliant and far-seeing. Everything he touched seemed to be a manifestation of his churning imagination as he dynamically changed the face of Vegas. His creativity commanded and compelled the attention of investment bankers, stockbrokers, gamblers, tourists, celebrities, and art dealers.

His success in Vegas grew from his involvement in his father's bingo parlor business. He is the son of Mike and Zelma Wynn. Mike's father changed the family's surname from Weinberg to Wynn to camouflage himself from anti-Semitism. Mike managed bingo parlors in several states, and he often took young Steve along with him. When Steve was ten years old, his father took him to Vegas, where Mike attempted to open a bingo parlor at the Silver Slipper. The parlor failed largely due to competition from the Golden Nugget, a future target of Steve's ambitions.

Years later, in a blaze of publicity that would have pleased Mike, Steve bought the Golden Nugget and immediately hired Frank Sinatra, the biggest name in Vegas, to appear in TV commercials with him. As if tipping a valet, Sinatra is seen pressing a $5 bill onto one of Steve's palms, then pinching one of his cheeks and asking that fresh towels be sent to his suite. Steve's eyebrows shoot up, and he exclaims in mock surprise, "Towels?"

Years later, Steve said that after he purchased the Golden Nugget his father would have been proud of him.

However, before Steve could venture forth on his mission to become a Vegas mogul, he had to deal with the unexpected death of his father during heart surgery. Steve had just graduated from the University of Pennsylvania with a degree in English literature. As the older of the two Wynn sons, Steve undertook to pay off his father's $350,000 gambling debts and support his family. Within a year, he had expanded the number of bingo parlors and generated significant profits.

In 1967, he moved with his wife, Elaine, to Vegas. The following year, the ambitious young man bought a wine distribution business. Then in short order, he purchased a small interest in the Frontier Hotel and Casino for $45,000 and went on to become the casino's slot machine manger.

At that time, he became acquainted with E. Parry Thomas, an influential banker and president of the Bank of Las Vegas. His bank was the only one in Vegas that was willing to lend money to casinos. Thomas took a special interest in the young Wynn and helped him by financing a number of land deals.

Around that time, Wynn began having vision problems. He was suffering from retinitis pigmentosa, a genetic disease that destroys the photoreceptor cells in one's eyes and leads to tunnel vision and finally to blindness. After he became a huge success, Wynn began donating $5 million per year to the University of Iowa's Institute of Vision Research. He hoped that his contributions would lead to a cure for his and other eye diseases. Though his eyesight became narrower and narrower as the years went on, he never lost sight of his ambition to be the biggest player in Vegas. And one of the properties he had his eyes on was the Golden Nugget, the casino that had been the obstacle to his father's success at the Silver Slipper when Steve was ten years old.

As noted above, Steve wanted the Golden Nugget. To finance it, he sold his interest in the Frontier and his wine distribution business. With the funds from those sales, he was able to satisfy his immediate ambition and buy a controlling interest in the Golden Nugget. Soon after becoming its principal owner, he wasted no time in completely renovating the old down-at-the-heels casino and hotel. He turned it into a luxurious modern resort that was successfully marketed to wealthy gamblers. And since Frank Sinatra was the biggest star in Vegas, he was the person whom Wynn wanted to promote the casino-hotel. To add to the place's glamour, Wynn arranged for Sinatra to perform there in sold-out shows. Sinatra proved to be a magnet for attracting the high rollers who identified with the swinging, swaggering singer. The Nugget quickly became one of the most profitable casino-hotels in Vegas. It would be only the beginning for Steve Wynn. In 1987, he sold it for $440 million and prepared for more ambitious conquests.

Years later when Wynn had become the biggest casino mogul in Vegas, owning the city's top resorts, he told reporter Mark Seal, "I'd give up everything for fifteen minutes with my father. To have him walk though [here] and see what happened. Now you're talking about something more than a number. I miss the thrill of showing my dad that it worked out OK. He would have been awful proud."[10]

For Steve Wynn, it was now time to move on. Following the sale of the Golden Nugget, Wynn's next big project would be the Mirage. He was prepared to spend $565 million and his friend, Michael Milken, was able to help finance the project by selling $525 million worth of mortgage bonds. The Mirage became known as the first resort that was built with the use of Wall Street junk bonds. However, the project went over budget at a cost of $630 million, thus becoming the most expensive casino-hotel in Vegas up to that time.

To no one's surprise, least of all to Steve Wynn, the investment paid off handsomely. When he opened the Mirage, he needed to take in $1 million a day to cover his overhead. Investors said it couldn't be done, but he exceeded that amount, taking in $40 million during its first month of operation.

The Mirage opened to the public in 1989. The local media swooned, and national magazines wrote adulatory stories accompanied by four-color photos. They reported that the Mirage was the largest hotel in the world, with 3,044 rooms, and with a tower that was twenty-nine stories high, built in a Y-shaped design. They noted that the top five floors, including the penthouse, would consist of elegant suites for high rollers. The resort also offered a little bit of old sin city by creating a poolside lounge where women could go topless and men age twenty-one or older could gaze.

The Mirage's South Pacific theme comprised a realistic replica of a volcano, a tropical indoor rain forest, and gorgeous gold windows that were made with genuine gold dust. Vegas had never seen anything like it, and tourists flocked to it like metal filings to a magnet. In addition to its beauty, the resort would feature popular televised boxing matches, which had been one of the attractions at Caesars Palace and the Las Vegas Hilton. Among the high-profile boxers who fought at the Mirage were Sugar Ray Leonard, Roberto Duran, Evander Holyfield, and Buster Douglas. They helped to make the Mirage the hottest destination in Vegas.

To keep ahead of the other casinos, the Mirage developed special acts that became world famous. One such act was the Siegfried and Roy Show, which was held in the resort's 1,500-seat showroom. Along with the magic acts that Siegfried and Roy performed, they excited their audiences, drawing oohs and aahs as well as spontaneous rounds of applause, for their audacious and dangerous performances with white lions and tigers. Unfortunately, the show closed in 2003 after Roy Horn was critically injured when Montecore, a six-hundred-pound white tiger, dragged him off stage, biting into his neck and severing his spine. While it lasted, the Siegfried and Roy Show was the biggest draw in Vegas.

It was impossible for casino owners not to see how Wynn had revolutionized Vegas architecture and earned millions of dollars for his efforts. They began to renovate their own hotel-casinos, thus making all of Vegas a more tempting vacation destination than it had been in years. Not one to stand still and take bows, his imagination flashing with new visions, Wynn began planning a new family-oriented resort. He named it Treasure Island Hotel and Casino. The $430 million resort opened on the night of October 26, 1993. It offered a 25,000-square-foot arcade and 2,900 hotel rooms for eager tourists, who were first welcomed by the resort's roadside sign that featured a 27.5-foot-high, 8,000-pound fiberglass pirate skull. Guests were then entertained by a free show titled the "Battle of Buccaneer Bay" that took place on a large, artificial lake in front of the hotel. The show was presented at regular intervals every night. The show featured the landing of pirates at a Caribbean village; the pirates then sacked the village before escaping. Nearby was a Royal British Navy ship that sailed the length of the lake before it and its doomed captain sank to the bottom. Spectators laughed and applauded. The entire show made guests happy to enter the casino and gamble away their money.

The resort cleverly combined the attractions of a carnival and Disneyland. As such, it attracted throngs of middle-class families, eager for fun. And their fun was not interrupted by worries about how the casino's gambling odds overwhelmingly favored, not them, but the casino. Fun-loving guests would go on to lose millions of dollars. It was the price for having all that fun. And Sin City now had a new come-on for attracting a new breed of gamblers. Though the guests spent millions at the slots, they had brought along all those kids who were not exactly big-time gamblers. So while kids enjoyed the pirate shows and arcade games, they produced little income for the casino. Improvements would have to be made.

As popular as the casino was, it did not attract high rollers, who did not want to gamble in a casino that was a kid's playground. The high rollers were serious gamblers, and when they wanted to relax after an intense night of gambling, they did not want to do so with kids underfoot, cannons exploding, and ships sinking. Their late-night expectations ran to dates with accommodating showgirls and beautiful prostitutes.

Wynn embarked on a complete makeover for Treasure Island. It would become sexy and seductive, exciting enough to attract high rollers. The major renovation that he initiated would end up costing approximately $150 million by 2003. Renovating just the hotel rooms cost $65 million. The arcade was shrunk to 1,200 square feet, and the front desk was placed in proximity to the pool. It worked: the resort was now an attraction for adults, though children still came with their parents. Even the pirate show was revamped to appeal to adults. It was described as a "sexy and beautiful, adult Broadway caliber show," by Treasure Island president Scott Sibella, who added that "we kept the pirate, Caribbean feel, and made it sexy."[11]

And there they were, the glamour of Sin City: bevies of sexy female dancers in revealing costumes who were in keeping with Vegas' showgirl history. While sexy dancers were added to the entertainment programs at Treasure Island, the giant welcoming pirate skull was taken down and donated to the Neon Museum. The museum, unique to Vegas, features enormous, once-glittering signs from old casinos, all displayed outdoors on 2.62 acres. Like the Mob Museum, it is a popular destination for tourists who want to partake of everything Vegas.

The remaking of Treasure Island having been completed, Wynn was headed in a new direction. He would build a casino more expensive, more luxurious than any other in the world. It was named the Bellagio and opened in 1998 at a cost of $1.6 billion. No other casino's costs came close. Famed for its elegance, the Bellagio features an artificial lake that houses the Fountains of Bellagio and a large dancing water fountain synchronized to music. Guests are also attracted to its beautiful botanical gardens and conservatory. The two towers of Bellagio offer guests a choice of more than four thousand luxuriously appointed rooms. So impressive was the Bellagio, it inspired a trend for building ultraluxurious hotels and casinos, many of which stand today, bold and commanding monuments to imagination and the love of gambling.

In addition to being the most expensively constructed hotel-casino in the world, its opening-night ceremony was more expensive than anything that had been done on the Strip. According to news reports, the ceremony cost $88 million. The opening event commenced with a forty-minute speech by Wynn to a specially invited audience, each of whom paid $1,000 to attend. Couples who paid $3,500 enjoyed spending opening night in the hotel's luxurious suites. Wynn donated the contributions from guests to the Foundation Fighting Blindness. (Through private individual contributions, corporate philanthropy, and community-based fund-raising activities, the foundation has raised more than $500 million since its founding and is the largest nongovernmental source of research funds for inherited retinal degenerative diseases.) Performing in Bellagio lounges on that opening night were cabaret and recording artists Michael Feinstein, George Bugatti, and John Pizarrelli.

Though the Bellagio had cost an eye-popping amount to construct, there was a new hotel-casino being drawn on a fresh Wynn blueprint. It would be the magnificent Wynn Las Vegas, a $2.7 billion casino built on the site of Moe Dalitz's Desert Inn.

Unlike Donald Trump, who put his name on everything he had built for himself, Steve Wynn had previously refrained from doing so. But then pollster Frank Luntz told him, after running focus groups, that the name Wynn would add $80 a night to the amount a guest would pay for a hotel room. And each of those rooms was magnificently luxurious. He had each room in Wynn Las Vegas designed to meet the most demanding expectations of affluent guests. Into each room that measured at least 640 square feet and into enormous suites went the dreams of top designers. In addition, so as never to be away from news and entertainment, guests in single rooms could enjoy a full range of TV channels. Each room had one large flat screen TV and another in the bathroom. Altogether, Wynn Las Vegas is like a small expensive city, spread out over 215 acres, that includes a casino, a convention center, and several thousand square feet of retail space. Within its forty-five floors, there are 2,716 rooms. Occupying the thousands of square feet of retail space are boutiques offering luxurious merchandise from some of the world's top designers, including Oscar de la Renta, Louis Vuitton, Cartier, Dior, Chanel, Manolo Blahnik, and Brioni. And if customers want to put their extravagant collections of treasures in vehicles befitting their hauls, there is a showroom that will sell guests the most dazzling Ferraris and Maseratis.

In addition to its casinos, entertainers, and expensive boutiques, Vegas is also known for its wedding chapels, some of which are drive-through operations. Wynn Las Vegas, however, makes it all very convenient, for there are three wedding chapels on the premises and twenty-two restaurants in which to celebrate nuptials.

Though gambling is the most popular activity at the casino, guests can take breaks from baccarat, blackjack, slots, dice, and roulette on the resort's 18-hole golf course, which features a thirty-seven-foot-high waterfall. At Wynn Las Vegas there is nothing too good for high-roller guests, many of whom are flown into town on the casino's private jets while sipping champagne and then whisked to their luxurious suites in swift, silent chauffeur–driven limousines. If those or other guests needed the use of conference rooms, their pleasure at being guests in the resort includes an added attraction, for the rooms overlook the topless section of a swimming pool. It is no wonder that Wynn Las Vegas has garnered five stars for its decor, its ambience, its luxury, its exclusivity, and its capacity for catering to the needs of its most affluent guests.

In her book, *Winner Takes All*, Christina Binkley writes

> Wynn Las Vegas's genius lies in social stratification, the way it guides its human traffic and creates safe zones for the kind of people who stay at the Georges V in Paris or the Pierre in New York. The resort functions something like the Hamptons. A hotel within the hotel, known as the South Tower, serves as Easthampton [*sic*], with its own exclusive lobby. This region connects salon via the discreet passageway.
>
> There exists an echelon of people with wealth in the world that is willing to spend almost any amount on amusement, as long as it is exclusive enough.[12]

And the name Wynn is not just associated with luxurious mega casino resorts, but also with a magnificent art collection. Wynn developed a well-deserved reputation for having an aesthete's fine eye for the best that major art auction houses have to offer. Whether in person or on the phone, he has bid for many of the world's most treasured works of art. Among the works that he has purchased for his casinos are paintings by van Gogh, Monet, Picasso, Degas, Vermeer, Giacometti, Warhol, Lichtenstein, de Kooning, Rauschenberg, Twombly, and others. They were placed in his most luxurious resorts, adding to the sense of luxury and exclusivity. Of all the paintings in his collection, one of the most celebrated was Picasso's *Le Reve* (The Dream). Wynn accidentally bumped his elbow into the painting, resulting in a small disfiguring puncture. It obviously had to be repaired and was done so at a cost of $90,000. It was worth it, for the painting later sold for

$155 million. Nevertheless, he loved touching some of his paintings, especially feeling the brushstrokes of one of his Van Gogh's.

In 2018, Wynn sold off his Wynn Resorts shares. First, he sold 12.1 million shares, then an additional 4.1 million shares, and finally 8 million shares. The sales occurred six and a half weeks after he stepped down as chairman and CEO of the company that bears his name. After Wynn sold off his Vegas holdings, he opened Wynn Fine Art. Its website notes that "Wynn Fine Art showcases noteworthy and historically significant pieces of artwork from the twentieth century, from museum-quality paintings to remarkable sculptures."[13]

He has sold many paintings from his highly prized collection. The following report appeared in the *New York Post*:

"Steve Wynn Is about to Unload Some Expensive Art"
  By Carleton English

Steve Wynn is in a selling mood.

The . . . casino mogul—who last month unloaded his entire stake in Wynn Resorts . . . now appears to be liquidating some of his art collection, according to a Monday report.

Modern art aficionados will have a chance to bid on at least two major pieces from Wynn's collection at a Christie's auction next month, *Artnet* reported, citing sources.

The artworks—Andy Warhol's *Double Elvis* and Pablo Picasso's *Le Marin*—are expected to take in at least $100 million at the famed auction house. *Artnet*'s sources say more sales are expected to be announced in coming weeks.

The motivation behind Wynn's reported sale isn't clear, as he just bagged $2.1 billion from the sale of his 11.8 percent stake in Wynn Resorts. *Artnet* sources speculated that some of Wynn's art holdings may in some way be tied to the holdings of Wynn Resorts, possibly necessitating the need to sell art as well.

At a current valuation of $30 million, Wynn would seemingly be taking a loss on the Warhol, which he bought at Sotheby's in 2012 for $37 million, including fees, *Artnet* reported.

However, the sale of the Picasso could be a big win for Wynn as it's a self-portrait of the artist that last sold for $8.8 million in 1997.

Both works are listed on Christie's "Impressionist and Modern Art Evening Sale," but the seller is not identified.

"As a matter of policy Christie's does not identify buyers or sellers by name without permission," a Christie's spokesperson told the *Post*.

The reported sales come months after Wynn resigned as chief executive at the company he founded, following accusations that he sexually harassed or assaulted several women. Wynn has denied the allegations.

Reps for Wynn did not immediately respond to requests for comment.[14]

Then in October 2021, *Artnet* reported that "former Casino Boss Steve Wynn's Picasso Collection Fetched $109 Million in a Special Sotheby's Event in Las Vegas. Sotheby's staged an action-packed event in Las Vegas for the occasion. The sale was short but action packed with all 11 Picasso lots easily finding buyers—making it a 'white glove' sale in auction parlance. It pulled in $109 million, exceeding the $100 million pre-sale estimate. All of the lots were guaranteed and three were backed by third parties."[15]

Wynn continues to reside in his $43 million mansion in Palm Beach, miles away from Vegas, but his hotel-casinos remain as monuments to his vision of Las Vegas not only as the entertainment capital of the world but also as a city of lavish luxury in all of its vivid manifestations.

SHELDON ADELSON

Sheldon Adelson, like Kerkorian, is a classic Horatio Alger story. The son of poor immigrant Jewish parents (his father emigrated from Lithuania, his mother from Wales) living in Boston, Adelson showed his first signs of being an entrepreneur when he was twelve years old. He had borrowed $200 from his uncle in order to buy a license to sell newspapers in Boston. Having succeeded at that business and having repaid his uncle, Adelson next borrowed $10,000 from his uncle to open a candy vending machine business. He was only fifteen years old. A few years later, he thought he might want to become a court reporter, but that was a poor fit for a budding entrepreneur. He was not the kind of person satisfied with sitting still and typing away for hours. Not sure what path to follow, he put his inchoate ambitions on hold and decided to join the army. After his uneventful service, the honorably discharged veteran briefly found a niche where the amount of money he earned depended on his success as a salesman: he marketed and sold a product named De-Ice-It, which when sprayed on a car's windshield would dissolve ice. He proved to be an effective salesman, but he wanted to be more and to earn a lot more. He next opened a charter tour business. That, too, was successful, and it served to add fuel to Adelson's hot ambition to be even more successful.

Prior to opening a casino, he opened fifty businesses, some of which failed. It didn't matter. He never accepted defeat. If one business failed, he would open another. He parlayed money earned from one business to fund another one. He made millions and lost millions. It was all part of being a never-satisfied restless entrepreneur. His imagination, drive, and energy were remarkable. He never doubted that he would one day hit upon the business that would make him a billionaire. Years later, he said that "entrepreneurship is essentially identifying the path that everyone takes; and choosing a different, better way."[16]

In 1979, he had a brilliant idea. It would be a trade show for the computer industry. He called it COMDEX (Computer Dealers Exposition), and under his direction, COMDEX became the largest computer trade show with the highest attendance record of any computer trade show in the world. It was so successful that Adelson had operations in twenty countries. In 1995, he and his partners sold COMDEX to SoftBank for $862 million. Adelson's share was $500 million.

Gambling, however, more than computers, would be the key to unlocking the vast wealth that Adelson was to obtain. Gambling has always been a unique business. It's the only one where one can open a store that sells nothing but the implicit (and unlikely) possibility of letting bettors win more money than they will lose. Own a casino and one will own a never-ending flow of profits. What budding entrepreneur would not want to own such a business? It was an ideal business for Adelson, and it would be the answer to his ambitions to be a billionaire. He would go on to build some of the world's most lavish hotel-casinos and then use his enormous wealth to effect political outcomes in the United States and Israel.

Before selling COMDEX, Adelson was investigating the possibility of buying a casino. An opportunity arrived, and Adelson and his partners quickly pounced like a pride of hungry lions. For $128 million, they purchased the Sands Hotel and Casino from Kirk Kerkorian. The Sands came with an awe-inspiring history. The place had been made internationally famous years earlier by Frank Sinatra and his Rat Pack. They had made the Sands the hippest, coolest casino on the Strip. However, once Adelson (now chairman and CEO of the Las Vegas Sands Corporation) and his partners took it over, their ambition was not to return to those days of old and build a showplace for entertainers whose careers might be short lived, but to create a world-class magnificent hotel and casino and make it the most profitable casino in Vegas, if not the world. But first, Adelson and his partners embarked on building the Sands Expo and Convention Center, which in 1989 was the only privately owned convention center in the country. Next on the agenda was the demolition of the old Sands and its replacement. But what kind of casino should replace it? While Adelson and his second wife, Miriam, were honeymooning in Venice, Italy, they had an inspiration: the old Sands should be replaced with a magnificent Venice-themed hotel and casino. It would be called the Venetian. It would take two years to build and cost $1.5 billion. The resort opened on May 3, 1999, with a burst of fluttering, flapping wings of white doves ascending skyward and the robust sound of stentorian trumpets, followed by costumed gondoliers singing romantic songs in Italian. Sophia Loren stood on a platform with Adelson as they christened a fleet of gondolas. A gambler, standing nearby, lamented to a reporter the death of the old Sands, then shouted, "Long Live the Sands."

Adelson and his partners soon enjoyed a prodigious return on their investment. As they had predicted, the Venetian soon soared into the financial stratosphere, becoming the world's most profitable casino. Tourists placed reservations weeks and sometimes months in advance for the hotel's 4,049 luxurious suites and many of its eighteen restaurants. To accommodate even more guests, the Venetian added the 1,013-room Venezia Tower, which was built on top of the garage parking lot. Since the Venetian's opening, guests have been drawn to its Venice-style canals that wind through the elegant mall of Grand Canal Shoppes. While window-shopping, they are entertained by gondoliers crooning romantic songs while steering motorized gondolas along the canals. In addition, the resort features copies of Venice's Rialto Bridge, the Campanile tower, and the Doge's Palace. In October 2001, the Venetian welcomed the Guggenheim Hermitage Museum. Ten years later, the Cantor Race and Sportsbook opened, which was the only Las Vegas sportsbook that was open twenty-four hours a day. Continuing the addition of attractions, the Venetian opened Carnevale, a summerlong festival that features a nightly 3-D projection show on the hotel's clock tower. As if all of that wasn't producing a tsunami of revenue, the resort's TAO nightclub contributed more than $50 million annually. The nightclub features a twenty-foot-high statue of Buddha, an infinity pool stocked with omnivorous koi fish, private skyboxes, a forty-foot terrace, and a pair of dance rooms. On top of the nightclub is the TAO beach, which offers guests private cabanas, each with a giant television screen and a safe for valuables.

Adelson and his partners were not finished. Next on the agenda was the creation of the Palazzo Hotel and Casino. Construction began in September 2004 by digging a four-story underground garage. The hotel's tower has thirty-five floors, and the casino offers guests a choice of one thousand rooms. When construction was completed in 2007, the costs had topped out at $1.6 billion. The Palazzo is an enormous edifice containing 6,948,980 square feet of floor space, making its floor space larger than that of the Pentagon.

Now that the former newsboy from Boston was as rich as Croesus, he would return to the world of newspapers. He not only owned a newspaper in Israel (*Israel Hayom*), but he purchased the *Las Vegas Review-Journal*, the largest daily newspaper in Nevada. He purchased it for $140 million. It would give him a platform for his political and business endeavors. Nevada politicians quickly came to respect the power of a *Review-Journal* editorial endorsement. The paper would also provide an opportunity for Adelson to voice his concerns not only about statewide politics but also about casino regulations. One of Adelson's major concerns was the growth of online gambling. In 2014, he was a force behind the formation of the Coalition to Stop Internet Gambling, an organization that focused on the negative impacts of online gambling and aimed to stop it throughout the United States. Adelson stated that online gambling was, "a threat to our society—a toxin which all good people ought to resist."[17] He did not note the irony of his statement as he was one of the world's most successful gambling moguls. He was most likely against online gambling because it posed a financial threat to his brick-and-mortar casinos.

In 2015, he backed a bill that was introduced in the House of Representatives named the Restore America's Wire Act. Republican representative Jason Chaffetz and Democrat representative Tulsi Gabbard introduced the Adelson-backed bill that would outlaw online gambling. Chaffetz claimed that he was against online gambling because it would target children. Senator Lindsey Graham of South Carolina also introduced a bill to ban online gambling. However, there were plenty of politicians of both parties who were not in favor of banning online gambling. And not all casinos were against it; MGM Resorts and Caesars Entertainment, for example, were in favor of online gambling. But as in most political disputes, positions were based on which constituency had the loudest voices and deepest pockets. Generous sums were spent on lobbying campaigns.

Fortunately for the online gambling industry, those who wanted to ban online gambling have thus far failed in their efforts. After all the money spent to influence politicians of various stripes, all forms of online gambling, including online poker, sportsbook betting, and casino gambling, are thriving in states where it is permitted.

Though the banning of online gambling was a defeat for Adelson, he continued to make billions from his brick-and-mortar casinos in Vegas, Macao, and Singapore. He did so right up to his death on January 11, 2021. He died as one of the richest investors and entrepreneurs in the world, whose estimated worth was $35 billion.

He, Sarno, Kerkorian, and Wynn completely changed the architecture, landscape, and skyline of Vegas. They also brought it out of the era of mob control, making Vegas the gaudiest, most popular entertainment capital of the world. More than New York or any other world-class city, Vegas is the city that never sleeps. Billions of dollars keep the city going twenty-four hours a day.

NOTES

1. Interview with September Sarno, January 6, 2022.

2. Interview with September Sarno, January 6, 2022.

3. Alan Hess, *Viva Las Vegas: After-Hours Architecture* (San Francisco: Chronicle Books, 1993), 84.

4. Interview with Jay Sarno Jr., January 6, 2022.

5. A. D. Hopkins, "Jay Sarno: He Came to Play," in *The Players*, ed. Jack Sheehan (Reno: University of Nevada Press, 1997), 99.

6. Hopkins, "Jay Sarno: He Came to Play," 100–101.

7. K. J. Evans, https://www.reviewjournal.com/news/jay-sarno/ (January 7, 1999).

8. K. J. Evans, https://www.reviewjournal.com/news/kirk-kerkorian/ (February 7, 1999).

9. William C. Rempel, *The Gambler: How Penniless Dropout Kirk Kerkorian Became the Greatest Deal Maker in Capitalist History* (New York: Dey St., 2018), 4.

10. Mark Seal, "Steve Wynn: King of Wow!" in *The Players*, ed. Jack Sheehan (Reno: University of Nevada Press, 1997), 175.

11. http://www.reviewjournal.com/lvrj_home/2003/Apr-22-Tue-2003/business/21158735.html (accessed January 5, 2022).

12. Christina Binkley, *Winner Takes All: How Casino Mogul Steve Wynn Won and Lost the High Stakes Gamble to Own Las Vegas* (New York: Hyperion, 2008), 244.

13. https://wynnfineart.com/about/ (accessed January 5, 2022).

14. https://nypost.com/2018/04/09/steve-wynn-is-about-to-unload-some-expensive-art/ (accessed January 5, 2022).

15. Eileen Kinsella, https://news.artnet.com/market/sothebys-sale-picasso-las-vegas-mgm-resorts-pulls-109m-2025286 (accessed January 5, 2022).

16. https://www.internetpillar.com/sheldon-adelson-quotes/.

17. https://www.freedomworks.org/content/lindsey-graham-moves-ban-online-gambling-benefit-casino-mogul-donor (accessed January 5, 2022).

BIBLIOGRAPHY

BOOKS/NEWSPAPERS

Anderson, Jack, with Les Whitten. "Hughes and Jean Peters." *The Gadsden Times*, April 13, 1976, p. 4.

Binkley, Christina. *Winner Takes All: How Casino Mogul Steve Wynn Won and Lost the High Stakes Gamble to Own Las Vegas*. New York: Hyperion, 2008.

Brill, Steven. *The Teamsters*. New York: Simon & Schuster, 1978.

Burbank, Jeff. *License to Steal: Nevada's Gaming Control System in the Megaresort Age*. Reno: University of Nevada Press, 2000.

Bush, Rudolph. "Lombardo Pleads Not Guilty to Charges—Appearance Has 'Clowning' Moments." *Chicago Tribune*, January 18, 2006, p. 7.

Fischer, Steve. *When the Mob Ran Vegas: Stories of Money, Mayhem, and Murder*. Las Vegas: Berkline Press, 2005.

Fischer, Steve. *When the Mob Ran Vegas: Stories of Money, Mayhem, and Murder*. New York: MJF Books, 2007.

Goldman, Albert. *Elvis*. New York: McGraw-Hill Book Company, 1981.

Goldsmith, Jack. *In Hoffa's Shadow: A Stepfather, a Disappearance in Detroit, and My Search for the Truth*. New York: Farrar, Straus and Giroux, 2019.

Gragg, Larry. *Bright Light City: Las Vegas in Popular Culture*. Lawrence: University Press of Kansas, 2013.

Griffin, Dennis N., and Frank Cullotta. *Cullotta: The Life of a Chicago Criminal, Las Vegas Mobster, and Government Witness*. Las Vegas: Huntington Press, 2007.

Hack, Richard. *Hughes: The Private Diaries, Memos and Letters.* Beverly Hills: Phoenix Books, 2007.

Hess, Alan. *Viva Las Vegas: After-Hours Architecture.* San Francisco: Chronicle Books, 1993.

Higginbotham, Alan (August 11, 2002). "Doctor Feelgood." *The Observer.* https://www.theguardian.com/theobserver/2002/aug/11/features.magazine27 (accessed September 10, 2021).

Higham, Charles. *Howard Hughes.* New York: St. Martin's Press, 2004.

Hopkins, A. D. "Jay Sarno: He Came to Play." In *The Players*, edited by Jack Sheehan. Reno: University of Nevada Press, 1997.

Hopkins, Jerry. *Elvis: The Final Years.* New York: Berkley, 1986.

"Jean Peters Asserts Hughes Secret Safe." *Register-Guard*, December 6, 1972, 5A. https://news.google.com/newspapers/p/register_guard?nid=4pF9x-cDGsoC&dat=19721206&printsec=frontpage&hl=en.

Jenkins, Gary. *Leaving Vegas: The True Story of How the FBI Wiretaps Ended Mob Domination of Las Vegas Casinos.* Scotts Valley, CA: CreateSpace Independent Publishing, 2016.

Jennings, Dean. *We Only Kill Each Other.* New York: Fawcett World Library, 1968.

Kaplan, James. *Sinatra: The Chairman.* New York: Doubleday, 2015.

Kelley, Kitty. *His Way: The Unauthorized Biography of Frank Sinatra.* New York: Bantam Books, 1986.

Konigsberg, Eric. *Blood Relation.* New York: Harper Collins Publishers, 2005.

Lacey, Robert. *Little Man: Meyer Lansky and the Gangster Life.* Boston: Little, Brown and Company, 1991.

Lalli, Sergio. "A Peculiar Institution." In *The Players*, edited by Jack Sheehan. Reno: University of Nevada Press, 1997.

Lalli, Sergio. "Howard Hughes in Las Vegas." In *The Players*, edited by Jack Sheehan. Reno: University of Nevada Press, 1997.

Moulden, Stuart. *The Kefauver Organized Crime Hearings, Abridged.* Scotts Valley, CA: CreateSpace Independent Publishing, 2013.

Newton, Michael. *Mr. Mob: The Life and Crimes of Moe Dalitz.* Jefferson, NC: McFarland and Company, Inc., 2007.

Otfinoski, Steven. *Bugsy Siegel and the Postwar Boom.* Farmington Hills, MI: Blackbirch Press, 2000.

Pileggi, Nicholas. *Casino: Love and Honor in Las Vegas.* New York: Simon & Schuster, 1995.

Puzo, Mario. *Inside Las Vegas.* New York: Grosset & Dunlap, 1976.

Rappleye, Charles, and Ed Becker. *All American Mafioso: The Johnny Roselli Story.* New York: Doubleday, 1991.

Rempel, William C. *The Gambler: How Penniless Dropout Kirk Kerkorian Became the Greatest Deal Maker in Capitalist History.* New York: Dey Street Books, 2018.

Roemer, William F. Jr. *The Enforcer*. New York: Donald I. Fine, Inc., 1994.

Russo, Gus. *The Outfit*. New York: Bloomsbury, 2001.

Russo, Gus. *Supermob: How Sidney Korshak and His Criminal Associates Became America's Hidden Power Brokers*. New York: Bloomsbury, 2006.

Sallaz, Jeff. *The Labor of Luck: Casino Capitalism in the United States and South Africa*. Oakland: University of California Press, 2009.

Scherman, Tony (August 16, 2006). "Elvis Dies." *American Heritage* 57, no. 4. https://www.elvisinfonet.com/spotlight_elvisdies.html (accessed September 16, 2021).

Seal, Mark. "Steve Wynn: King of Wow!" In *The Players*, edited by Jack Sheehan. Reno: University of Nevada Press, 1997.

Server, Lee. *Handsome Johnny: The Life and Death of Johnny Rosselli*. New York: St. Martin's Press, 2018.

Sheehan, Jack, ed. *The Players: The Men Who Made Las Vegas*. Reno: University of Nevada Press, 1997.

Shnayerson, Michael. *Bugsy Siegel: The Dark Side of the American Dream*. New Haven, CT: Yale University Press, 2021.

Sifakis, Carl. *The Mafia Encyclopedia*. New York: Checkmark Books, 1999.

Sloane, Arthur A. *Hoffa*. Cambridge, MA: MIT Press, 1991.

Smith, John L. *Las Vegas Review-Journal*, February 7, 1999, p. 3. www.review journal.com/news/moe-dalitz/ (accessed May 15, 2021).

Smith, John L. "Moe Dalitz and the Desert." In *The Players*, edited by Jack Sheehan. Reno: University of Nevada Press, 1997.

Summers, Anthony, and Robbyn Swan. *Sinatra: The Life*. New York: Alfred A. Knopf, 2005.

Sussman, Jeffrey. *Big Apple Gangsters: The Rise and Decline of the Mob in New York*. Lanham, MD: Rowman & Littlefield Publishers, 2020.

Swanson, Doug J. *Blood Aces: The Wild Ride of Benny Binion, the Texas Gangster Who Created Vegas Poker*. New York: Viking, 2014.

Thomas, Evan. *Robert Kennedy*. New York: Simon & Schuster, 2000.

Time-Life Editors. *Mafia*. New York: Time-Life Books, 1993.

Velotta, Richard N. *Las Vegas Sun*, August 25, 2012. https://lasvegassun.com/news/2012/aug/25/harry-reid-pat-mccarrans-name-shouldnt-be-anything/ (accessed May 4, 2021).

Wilkerson, W. R. III. *Hollywood Godfather: The Life and Crimes of Billy Wilkerson*. Chicago: Chicago Review Press, 2018.

Wolfe, Tom. "Las Vegas (what?)." In *Smiling Through the Apocalypse*, edited by Harold Hayes. New York: McCall Publishing Company, 1969.

Woo, Elaine. "Jean Peters; Actress in Film, TV Married Howard Hughes." *Los Angeles Times*, October 21, 2000. https://www.latimes.com/archives/la-xpm-2000-oct-21-me-39956-story.html.

Zoglin, Richard. *Elvis in Vegas*. New York: Simon & Schuster, 2019.

MOVIES

Casino
Hoffa
Mr. Lucky
Once Upon a Time in America
Showgirls
Stripper
Viva Las Vegas

INDEX

ABOUT THE AUTHOR

Jeffrey Sussman is the author of sixteen nonfiction books, six of which have been published by Rowman and Littlefield. In addition to *Sin City Gangsters*, Sussman is the author of two other books that deal with the mob: *Big Apple Gangsters: The Rise and Decline of the Mob in New York* and *Boxing and the Mob: The Notorious History of the Sweet Science*. He lives in New York City.